ADULT EDUCATION IN A MULTICULTURAL SOCIETY

ROUTLEDGE SERIES ON THEORY AND PRACTICE OF ADULT EDUCATION IN NORTH AMERICA

Edited by Peter Jarvis,
University of Surrey

ADULT EDUCATION IN A MULTICULTURAL SOCIETY

Edited by

Beverly Benner Cassara

London and New York

First published 1990
by Routledge
11 New Fetter Lane, London EC4P 4EE

Simultaneously published in the USA and Canada
by Routledge
a division of Routledge, Chapman and Hall, Inc.
29 West 35th Street, New York, NY 10001

Printed and bound in Great Britain by
Biddles Ltd, Guildford and King's Lynn

British Library Cataloguing in Publication Data

Adult education in a multicultural society. – (Theory and
    practice of adult education in North America series).
    1. United States. Adult education
    I. Cassara, Beverly Benner, *1922*–
    I. Title II. Series
    374′.973

    ISBN 0-415-03644-5

Library of Congress Cataloging in Publication Data is available

CONTENTS

Contents

FIGURES

TABLES

CONTRIBUTORS

Thelma Barer-Stein is the founder and director of the consulting firm, Cultural Concepts, Inc. With her Ph.D. from the University of Toronto, she has been involved in developing and teaching cross-cultural curriculum in adult education at Toronto University's Ontario Institute for Studies in Education.

Peter S. Cookson directs the adult education graduate program at the Pennsylvania State University. His work has included studies of the rural highland Indians in Peru, and of the achievement of Mexican American small businessmen in Chicago. He is a leader in the developing field of international adult education.

Philip T.K. Daniel is a professor in the Department of Leadership and Educational Policy Studies at Northern Illinois University, DeKalb. His international publications include the fields of the history of education and multicultural education with emphasis on adult populations.

Vesta A.H. Daniel is a professor in the School of Art at Northern Illinois University. Her publications include the areas of multicultural art education and African art history. Her research has taken her to countries in Europe and Africa.

René Díaz-Lefebvre teaches psychology and counseling at Rio Salado Community College in Phoenix, Arizona, a college-without-walls serving the adult learner, where he received the Outstanding Teacher Award in 1987. He serves on the College Board's Adult Learning Services National Advisory Committee.

C. Ray Graham is an associate professor of linguistics and ESL at Brigham Young University, Provo, Utah. His extensive work in teaching linguistic minority adults has led to the publishing of a teacher's guide and various articles dealing with the teaching of English as a Second language.

Cornelius (Neal) Grove, Director of the American Field Service Center for the Study of Intercultural Learning, has taught at Teachers College, Columbia University, and Beijing Foreign Studies University, Beijing, China. He is author with Chancellor Hu Wenzhong of Beijing Foreign Studies University of a forthcoming book on the differences between Chinese and American social and communicative behavior.

Bettina Hansel is an Associate of the American Field Service Center for the Study of Intercultural Learning. Her research concerns the extent of learning and growth achieved by adolescents participating in intercultural homestay experiences. She is the Associate Editor of AFS's monograph series, *Occasional Papers in Intercultural Learning*.

Kimerly Miller serves on the Steering Committee for the AFS Service Urban Scholars Program in New York, where she advises on program development and volunteer recruitment and management. She has carried out volunteer training and management programs for various national organizations. She is also a consultant to the AFS Center for Intercultural Learning.

Martha Montero-Sieburth teaches at the Harvard Graduate School of Education in the area of curriculum development and multicultural education. Currently she is conducting research on the educational processes of bilingual teachers who are working with immigrant students in an urban school district.

Charlotte T. Morgan is the Chair of the Black Studies Program at Lehman College, The City University of New York. Her published articles feature Black adult education and international education. Her current research interests include the role of adult education in African and African-American women's groups, and research on local Black women's history in the Bronx and downstate New York.

Don Toshiaki Nakanishi teaches at the Graduate School of Education at the University of California in Los Angeles, where he is also Associate Director of the Asian American Studies Center. He has published books and articles on issues of educational access and political participation of Asian Pacific Americans and other minority populations. He is a member of the College Board's Minority Advisory Committee.

Young Pai is Chairman of the Division of Social-Philosophical Foundations of Education, School of Education, University of Missouri-Kansas City. He has published three books on the philosophy of education, and is currently doing research on the cultural foundations of education. He is past president of the Philosophy of Education Society and the Council of Learned Societies in Education.

Joan S. Reeves, clinical Assistant Professor, Department of Public Health, University of Illinois at Chicago, College of Nursing, has also taught in the Department of Nursing Education at the University of Botswana in Gaborone, through a Kellogg Foundation faculty exchange program. She has been heavily involved in primary health care programs for various ethnic communities in the United States.

Charles A. Tesconi Jr, Dean of the School of Education at the American University, Washington, DC, is the author and co-author of several books and articles. He is currently involved in research on the policy characteristics of a number of particularly successful high schools. He has served as Dean of the College of Education at the University of Vermont.

John W. Tippeconnic III, on the faculty of Education at Arizona State University in Tempe, has served as Vice President of Academic Affairs at Navajo Community College, Tsaile, Arizona. He also has served as Associate Deputy Commissioner for Indian Education, US Department of Education, Washington, DC. He is the editor of the *Journal of Indian Education* and has published many articles on the education of American Indians.

EDITOR'S NOTE

Theory and Practice of Adult Education in North America is a series of books which provides scholars and students with an informed collection of studies by eminent scholars on all aspects of adult education throughout the continent. The books thus far have included studies of history, planning, and adult learning, and cover both a theoretical and a practical dimension.

This book, edited by Beverly Benner Cassara, is an important addition to this series, since it focuses upon an area of adult education in which there have been few serious studies — the recognition that America, like many other countries in the world, is a multicultural society and that adult education functions within it. That it has a place is not surprising, but the fact that the work that it does with different cultural groups remains little studied is much more surprising. Beverly Benner Cassara has provided an important and stimulating series of papers.

There is a companion series of books published by Routledge, the International Series, and together they offer the field of adult education a library of books that seeks to cover a wide variety of topics of interest and concern to adult educators.

Peter Jarvis
Series Editor

ACKNOWLEDGMENTS

The research which resulted in this book was supported in part by a grant from the University of the District of Columbia. I also gratefully acknowledge the support over the years of my colleagues on the faculty and the administration of UDC, for my intercultural and international adult education efforts.

In two cases, contributors to this book have adapted ideas used in earlier publications. Young Pai has been granted permission to use selections from *Philosophy and the American School*, Second Edition, by Van Cleve Morris and Young Pai, copyright 1976 by Houghton Mifflin Company. He also has received permission from the American Association of Adult and Continuing Education to quote from an article in *Lifelong Learning* (January 1984), 'Cultural diversity and multicultural education.' Charles A. Tesconi Jr has incorporated ideas published earlier in 'Multicultural education: a valued but problematic ideal,' in *Theory into Practice* (spring 1984).

I thankfully acknowledge the expert advice and technical editing provided by Ernest Cassara.

Finally my thanks are due to Dr Peter Jarvis of the University of Surrey who urged me to undertake this project. As General Editor of this series his counsel has been invaluable.

Beverly Benner Cassara

INTRODUCTION

Beverly Benner Cassara

> Adult education will become an agency of progress if its
> short-time goal of self-improvement can be made compat-
> ible with a long-time, experimental but resolute policy of
> changing the social order.
>
> (Lindeman 1926: 166)

By the year 2020, there will be forty-seven million Hispanics
in the United States.[1] The 1980 Census reported a 72 percent
increase of American Indians over those counted in the 1970
Census.[2] While 13 percent of the English-speaking population
in the United States is illiterate, the percentage of illiterate
Black youths is 47 percent.[3] By 1990 the Asian Pacific
population of California will be larger than the Black population, and be second only to the Hispanic.[4]

There is a new urgency to meet the needs of the ever-
increasing numbers of newly arrived minorities in the United
States, as well as the continuing needs of American Indians
and Blacks. Will it be possible for these people to become fully
functioning members of their communities, and nevertheless
retain their prized cultural distinctiveness? Failure in this
regard may well lead to increasing polarization with its
inherent dangers. This book invites adult educators and policy
makers to take a new look at an old question, namely, the
adult education needs of minority ethnic groups in the United
States.

Should adult educators attempt to change the social order,
to improve the quality of life? Social consciousness, after all,
has been a hallmark of the adult education movement. If it
goes without saying that adult educators are only one small
group of players on the national scene responsible for the
optimal inclusion of ethnic persons in American society,
nevertheless, they do have a great responsibility, which
includes influencing national policy.

1

To take one example: is the main reason for teaching English as a second language to enable a person to buy a loaf of bread or to get a job as a dishwasher? Or should adult education be concerned with developing a framework for a comprehensive, humanistic education for members of ethnic groups, so that they may share equally in the opportunities which American society affords? There are further, perhaps more important, questions, which go beyond the issue of social justice for the individuals in minority groups to the underlying concern for the very nature of the society which is developing. Is the purpose of adult education only to aid minority persons to share the *status quo* of the dominant culture, with its strengths, but also its many weaknesses?

These are not simple issues, to be decided in a vacuum. There are a number of social, economic, and political implications. The economic picture, for instance, is complicated by the fact that society has become dependent on undereducated immigrants to take the lowest level jobs, without security and benefits. Politically, is it acceptable that strong ethnic groups control certain regions of the country?

There are millions of adults in various ethnic groups in the United States who are not well served — if served at all — by educational institutions. To be sure, there are any number of special programs attempting to meet the needs of various groups, but many of these are ephemeral, depending as they do on uncertain funding, or the individual initiative of certain leaders. What are these programs trying to achieve? Is there a national policy, or only stop-gap answers to specific situations?

America has been multicultural since the European settlers migrated to the land of the American Indians, who themselves did not share a monolithic culture. If today there are people from every country in the world living in the United States in a condition of at least minimal harmony, it is at best an uneasy accommodation. Mr Justice Thurgood Marshall of the Supreme Court has warned that racism is only thinly disguised. Some dismal chapters in history, and recent events confirm this.

The suffering of the Black people may be the most obvious, but the treatment of the American Indians has been equally inhumane. The Chinese, who provided much of the hard labor in the last century, were thanked by being excluded from immigration in 1882. Fear of the 'yellow peril' led to the exclusion of the Japanese in 1924. Mexicans, who have always crossed the border, legally and illegally, and have contributed much labor to American agriculture, have had to meet the amnesty rules of the 1986 Immigration Law, leave the country, or continue to reside illegally. This law, of course, applies to other immigrant groups as well.

While the issue of immigration is a serious national problem, it is not the subject of this book. Nevertheless, adult educators have the responsibility to work with the persons who are in the country at any given time. The migration of large numbers of peoples across borders in all parts of the world today is not an aberration, but probably the wave of the future. It is important to adult educators because it poses a major challenge. In so far as adequate government funding for programs is not available, adult educators need to play a larger role in influencing policy.

Earlier defenses of the ideal of 'the melting pot,' 'assimil-ation,' and 'acculturation,' are being questioned, since their assumptions were that ethnics would surrender their various heritages in order to join the dominant culture. The 'melting pot,' while taken for granted earlier, has become controversial. In so far as immigrants, such as the Europeans, desired to become one with the dominant culture, the concept served well. Today, however, with a new emphasis on the conserva-tion of ethnic heritages, it is rejected by some groups, such as the American Indians and Blacks, who do not desire to lose their ethnic distinctiveness. Bayard Rustin writes: 'There never was a melting pot; there is not now a melting pot; there never will be a melting pot; and if there were, it would be such a tasteless soup that we would have to go back and start all over' (Novak 1973:13).

'Cultural pluralism,' which idealistically allows all groups to live and work together while maintaining their cultural identities, raises a problem of possible contradiction. Accord-ing to the views of some, emphasis on cultural distinctiveness works against allegiance to a common American culture, has the possibility of promoting divisiveness, and enhancing social segregation. Proponents, on the other hand, see 'cultural pluralism' as the only tenable basis for ensuring equality and human rights for all.

A search through education literature with descriptors such as 'multicultural,' 'cross-cultural,' 'multiethnic,' and 'trans-cultural' brings up many articles, but almost all are related to grades K through 12. However, even here, the terms are not very meaningful. They are often defined ambiguously and inconsistently, and at times overlap. Probably the clearest and most comprehensive elucidation is that of James A. Banks in his *Multiethnic Education* (1988), but his work does not go to the field of adult education. Multiethnic education requires that all students, both of the dominant culture and ethnic minorities, learn to know and respect all cultures. Other authors describe this as 'transcultural' education.

Two adult educators who have concerned themselves with the subject of multiculturalism in adult education are Horace M. Kallen and Robert A. Carlson. Carlson's recently revised work, also in this publication series, *The Americanization Syndrome: A Quest for Conformity* (1987), presents a controversial analysis of education for Americanization. He argues that most Americanization programs have been 'no more and no less than attempts at cultural genocide' (p.12). On the other hand, Kallen, writing in the early part of this century, looked to 'cultural pluralism' as the most democratic framework for making newcomers at home in America. He is quoted by Carlson on this: '... democracy involves, not the elimination of differences, but the perfection and conservation of differences. It aims through union, not at uniformity, but at variety' (p.97).

As ideal as 'cultural pluralism' may sound, there is not only no consensus on its meaning, but the problems inherent in implementing it in the educational setting raise questions of economic, social, and political importance way beyond the power of the public school to control. In so far as 'cultural pluralism' suggests all students learn about many cultures, the possibility of controversy is very clear. Community approval, the *sine qua non* for such curriculum development, may not be forthcoming, not to mention the financial backing needed for significant alteration of the public school curriculum. Adult education activities, occurring as they do, in a wide variety of situations, have a better opportunity to implement 'cultural pluralism,' in that they are more free from community control. The question is, do adult educators have the vision and the training to implement 'cultural pluralism?'

What is the philosophy of the individual adult educator working with ethnic persons? Who is writing and speaking out, explaining the complications, the problems, the challenges, and the opportunities? Many dedicated practitioners are involved in the education of ethnic adults, often working in the face of great difficulties. Their efforts, however worthwhile, do not add up to a comprehensive policy.

This book is designed to raise some of the issues that must be considered in the development of such a comprehensive policy. It is divided into three parts. Young Pai discusses various possible approaches to the integration of ethnic groups in the United States and the responsibilities of the dominant culture in the process.

Charles Tesconi compares, among others, the concepts of

the melting pot, multiculturalism, and cultural pluralism, and the possible consequences of the adoption of each approach.

Ray Graham and Peter Cookson advocate the practice of bilingualism, which they believe provides the illiterate linguistic minority adult with a more effective transition from one culture to another. The policy, of course, has created controversy in the United States, so much so that California passed a law in 1986 explicitly making English the official language of the state, and, as of the 1988 elections, Colorado, Arizona, and Florida have followed suit.

In the second part of the book, four authors set forth the present-day situation of adult education in the treatment of four major ethnic groups, tracing it to its historic roots. Charlotte Morgan describes present efforts to provide adult education for Blacks in Manhattan. In a series of vignettes she shows that, despite racist attitudes of white leaders that affected earlier efforts, Blacks have achieved a measure of success in devising a strategy to help themselves.

John Tippeconnic III describes federal government policies on education of the Native Americans over the years. Although some of the federal approaches deprived the American Indians of equality of education, they have developed a sophistication in dealing with the bureaucracy. This promises a greater control over their educational programs.

Martha Montero-Sieburth pictures the diversity of the groups within the Hispanic community and explains why some adult education efforts are not serving them effectively. She describes a number of present efforts across the country, however, which provide models for more effective approaches.

Don Nakanishi reviews the literature on adult education for Asian Americans. Citing the diversity of groups within that community, and using the criterion of electoral participation, he points out that adults from countries with authoritarian governments need political education in the United States, as well as ESL, literacy, and vocational education.

The third part of the book presents examples of innovative action and research projects which represent forward thinking on the part of some concerned adult educators. Philip and Vesta Daniel explain the work of the Northern Illinois University in making graduate study available to minority persons at the same time that it uses graduate study and research as a means of understanding how adult education can serve the needs of ethnic communities.

Thelma Barer-Stein has used a phenomenological approach in her research, in an attempt to understand culture. Her purposefully subjective concern with one individual, as illustrated in her chapter, is in sharp contrast to the quantitative research found in much of the adult education literature today.

Joan Reeves gives a first-hand account of participatory research in a project at the University of Illinois-Chicago. She and her associates worked in ethnic communities to help women learn to become more responsible for primary health care, the purpose being not to solve their problems for them but to develop with them a useful process.

Kimerly Miller, Neal Grove, and Bettina Hansel report on the experiences of families who play host to students from other countries. Their study shows how personality, as well as cultural differences, influence the chances of success in these home-stays.

René Díaz-Lefebvre describes a community project he initiated at a community college, by which ethnic persons had an opportunity to become acquainted with the services of the college, to assess their own educational needs, and to be convinced that it was possible for them to attend the college.

The reader will, of course, know other cogent examples of adult educators involved in innovative and effective practices for the education of members of ethnic groups, such as innovative entrepreneurial training, career change opportunities, etc. These efforts are commendable. However, creators of these programs are often working on their own individual initiative, apart from the mainstream. In so far as this is true, two major problems must be faced. The immediate problem is the question of funding, which is unstable and thus causes the demise of effective programs. The achievement of more secure funding will require a better understanding of the educational needs of ethnic minority persons by adult educators, politicians, and the general public.

The challenge of providing effective education for ethnic minorities is not peculiar to the United States. Many countries are facing the same problem. A conference on this subject in the Federal Republic of Germany in the summer of 1985, sponsored by the University of Frankfurt, the Folk High School at Falkenstein, and several adult education agencies from the city of Frankfurt, brought together adult educators from Germany, England, and the United States. Members presented papers on political, economic, and social forces at work in each of the countries as they confronted the education of groups as diverse as the foreign workers from Turkey and southern and eastern Europe in Germany, Blacks from former colonies in the Caribbean and Africa in the United Kingdom, and various minority groups in the United States. This book was inspired by the experience of the editor, who was one of the coordinators of the conference. Three of the authors in this collection — Morgan and the two Daniels — also attended and presented papers. One significant conclusion at that conference echoed Lindeman's challenge to adult educators to develop a 'long-time, experimental but resolute policy of changing the social order,' if adult education is to become 'an agency of social progress.'

NOTES

1. See Chapter 6, p. 97.
2. See Chapter 5, p. 78.
3. See Chapter 4, p. 63.
4. See Chapter 7, p. 122.

REFERENCES

Banks, James A. (1988) *Multiethnic Education: Theory and Practice*, Boston, Mass.: Allyn & Bacon.

Carlson, Robert A. (1987) *The Americanization Syndrome: A Quest for Conformity*, London: Croom Helm.

Lindeman, Eduard C. (1926) *The Meaning of Adult Education*, New York: New Republic.

Novak, Michael (1973) *The Rise of the Unmeltable Ethnics*, Toronto: Macmillan.

Part One

DIMENSIONS OF THE PROBLEM

Chapter One

CULTURAL PLURALISM, DEMOCRACY AND MULTICULTURAL EDUCATION

Young Pai

The demand for cultural pluralism in America is based partly on the belief that it is intrinsic to democracy. Yet, its proponents have not always clearly articulated the meaning of cultural pluralism or its social, political, and educational implications or its alleged connections with democracy. Clearly, the kind of cultural pluralism believed to be consistent with democracy is much more than the separate or independent existence of disparate ethnic groups without any contact between institutions or individuals. Rather, it is an ideal that seeks to establish and encourage cultural diversity as a basis of unity, so that America can become a cohesive society whose culture is enriched by sharing widely diverging ethnic experiences. Hence, cultural pluralism is based on the belief in equality of opportunity for all people, respect for human dignity, and the conviction that no single pattern of living is good for everyone. In this context, the traditional notion of tolerance for different cultural patterns is said to be patronizing, for it suggests an attitude in which the dominant group regards human dignity as a grant bestowed by 'me' on 'you' or 'you' on 'me' (Hazard and Stent 1973:15).

Cultural pluralism, then, must include the belief that in the coexistence of people with diverse cultural backgrounds, to be different is not to be inferior. While this pluralistic view necessitates the acceptance of the intrinsic worth of all human beings and their unique individuality, it should not prevent one from learning new cultural patterns. On the contrary, the individual life or the culture of a group or a nation may be enriched by preserving and sharing different socio-cultural patterns.

In a similar vein, Horace N. Kallen asserted that ethnic groups should develop a positive self-image and pride in their respective group's cultural heritage and communal values, but still function as partially integrated political and economic

11

entities in American society. He was convinced that America would be richer as a result of cultural diversity. Accordingly, he likened the American way as

> the way of orchestration. As in an orchestra, the different instruments, each with its own characteristic timbre and theme, contribute distinct and recognizable parts to the composition, so in the life and culture of a nation, the different regional, ethnic, occupational, religious, and other communities compound their different activities to make up the national spirit.
>
> (Kallen 1949:117)

Thus the American way was to be sustained by equality of different ethnic groups and the interactions between the 'different but equal.' No single group would dominate the rest and all would function as partially integrated political and economic entities within the boundaries of a common national aspiration and spirit.

THE NEW PLURALISM

Since the mid-1960s there has been a resurgence of the concept of cultural pluralism with a different thrust. As Harry S. Broudy points out, the 'new pluralism' grew out of the attempts to translate the civil rights and Great Society legislation into educational and economic programs. While the new pluralists, as did Kallen, held that the different in our society will be unified into a cohesive democratic nation, their arguments were heavily skewed in favor of demanding that minority cultures, as different but equal groups, be allowed to participate in the various activities of the country on their own terms. Further, the social institutions, particularly schools, were asked to 'take into account the linguistic and other cultural differences that children of minority groups bring to the classroom, and that the schools refrain from imposing the majority culture both in its language and ethos on these children' (1981:232).

Advocates of the new pluralism insisted that participatory democracy is fundamentally pluralistic and that it entails the acceptance of the intrinsic worth of all human beings and their unique individuality. This means that cultural differences between persons should be viewed as differences but not as deficits. Stephen S. and Joan C. Baratz echoed the same sentiment, when they noted that many social science research efforts with minority groups 'have been postulated on an idealized norm of "American behavior" against which all behavior is measured. This norm is defined operationally in terms of the way white-middle-class America is supposed to behave' (1970:31-2). They go on to point out that acceptance of such a norm, in place of legitimate values of a minority group, leads to the belief that to be different from white is to be inferior. And, thus, 'differences in behavior are interpreted as genetic pathology or as the alleged pathology of the environment' (pp.31-2). The deficit view, it is argued, denigrates the worth and dignity of the individual by unjustly and erroneously judging human potentialities and the different ways in which people of other cultures think, learn, communicate, and act.

The notion that 'a difference is not a deficit' is useful in exposing ethnocentric assumptions underlying various social and educational programs in our society. But it is not without difficulty, for it is not always clear just how far the notion should be carried. For example, are we willing to grant that practices of all cultural groups are different but equally valid, and, therefore, we should render no judgments about them? Are we then also willing to admit that the racist practices of the Ku Klux Klan are nothing more than cultural practices different than our own? Here Broudy is right in pointing out

> that social organization necessitates varying degrees of interdependence, whereas cultural diversity that claims complete autonomy for each cultural group can only result in an aggregate of groups with a minimum dependence on each other. Taken seriously and interpreted strictly it leads to cultural separatism or atomism.
>
> (1981:232)

He goes on to say that the advocates of cultural pluralism do not agree on how far toward such separatism they wish to go. Even James Banks, who has written widely in support of cultural pluralism and multicultural education, warns us that 'if carried to its logical extreme, the cultural pluralism argument can be used to justify racism, cultural genocide, and other cultural practices which are antithetical to a democratic society' (1981:229).

While it is not clear what Banks means by 'the cultural pluralism argument,' it is clear that building a cohesive democratic society cannot follow from an argument that, (1) all cultures are equally valid in their own context; (2) there can be no objective standards by which to judge other cultures; and, (3) therefore all cultural groups should be permitted to practice their own ways, regardless of the consequences to the larger society. This, of course, is not the kind of reasoning the supporters of cultural pluralism are advocating. Yet, educators often view cultural pluralism and multicultural education as representing this extreme cultural relativist view, which would allow anything and everything. It is not unusual to find that multicultural education is misunderstood by many to be concerned exclusively with minority problems and/or ethnic studies. The fact that different cultures have different norms does not necessarily imply that values ought to be relative or that there cannot be some objective way of justifying value judgments. Richard Pratte cautions us:

> While it is true that the same action or thing is judged differently in different cultures, it is a major and unwarranted jump from the description of existing relativism to the claim that no objectively valid rational way of justifying basic ethical or value judgments exists.
>
> (1979:51)

In point of fact, those of us who value cultural diversity, and support cultural pluralism, do not view religious bigotry and racial discrimination as practiced by certain groups in America as a matter of cultural difference; rather, we judge them to be unethical and undemocratic.

DEMOCRACY: BASIS FOR CULTURAL PLURALISM

Is cultural pluralism intrinsic to American democracy? The fundamental principles of democracy, as articulated in the Declaration of Independence and the Constitution of the United States, clearly indicate that the founders of the United States believed that each person is to be regarded as an end. It is for this reason that exploitation of any individual or group violates a fundamental democratic maxim. Institutions in American society must be made to serve the individual, not vice versa. In John Dewey's words:

> Democracy has many meanings, but if it has a moral meaning, it is found in resolving that the supreme test of all political institutions and industrial arrangements shall be the contribution they make to the all-around growth of every member of society.   (1939a:127)

To regard each individual as an end is to accept the belief that there is an 'intrinsic connection between the prospects of democracy and belief in the potentialities of human nature — for its own sake' (p.127). In building democracy we must begin with the faith that all people have the capacity to develop and exercise their own intelligence in shaping their own future (Dewey 1939b:49). It is not that these capacities are already formed and ready to be unfolded, but, if given the opportunity, individuals can grow socially, emotionally, and intellectually, so that they cannot only decide what is good for them, but also find the most effective means of attaining it. Hence, democracy 'denotes a state of affairs in which the interest of each in his work is uncoerced and intelligent: based upon its congeniality to his own aptitudes' (Dewey 1961:316). Consequently, freedom of all kinds is essential to democracy, and 'the cause of democratic freedom is the cause of the fullest possible realization of human potentialities' (p.129).

A democratic society is necessarily pluralistic culturally, politically, intellectually, and socially, because it is founded on a belief in the intrinsic worth of individuals and their unique capacities to become intelligent human beings. In this sense, the unique qualities of individuals or groups become assets rather than hindrances. Accordingly, 'there is no physical acid which has the corrosive power possessed by intolerance directed against persons because they belong to a group that bears a certain name' (1939b:127). In a more revolutionary vein, Paulo Freire points out that

[the oppressed or minorities] are treated as individual cases, as marginal men who deviate from the general configuration of a 'good, organized, and just,' society, which must therefore adjust these 'incompetent and lazy folk' to its own patterns by changing their mentality. These marginals need to be 'integrated,' 'incorporated' into the healthy society that they have 'forsaken.'

(1984:106-7)

For Freire, the oppressed — minorities of all sorts — are not 'marginals,' i.e., people living 'outside' society. They have always lived 'inside' the socio-cultural structure which made them 'being for others,' because they did not conform to the norms of the dominant culture. Hence, they were not treated as ends in themselves but, rather, as a means to someone else's end, i.e., objects of exploitation and oppression. The solution, Freire concludes, is not completely to absorb or assimilate minorities into the dominant social structure, but to transform that structure, so that they can enjoy the status of 'being for themselves.' A corollary of this solution, from Dewey's perspective, is that a society must provide the equality of opportunity that will enable individuals to develop their capacities to the fullest possible extent. Hence, 'all individuals are entitled to equality of treatment by law and in its administration. Each one is affected equally in quality if not in quantity by the institutions under which he lives and has an equal right to express his judgment' (Dewey 1939b:403).

While democracy requires an emphasis on personal needs and interests and on varied points of shared common interest, it also demands a recognition of mutual interest as a means of social control. A democratic society should not only encourage free interactions among individuals and groups, but also changes in social habits, that is, continuous readjustment through meeting new situations produced by a wide variety of interactions with others. It is essential that the members of democratic society recognize that the needs of others are as important to them as their own are. This recognition is a necessary prerequisite for effective handling of conflicts among individuals and groups.

Conflicts in interests and values are bound to arise in a society which has diverse cultural elements. But, since no single group is to rule over others, and because of our implicit faith in the human capacity for intelligent behavior, democracy requires a method of resolving conflicts by inquiry, discussion, and persuasion, rather than by violence. This approach to conflict resolution is reminiscent of Jurgen Habermas's notion of an 'ideal speech situation,' in which all persons have equal opportunity to express their views, so that all sides of an issue can be heard, and that the validity of the consensus thus reached is dependent upon the soundness of what has been said, but not on the authority nor the social status of the speakers. Hence, education that befits this kind of society must cultivate reflective thinking and critical inquiry, which will enable a person to raise questions about the meaning of what has been learned, as well as the assumptions upon which our knowledge and socio-cultural practices are founded.

A central problem of cultural pluralism is how minority groups can maintain enough separation from the dominant culture to perpetuate and develop their own ethnic traditions without, at the same time, interfering with the execution of their standard responsibilities to the American society of which they are also members. That is, how can cultural diversity and unity be maintained simultaneously, particularly when conflicts arise between the society at large and these sub-units?

DIFFERENCES ARE NOT DEFICITS

According to Clifford Geertz, 'Culture is best seen not as complexes of concrete behavior patterns — customs, usages, traditions, habit clusters, as has, by and large, been the case up to now, but as a set of control mechanisms — plans, recipes, rules, instructions (what computer engineers call "programs") — for governing behavior' (1973:44). Hence, the culture of society consists of the standards and control mechanisms with which its members assign meaning, values, and significance to things, events, and behaviors. These standards and controls have been established because they enable the members of that society to deal with the needs and problems which arise out of their environment and association with others. Cultures, then, can be seen as different ways of dealing with essentially similar problems and needs. They represent the successful experiments in living of various societies which have been built over time. Human beings become individuals 'under the guidance of cultural patterns, historically created systems of meaning in terms of which we give form, order, point, and direction to our lives' (Benedict 1934:278). The culture to which one belongs, then, becomes the root of the individual's identity. Hence, to reject or demean a person's cultural heritage is to do psychological and moral violence to the dignity and worth of that individual.

If we conclude that cultures are successful experiments in living of various societies, we can argue that the patterns of beliefs and behaviors found in various societies have no intrinsic meanings apart from their cultural context, for such patterns are reflections of unique world views and value orientations belonging to individual societies. In this sense, as Ruth Benedict (1934) and Melville Herskovits (1973) have pointed out, cultures are equally valid patterns of life and every set of cultural norms is valid only for the people who have them. Hence, it would be unreasonable to argue that any one set of cultural norms is universally good for all societies or is inherently superior to all other cultures.

As was suggested earlier, we become individuals through our culture. And because our culture is so much a part of what we are and what we do, we often view it as if it were innate, or an absolute by which all individuals must guide their lives. Thus, ethnocentrism leads us to judge others in terms of our own cultural norms, which makes it difficult for us to see that other cultures are also effective means of dealing with the needs and problems of the respective societies. This attitude, of course, inclines us to conclude that those who do not conform to our norms must be stupid, depraved, irresponsible, psychopathic, inferior, or sinful, to a point beyond all redemption, and to define American culture in terms of being white and competent, in terms of the stereotypic Anglo-American traits. It is this implicit but pervasive deficit view in the American culture which forces many minority individuals to be ashamed of their ethnicity and cultural heritage. At best, ethnocentrism and the deficit view rob society of richness.

Cultural diversity is enriching in at least two ways. One is that human life becomes much more interesting, stimulating, and even exciting, when there are many varied ways of thinking, feeling, expressing, acting, and viewing the world. Second, and perhaps more importantly, given the range in kinds and complexity of human needs and wants, the more alternative problem-solving approaches there are the more we are likely to find solutions which may enable us to live our lives in an increasingly effective way. Cultural differences as alternative ways of dealing with essentially similar problems present us with a wide variety of options from which we can learn. Thomas Green concurs in saying that no one person or group's way of life is so rich that it may not be further enriched by contact with other points of view: 'The conviction is that diversity is enriching because no man has a monopoly on the truth about the good life. There are many ways. Diversity is further valued because it provides any society with a richer pool of leadership from which to draw in times of crisis' (1966:10).

In sum, the deficit model of viewing minority cultures is unfair to groups and individuals, for it not only leads to erroneous judgments about human potentialities and their realization but it impedes the development of a just cultural democracy. What is tacitly implied in all this is the view that the worth of a culture is not based solely on the fact that it is 'ours,' but that our cultural patterns (norms) have enabled us to achieve our purposes.

DIFFERENCES ARE NOT MERE DIFFERENCES

On the basis of the foregoing, we may conclude that all cultures do their job. However, from the fact that particular behaviors and belief patterns have been worked out by a given culture as a means of dealing with its problems, we should not conclude that such patterns are necessarily the best possible ways of meeting the human needs in that society. Nor should we even insist that a particular practice which has worked well in one cultural setting will be equally effective in a different cultural setting.

Ample evidence exists to suggest that some cultural practices, particularly in highly technological societies, while fulfilling immediate needs, have long-term consequences which are counterproductive. The culture of a society that selects its means of problem solving chiefly in terms of its immediate utility may face many complex and unsuspected outcomes which may be self-defeating to the fundamental goals of that society. That is, cultural patterns can be judged in terms of the effectiveness with which they enable the members of that society to deal with their problems. This implies that some cultures may be more effective than others. Similarly, some cultures may be more maladaptive and self-defeating than others and that those cultural practices which tend to be self-defeating need to be modified, abandoned, or even prohibited. Clearly, tenacious adherence to one's own cultural practice in a radically different cultural context may be self-defeating. We should not consider the use of maladaptive and self-defeating patterns as merely a matter of applying different but equally valid cultural norms.

As Harry Broudy (1981) pointed out above, social organization necessitates varying degrees of interdependence. Members of a democratic society (no matter how imperfect it may be) must be concerned about the consequences of actions performed for the purpose of achieving personal objectives. The merit of actions should be tested in terms of personal goals, which, in turn, should be examined according to the fundamental principles upon which American democracy is founded, i.e., the principle of freedom and equal opportunity, justice, and rights for all. In the final analysis, personal or cultural practices which are contradictory to these ideals of participatory democracy will affect everyone's life. If one's own cultural norms sanction exploitation of others, limit their freedom and equality, such practices can no longer be justified in the name of cultural pluralism, because they are self-defeating, both at the personal and societal levels. Indeed, the degree to which our actions violate the rights and freedom of others, to that degree our own freedom and rights are diminished. It is in this sense that certain practices of various cultural groups may not be viewed as simply cultural differences.

In the context of our discussion, all sorts of cultural practices are permissible, in so far as they do not violate the basic tenets of participatory democracy, because 'cultural pluralism is characterized by a commitment to the worth of cultural diversity and factions promoting an agenda of politics, but it goes beyond the promotion of the values of cultural subgroups to the forming of a public as the result of a recognition of a problematic situation having direct and indirect consequences' (Pratte 1979:151). Democracy requires not only an emphasis on personal needs and interests and on various points of shared common interest, but also a recognition of mutual interest as a means of social control. A democratic society should not only encourage free interactions among individuals and groups but also changes in social habits; that is, continuous readjustments through meeting new situations produced by a wide variety of interactions with others.

ROLE OF THE DOMINANT GROUP

While value conflicts between groups should be resolved according to majority rule, society should avoid such conflicts as much as possible by giving the groups many alternatives from which to choose their own courses of action. For example, one can choose to learn the dominant language and behavior patterns and work outside of one's ethnic group, or one can choose to remain in the ethnic enclave and carry on a trade that would serve primarily the members of that community. A constantly recurring theme of cultural pluralism is the belief that no single group should impose its own pattern as the only idealized norm for every other group.

Cultural pluralism, as a social ideal to preserve each ethnic group's cultural distinctiveness within the context of American citizenship, may be viewed as involving contradictory social practices. To maintain one's unique cultural traits, a person must maintain the most meaningful personal relationships with his or her group. But, if an individual is to achieve social, political, and economic status in the larger society, he or she must also participate in the processes of the dominant culture. Whether or not these practices are contradictory to each other is quite debatable. What seems to have happened in America is that many members of minority groups have shed much of their cultural distinctiveness. Yet they carry on only minimal interactions with other minority groups or with the dominant society.

On the basis of the foregoing discussion, it would be quite legitimate to ask if cultural pluralism is in fact an achievable ideal. Some argue that America is approaching an open society, rather than a culturally pluralistic society (Green 1966:25). That is, while a pluralistic society encourages cultural differences, an open society regards cultural differences as no longer relevant in determining the worth or merit of individuals. Hence, America as an open society should emphasize individual equality and national unity rather than cultural diversity, so that each member of any given minority group can form his or her identity as a citizen of the country rather than as a member of a subculture.

While America may be approaching the state wherein the individual's position and merit are evaluated in terms of equality and competence, it is little help to tell nonwhite minorities that their identity should be achieved in terms of their status as citizens of the nation. They find that their status as Americans is still affected by their color and ethnic backgrounds. At the same time, many discover that they belong to neither the dominant white culture nor their own ethnic group and consequently they see themselves as dislocated and alienated. This condition is particularly common among today's younger generation of minority cultures, whose self-image is not intimately bound up with their legal citizenship in the United States. Members of ethnic minority groups must be helped to develop pride in their own racial and cultural heritages, to achieve their identity as unique human beings. This is nearly impossible to achieve without the earnest and persistent attempts by the dominant group, not only to appreciate the worth of other cultures but, also, critically to examine the fundamental assumptions upon which the dominant norms rest, for the deficit model of viewing others is deeply embedded in the dominant culture. As Henry A. Giroux (1983) expressed it cogently:

> Culture as a political phenomenon refers to the power of specific meanings, message systems, and social practices in order to 'lay the psychological and moral foundations for the economic and political system they control.' Within the dominant culture, meaning is universalized and the historically contingent nature of social reality appears as self-evident and fixed....
>
> (p.196)

In a multicultural and democratic society, such as America,

it is not enough to propose that an individual be evaluated according to merit and competence alone, for the criteria of merit and competence are defined in terms of the dominant norms alone. Indeed, we must regard cultural diversity as an asset to be developed, for no one can escape from the racial and cultural backgrounds that inexorably govern one's view of oneself. Hence, the willingness of the dominant group to understand and analyze its own culture critically is equally important in building a democratic society which is open and self-correcting.

Finally, a sound concept of cultural pluralism should not be based on the desirability of cultural diversity alone; it should be founded on unity as a basis. This unity should not come from establishing the linguistic, ethical, and behavioral patterns of the mainstream culture as the only idealized norms for all individuals. Rather, the unity should be based on the acceptance by the members of both minority and dominant cultures of the belief that all human beings are to be regarded as ends in themselves, so that no person can be exploited by other individuals or institutions.

MULTICULTURAL EDUCATION

The belief that multicultural education is necessary to a democratic society is based on the implicit assumption that a person's basic intellectual and emotional disposition toward nature and others can be formed or changed through education. In other words, cultural pluralists hope to bring about a fundamental change in the attitude of American people toward cultures that are different from their own through 'establishing a mutually supportive relationship within the boundaries or framework of one nation of people of diverse cultures' (Hazard and Stent 1973:14). Such an education must provide a genuinely representative and balanced account of the contributions made by diverse culture groups in the making of this country in the context of a critical understanding of the past and the present. It is especially essential to help learners abandon the belief that there is a single style of living that befits everyone. One way to do this is by cultivating the attitude that their own modes of behavior and belief are as important and functional to them as other patterns are to others.

PRIVATE CULTURE, SYNCRETISM, AND MULTICULTURAL EDUCATION FOR ADULTS

In order to live effectively and in an enriching way, one not only needs to know about other cultural patterns but also how to reconcile the diverse patterns, so that a new and unique approach to life may emerge. Here we find the concepts of private culture and syncretism to be useful.

As every society has a culture, so may we speak of each person as having his/her own private 'culture,' which may include awareness of several distinct 'cultures' of other individuals. These cultural awarenesses within a person's private culture represent the individual's perceptions of how other human beings have organized their experiences, based on the standards by which others perceive, predict, judge, and act (Goodenough 1963). It is through our knowledge of the private cultures of our associates that we learn to accomplish those goals that are best achieved through working together. Hence, a person's private culture may include knowledge of several language patterns, norms of conduct and valuation, and procedures for getting things done. Depending upon the nature of one's purpose and its context, the individual often moves from one set of cultural concepts to another within one's repertoire. For example, if this paper had been written for a sixth-grade audience, the author would have used a different 'language.'

If a person operates rigidly in terms of a single culture (e.g., using standard English in a multiethnic community), he/she will be less effective in accomplishing desired purposes. This suggests that the greater one's breadth of cultural awareness, and the more flexible a person is in shifting from one appropriate cultural context to another, the more successful that person will be in achieving desired outcomes. Frequent inter-ethnic contact is important, for it tends to increase the number of other cultural orientations within the private culture of an individual.

Typically, a person uses only a limited number of cultural orientations in his/her repertoire. If the dominant culture views other cultural patterns as deficits, the number of alternative cultural orientations that an individual could use would be limited to those the mainstream culture regards as legitimate. Minority children, for example, may be pressured, implicitly or explicitly, to reject their own language and use only standard English. Rejection of their language patterns as a low-status form reinforces the negative image minority children have of their own culture and personal identity. One of the problems of the deficit view for minorities is that, the more one conforms exclusively to the dominant (the 'right') norm, the more one crushes self-esteem and pride in one's own identity. Ethnocentrism (the deficit view) not only robs richness from both the dominant and minority cultures, but also increases alienation and socio-psychological conflicts.

If the goal of democratic education is to develop each individual's potential and to aid in building a social order that can make life secure and enriching for all, then neither total assimilationism nor separatism is the answer. Notwithstanding the importance of minority cultures to many Americans, the norms of the dominant culture are likely to prevail in many activities of the larger society. It would indeed be unrealistic to suggest that minority groups ignore the dominant culture, but it is equally unreasonable to demand that members of minority cultures divest themselves of their own distinctiveness. What is needed is the preservation and enrichment of minority cultures, as well as reconciliation of these patterns with those of the dominant culture. However, the notion of 'preservation and extension' should not be understood as a reactionary, 'back-to-the-blanket' move; rather, it should be seen as a syncretic process.

'Syncretism is the reconciliation of two or more cultural systems or elements, with the modification of both' (Burger 1966:103). This conception is not the same as the 'melting' of distinctive cultures into one allegedly superior one. Syncretism refers to the development of a new and unique culture (private or societal) and a new personal identity by interweaving different cultural elements together. For example, an Asian-American youth may discard the unquestioning obedience to elders and become more self-assertive, but may retain the part of Asian culture that encourages one to be less egocentric and think in terms of relationships with others. This person is neither an Asian in America, nor an imitation of the white American, but has emerged as a new Asian-American.

What we learn about other cultures is not classified neatly into different cultural pigeon holes in our mind and that a right pattern is pulled out of an appropriate category when a situation calls for a particular way of acting. In consonance with the preceding discussion, our knowledge of, and experience in, other cultures become integrated into the complex terrains of a private culture. Hence, acting appropriately in different situations (acting biculturally or multiculturally) requires not only knowledge of divergent patterns, but also an ability to evaluate the situation, formulate possible options available in relation to one's goals, and then to make a critical judgment, choosing that option which will help us achieve the present objective as a means of accomplishing future goals. Multicultural education should be seen as the process by which each individual can learn to live in a progressively effective and enriching way by acquiring cognitive understanding and significant experiences of a wide range of cultural patterns. Thus, a primary objective of multicultural education should be the increase of the individual's cultural repertoire in his/her private culture, as well as developing the skill with which one can reconcile divergent patterns so that a new and unique approach to life may emerge. This should indeed be a central goal of lifelong learning.

The above view of multicultural education, based on the preceding discussions of private culture and syncretism, implies the centrality of critical and reflective thinking about one's own ways and those of others in selecting and developing the most appropriate and effective means to achieve one's many varied ends. In a sense, this approach to multicultural education is similar to what Jack Mezirow (1984) calls 'perspective transformation.' According to Mezirow, this is the process of becoming aware of the ways in which existing socio-cultural and psychological assumptions, processes, and patterns, have inhibited the development of human potentialities. 'It is the learning process by which adults come to recognize their culturally induced dependency roles and relationships and the reasons for them, and take action to overcome them' (p.124).

Mezirow explains that this process of perspective transformation could occur as a result of a sudden insight into the cultural and psychological assumptions and patterns which limit our role and development or 'by a series of transitions which permit one to revise specific assumptions about oneself and others until the very structure of assumptions become transformed' (pp.125-6). This process of transformation is much more than simply identifying oneself with a new reference group or accepting a different set of norms by which one acts and relates to others. It is the process in which one's experiences and thinking become more inclusive, discriminating, and integrating, as well as becoming 'sufficiently permeable to allow one access to other perspectives' (p.127). This is, and should be, an important characteristic of adult education. One cannot help but think that increasing the number of cultural orientations in one's repertoire, through culturally diverse experiences, is an essential prerequisite to the process of perspective transformation (emancipatory action).

Conflicts in interest and values are bound to rise in a society like America that has many diverse cultural elements. Hence, we are constantly in a position of having to interact with individuals who do not share our own system of norms and beliefs. Thus, we can no longer depend on our own cultural ways to gain reliable reading of what others are going to do next or how we can deal effectively with our own life problems. In a culturally diverse society, all of its members may need to modify some of their ways by going beyond their own culture. To do this, we need to understand the dominant as well as minority cultures in terms of their points of agreements, disagreements, and even conflicts with our own norms, so that there may emerge new and unique cultural patterns consonant with the fundamental ideals of participatory democracy. But we cannot normally go beyond our own culture without 'first exposing its major hidden axioms, and unstated assumptions concerning what life is about — how it is lived, viewed and analyzed, talked about, described and changed' (Hall 1976:195). 'Helping adults construe experience in a way in which they may more clearly understand the reasons for their problems and understand the options open to them [through critical understanding of their own culture and those of others] so that they may assume responsibility for decision making is the essence of [multicultural] education' (Mezirow 1984:135).

REFERENCES

Banks, James (1981) 'Cultural pluralism and the schools,' in J.M. Rich (ed.) *Innovations in Education*, Boston: Allyn & Bacon.

Baratz, S.S. and Baratz, J.C. (1970) 'Early childhood intervention: the social science base of institutional racism,' *Harvard Education Review* 40.

Benedict, Ruth (1934) *Patterns of Culture*, Boston: Houghton Mifflin.

Broudy, H.S. (1981) 'Cultural pluralism: new wine in old bottles,' in J.M. Rich (ed.) *Innovations in Education*, Boston: Allyn & Bacon.

Burger, H. (1966) 'Syncretism, an acculturative accelerator,' *Human Organization* 25.

Dewey, John (1939a) *Freedom and Culture*, New York: Capricorn Books.

——(1939b) 'The modes of social life,' in Joseph Ratner (ed.)

Intelligence in the Modern World, New York: Random House.

——(1961) *Democracy and Education*, New York: Macmillan.

Freire, Paulo (1984) 'Pedagogy of the oppressed,' in Sharan B. Merriam (ed.) *Selected Writings on Philosophy and Adult Education*, Malabar, Florida: Robert Krieger.

Geertz, C. (1973) *The Interpretation of Cultures*, New York: Basic Books.

Giroux, Henry A. (1983) *Theory & Resistance in Education*, South Hadley, Mass.: Bergin & Garvey.

Goodenough, W. (1963) *Cooperation in Change*, New York: Russell Sage Foundation.

Green, Thomas (1966) *Education and Pluralism: Ideal and Reality*, Twenty-Sixth Annual J. Richard Street Lecture, Syracuse, NY: Syracuse University School of Education.

Hall, E.T. (1976) *Beyond Culture*, Garden City, NY: Anchor Press/Doubleday.

Hazard, William R. and Stent, M.D. (1973) 'Cultural pluralism and schooling: some preliminary observations,' in William R. Hazard, Madelon D. Stent, and Henry N. Rivling (eds) *Cultural Pluralism in Education*, Englewood Cliffs, NJ: Prentice-Hall.

Herskovits, M.J. (1973) *Cultural Relativism*, New York: Vintage Books.

Kallen, Horace N. (1949) *The Education of Free Men*, New York: Farrar & Straus.

Mezirow, Jack (1984) 'A critical theory of adult learning and education,' in Sharan B. Merriam (ed.) *Selected Writings on Philosophy and Adult Education*, Malabar, Florida: Robert Krieger.

Pratte, Richard (1979) *Pluralism in Education*, Springfield, Ohio: Charles Thomas.

Chapter Two

MULTICULTURALISM IN EDUCATION:
THE IMPORTANCE OF MEANING

Charles A. Tesconi Jr

In 1782, when *E Pluribus Unum* was adopted as a motto, it
referred to the confederation of the original thirteen colonies.
Today, it is invoked to affirm the ties that seemingly bind the
diverse people who make up this country. 'One from many,'
however, evokes a plethora of issues and concerns about
cultural diversity and its place and prospects in the making of
a healthier America. The issues have a long history, given
diversity as a fact of American life since its beginnings.

The original colonies of the seventeenth century were
made up of various nationalities, religious traditions, and cults.
It has been estimated that among the total white population at
the time of the Revolution, some 2.5 to three million people,
as much as one-third may have been foreign born. This
estimate, derived from the first federal census taken in 1790,
did indicate a clear predominance of English stock in the
white population. Upwards of 50 percent had English and
Protestant origins. Though comparatively fewer in number,
there were, nevertheless, substantial groups of Germans,
Scots-Irish, Dutch, French, Canadians, Belgians, Swiss,
Swedes, Poles, and a scattering of people from other primarily
European countries. Catholics were represented in small
numbers, concentrated mostly in the middle colonies, and a
small number of Jews were scattered throughout the colonies.
The French were both Huguenots and Roman Catholics; the
Germans were primarily Lutherans, Moravians, and Dunkers;
the Dutch were Calvinists; the Swedes Lutheran; and the
English, Scots, Welsh, and Scots-Irish populations embraced
Episcopalians, Congregationalists, Presbyterians, Methodists,
Quakers, and a few Jews and Roman Catholics.

This diversity was not seen as a threat to, nor an assimilative problem for, the dominant and presumed American
cultural standard — the Anglo tradition. It was thought that
non-Anglo whites would easily adjust to, and assimilate in, the

dominant mainstream, given the wide-open spaces of the new nation, in such a fashion as to be non-visible and, hence, non-threatening. In short, the rich and vast wide open spaces became thoroughfares of escape for both those who refused to assimilate and, figuratively, for the young country not wishing to confront the problem directly. Blacks, who at the time of the Revolution comprised nearly one-fifth of the total population (757,208 were recorded in the 1790 Census), and Native Americans, contributed to the diversity but, as we all know, they were disdained as candidates for citizenship and, thus, ignored in these matters.

This comparatively modest diversity, however striking, because of the inattention to it in our school textbooks, was to grow in complexity in subsequent years, given, among other things, the so-called First and Second Waves of Immigration (around 1830 to 1860, and 1890 to 1920). The continuing steady flow of newcomers — Hispanics and Asians most visibly in recent years — points to an apparent American tolerance for diversity (life styles, dress, regional subcultures, etc.) beyond that typically associated with ethnic and cultural groupings.

In any case, it seems that perennial and new issues and concerns about ethnic, cultural, and other kinds of diversity, emerge during periods when newcomers arrive in what appear to be inordinately high numbers, under odd or politically disputatious circumstances (Haitian, Cuban, Laotian, Cambodian, and Vietnamese 'boat people'), and/or when they reveal attachment to ways seemingly quite alien to what is familiar to the settled population and appear impervious to assimilative forces.

The old and new concerns force renewed attention to the most central question: How does a nation with no one clear cultural standard, no one race, no one history, no one ethnic stock, and with numerous languages, continue to exist as one? This, in turn, evokes other questions. Should the diverse ethnic and other cultural groups be treated in ways which might generate a new monoculture out of that diversity? Have these groups, in fact, been treated in ways which indeed did produce a new culture out of the diversity? Should diverse groups be expected to reject their cultural trappings, in favor of some larger and dominating cultural standard? Is it historically the case that these groups have indeed been expected, as a prerequisite for entering the mainstream of society, to reject their cultures? Should the many different ethnic and cultural groups be treated in ways which serve to preserve, and locate as a social and cultural resource, the various cultures they represent? Or has this in fact been the case, historically, in our country? How should schools function relative to cultural diversity?

While each era raised these important questions, it also seems to be the case that a particular set of descriptive and prescriptive answers has come to prevail, in the midst of others, during each era. In short, each era seemed to favor a set of descriptors and prescriptors which purported to explain what was happening, and what had happened historically, while offering a prescription for what should happen. Each of these, in turn, came to represent a convergence of ideas, ideals, sentiments, and sanctions, which, by implication if nothing else, spoke to how public and education policy ought to function in regard to diversity.

ANALYSIS OF CONCEPTS

The assumptions suggested above regarding the presumed Anglo and northern European standard provided the foundation for what has come to be known as the Anglo-Core Culture Conformity (ACCC) paradigm. Partly descriptive and partly prescriptive, ACCC saw the American culture as an essentially finished product, in an Anglo-Saxon-Teutonic mold. Indeed, the mere expression of concern which we hear every now and then that some elements in the population might not become 'Americanized' implies the existence of some settled standard of what is 'American.' ACCC suggests that the essentials of that standard were and are demarcated by heavy lines.

Some people contend that finding that 'standard' is difficult, if not impossible. Many reasons are offered to support this claim, but pre-eminent among them are those associated with another descriptor and prescriptor, one that has also been around for quite some time, but which seems to have been best articulated when a 1909 hit Broadway play, *The Melting Pot*, written by Israel Zangwill, gave it a name.

As early as 1782, the French-born American farmer, J. Hector St John de Crèvecoeur, after several years of residence in America, expressed, in what has become a classic statement, the essence of the conception of America as a melting pot. In characterizing the nature of the American, Crèvecoeur observed:

> He is either European, or the descendant of a European; hence that strange mixture of blood, which you will find in no other country. I could point out to you a family

whose grandfather was an Englishman, whose wife was Dutch, whose son married a French woman, and whose present four sons have now four wives of different nations. He is an American, who leaving behind him all his ancient prejudices and manners, receives new ones from the new mode of life he has embraced, the new government he obeys, and the new rank he holds. He becomes an American by being received into a new race of men, whose labours and posterity will one day cause great changes in the world.

(1925:54-5)

The notion that the various ethnic, racial, and cultural groups would fuse together, producing a new people and a new civilization, has had compelling appeal since the earliest days of the United States. Its enduring allure has been sustained by the view that America, as a continuous experiment in democratic living, leads quite naturally into a melting pot process. The rich and spacious environment, the formal checks and balances over political institutions, the traditions associated with liberty, the informal but cherished balances which come from the push and pull of competing interest groups, the varieties of peoples from all over the earth — all these elements are contained in the appeal of the Melting Pot (MP) ideal. It evokes a sense of the might and beauty of America that inspires reverence.

Support for the MP, as both a descriptive and prescriptive conception, is not limited to the sanctimony of the 'experiment in democratic living.' This perspective gains in credibility when one considers, for example, the elementary fact that, from the beginning, conditions in America obviously modified the institutions, values, etc., which immigrants brought with them. This has held true, to some extent, through all the periods of immigration. 'Resident' Americans had an impact on the newcomers and the latter, in turn, had an impact on their hosts. It was, and is, impossible to transport, unmodified, one culture to another society. Was, and is it not possible, then, to think of American civilization as one in a continual process of evolution, not a slightly modified England, but rather as a totally new blend, culturally and biologically, in which the society and cultures brought by all immigrants merge with each other and with that of the receiving hosts in a continual process of 'becoming?' Many observers of the American scene, early and recent, saw what was happening as just this and proposed that it be recognized and prescribed in matters of education and public policy.

The MP notion remains much more attractive to most thinkers than the Anglo-Core Conformity model. The latter connotes imposition and superiority; the former accommodation, egalitarianism, and destiny. However, many see both as at least implying policies and strategies which eventually rob America of a richness otherwise found in the mere social fact of diversity and an educational and cultural resource in the celebration of it. The MP might be close to being a natural process, but, say these thinkers, it ought not to be allowed to proceed apace by supportive public and education policies. Indeed, these would argue that it should be put to rest by a public and social philosophy which supports 'cultural pluralism.'

Cultural Pluralism (CP) as an answer to the issues and concerns of diversity was first presented in an article by Horace Kallen, 'Democracy versus the Melting Pot,' in the *Nation* in February 1915. It was at once an attack upon the ACCC model and an expression of disdain for the MP notion. The former was seen as an unwelcome imposition, the latter as a kind of preposterous alphabet soup denouement. Intellectuals who have advocated CP see it as an expression of the democratic ideal which, if put into practice, could only serve to enrich the civilization of America.

CP as an expression of democracy, and as an attempt to reconcile the contradictions of, or totally eliminate, the influence of the melting pot and Anglo-conformity conceptions, was rooted in the conviction that:

> There is no such thing as humanity in general, into which the definite, heterogeneous, living creature can be melted down.... There is no human mould in America to which the spiritual stuff of the immigrant is to be patterned. Not only is there as yet no fixed and final type, but there never can be.... The very genius of democracy, moreover, must lead us to desire the widest possible range of variability, the greatest attainable differentiation of individuality, among our population.... The business of America is to get rid of mechanical uniformity, and, by encouraging the utmost possible differentiation through mental and psychic cross-fertilization to attain a higher level of humanity.
>
> (Horace J. Bridges, quoted in Handlin 1959:155-6)

Those who advocated CP argued that the melting pot and Anglo-conformity conceptions led to ethnic self-hatred, with all its debilitating social-psychological consequences, including family disorganization, crime, and juvenile delinquency. Both were regarded as lacking any shred of insight into the needs of the ethnics. The melting pot, like Anglo-conformity, moved one to turn one's back on that which made one a person. Cultural groups, claim the cultural pluralists, are adversely affected by both conceptions, for each, ultimately, constitutes an attack upon their language, institutions, and their very conceptions of themselves as individuals and members of a particular group. Cultural pluralists argue that one's group must be free to bring its contributions, its strengths, its values, etc., to a larger democratic process. If the group is not permitted to do this, because of Anglo-conformity or melting pot demands, then democracy does not exist. Kallen put it this way:

> [Cultural pluralism as following from the democratic ideal] neither deprives the human person of his dynamic relations with his neighbors, nor converts the ever-ongoing communications between them to a pre-ordained ineluctable harmony. On the contrary, it recognizes that the relations do relate with identifying; that the communications do truly inform and persuade without coercing. It signalizes them as the ways that people who are different from one another do, in fact, come together and move apart, forming and dissolving the groups and societies wherewith they secure to one another their diverse safety and happiness.... It is what the Democratic Idea intends, and designates the cultural idea natural to a free world.
>
> (1956:51)

Kallen's argument speaks not only to the reality of ethnic communities, in spite of the drives for assimilation, but it recognizes how members of these communities, while learning the language of general communication and participating in the larger society, nevertheless express their desire and need for group identification. It is interesting to note in this regard that advocates of CP have addressed themselves to the existence of ethnic communities and cultural diversity as a social reality, as evidence of both the impracticality of assimilation efforts and the human desire for belonging.

It is probably safe to say that each of these perspectives contains some truths. Given the major language of the United States, its English tradition of liberty and institutional limitations on the powers of government, its values, and the like, it can be said that Americans are Anglo in many ways. It is also true that they are unique culturally and otherwise and, thus, that a melting process or stewing process of some sort has been, and is, at work. One might even argue, given such contingencies as an ultimate limit on the varieties and numbers of cultural groups that can be brought to American shores, that, in some far distant time, Americans might be able to claim without reservation that a melting pot indeed had been at work. If nothing else, the melting pot notion bespeaks of open-endedness, of becoming. Perhaps it is in process and Americans just cannot fathom it all — yet. On the other hand, the reality of ethnic and other cultural diversity lends truth to the perspective of cultural pluralism. We all know just how persistent ethnic and cultural identity are, how much has not melted through imposition or otherwise. Consider some features of American diversity:

— Americans worship in over 220 denominations.
— Many Americans do not worship at all.
— There are at least three prominent categories of racial membership.
— There are well over 120 national groups.
— Within each national group numerous subdivisions exist (over 100 among Native Americans alone).
— There are at least six, perhaps more, regional subcultures, often with large differences in dialect and life style.
— Individuals hold membership in many of these groups simultaneously.
— There are numerous subcultures of age, socioeconomic class, and sex.

In any case, truth or partial truth in the descriptive aspects of these perspectives is one thing; deciding upon which one ought to prevail as a guiding philosophy is another.

ASSUMPTIONS OF MULTICULTURAL EDUCATION

The diversity alluded to above has been the basis of efforts to re-invoke the cultural pluralism prescription, albeit with a new term. Congress, the courts, educational organizations, and numerous professional and citizen groups, have argued in the light of it that public schools must prepare individuals to appreciate, value, and function effectively, in a diverse society. This recognition has been translated into educational policies and practices which reflect the conviction that individuals must have a deeper understanding of their cultural heritages and those of others, that prejudices must be minimized, and the appreciation of all differences maximized.

These and other related efforts, it is claimed, will create a more 'harmonious, patriotic, and committed populace' (Title IX, Ethnic Heritages Act, 1974).

'Multicultural education' is the currently favored term employed to label these efforts. As set forth by the National Council for the Accreditation of Teacher Education (1979), multicultural education is

> preparation for the social, political, and economic realities individuals experience in culturally diverse and complex human encounters. These realities have both national and international dimensions. This preparation provides a process by which an individual develops competencies for perceiving, believing, evaluating, and behaving, in differential cultural settings. Thus, multicultural education is viewed as an intervention and an ongoing assessment process to help institutions and individuals become more responsive to the human condition, individual cultural integrity, and cultural pluralism, in society.

Educational policies and practices derived from this broad concept vary widely, as would be expected. But all tend to subsume matters associated with the following:

— knowledge of cultures and subcultures, with emphasis on significant minority groups,
— awareness of how specific cultures shape student responses to schooling,
— minimization of prejudice and maximization of tolerance for different others,
— adjustments in curricula aimed at promoting non-assimilationist strategies and values.

'Multicultural education' is derived from the term 'multiculturalism.' It is important to recognize that the latter term possesses a descriptive meaning, carrying ideological connotations, and suggesting a particular forging of social and educational policy. Multicultural education is one derivative of the prescriptive meaning. In these ways, the term multiculturalism is not unlike the other terms, concepts, and paradigms, employed in American social, political, and educational discourse regarding the state of cultural differences in American society. Specifically, multiculturalism, as with ACCC and the MP, is at once offered as a descriptor regarding the state of cultural differences in American society and as a prescriptor in terms of what should be done relative to such differences.

As a descriptive term, multiculturalism speaks to a condition of numerous ways of living, numerous and different values and belief systems. It points to a condition of living, wherein a society is a complex interlocking of numerous and diverse cultural groups whose members pursue diverse interests through the medium of private associations, which in turn are coordinated, negotiated, encouraged or discouraged, guided or misguided, through the push and pull of interest group politics.

As a prescriptive term, weighted with ideological values, multiculturalism borrows heavily from the theory of cultural pluralism and holds that any human society is best served by maximizing, or at least maintaining, the distinctiveness of different tastes and values, not only in the political and economic realms, but in the religious, ethnic, racial, and linguistic, as well. In this sense of the word, the cultural differences pointed to in the descriptive sense are held to have equal validity.

Several premises provide the foundation for translating the descriptive and prescriptive meanings of multiculturalism into education policy and practice:

— Multiculturalism is a fact of American civilization (the descriptive meaning of the term).
— Multiculturalism is a resource that ought to be preserved, if not extended, in American society (the prescriptive and ideological meaning of the term).
— By treating diverse cultural groups and ways of life as equally legitimate, by teaching about them in positive ways, and by legitimizing these differences through various education policies and practices, we promote self-understanding, self-esteem, and intergroup understanding and harmony.
— The school is society's major socialization agent and it is the logical, if not natural, place (prescriptive/ideological) to preserve and perhaps extend this resource.

It is interesting to note that these premises are virtually the same as those embedded in cultural pluralism ideology and in efforts to ensure such pluralism is accommodated in educational policy and practice. In short, proponents of multicultural education have wittingly or unwittingly embroidered their advocacy with the tenets of cultural pluralism.

The heavy reliance on CP reflects the need for multicultural education proponents to carve out a unique theoretical foundation for multiculturalism and multicultural education. Otherwise, multicultural education advocates are vulnerable to the limitations which inhere in CP; that is, questions and challenges which can be directed at CP are also appropriately raised relative to multiculturalism and multicultural education. It is to these that we now turn.

It should come as no surprise that multiculturalism (in its prescriptive sense), and multicultural education, are causing controversy and confusion. After all, the term 'cultural pluralism' and its ideology are as controversial and illusive today as they were in the 1950s, when Horace Kallen sought to clarify their meaning some five decades after he had introduced them (Kallen 1956). Kallen recognized that the wide-ranging sociopolitical implications of CP would attract much attention and criticism. CP speaks primarily to the way in which a society should be organized, and the manner in which oncoming generations should be socialized. Most significant, the term and ideology were introduced during a time when assimilationist ideology fueled public and education policy.

Despite a growing body of literature calling for the incorporation of cultural pluralism theory in all institutional sectors, particularly those which serve as major agents of socialization, there is no comprehensive, systematic analysis of this theory. Indeed, the effects of living in a culturally pluralistic society upon the developing, as well as the adult human being, are, for the most part, unknown. Milton Gordon pointed out in 1961 what remains essentially accurate today, in spite of the wider use of the term cultural pluralism, and its central role in the formation of education policy, 'No close analytical attention has been given either by social scientists or practitioners of inter-group relations to the meaning of cultural pluralism, its nature and relevance for a modern industrialized society, and its implications for problems of prejudice and discrimination' (1961:90).

Nevertheless, demands for promoting a greater cultural pluralism, heard today largely in terms of multicultural education, grow louder every day. And the promises of cultural pluralism ideology, in spite of reliance on untested assumptions, are used to legitimize these demands.

Several interrelated assumptions underlie cultural pluralism ideology and hence its step-child, multiculturalism. We shall look at five of these which relate directly or indirectly to socialization processes and goals and to group diversity.[1]

The first assumption of cultural pluralism ideology, and

hence multiculturalism, is that an individual's membership in, and attachment to, primary ethnic or cultural group life, and the socially encouraged involvement in it, promote those characteristics in a person usually associated with a healthy personality type — self-esteem, sense of belonging, respect for others, purposefulness, and critical thinking (Kallen 1956:251).

This assumption must be counted among the least controversial of cultural pluralism ideology; yet, some major questions present themselves. Although few of us would take issue with the claim that strong primary group ties lead to a sense of security and 'rooted' identity, is it true that respect for others follows from such ties? What happens to individuality in organic communities? Under what conditions do such ties lead to respect for others?

This latter question suggests another assumption, namely, that a personality characterized by tolerance of, and openness to, different others — necessary to a truly democratic society — is dependent upon the opportunity of individuals to encounter and interact with a variety of culturally different others. As Kallen argued, the more groups an individual can encounter, join, or leave, the more varied their characters and functions, the more civilized is likely to be the individual and society as a whole (1956:251).

This second assumption serves partially to answer the question raised previously regarding respect for others following primary group attachment. Specifically, intergroup fluidity protects against what otherwise could be negative consequences following socially encouraged group membership, especially if that membership means parochialism, is not open to change, and/or does not allow contact with other groups. However, consideration should be given to the possibility that intergroup fluidity in the context of potent assimilative pressures, or in the absence of strong reinforcements for ethnic group identification, could lead to, indeed often does lead to, acculturation, or assimilation. This poses a serious question for cultural pluralism advocates: What does freedom of association and intergroup fluidity do to the culture which binds one to a primary group? What does it do, ultimately, to the cultural differences so highly valued?

Before these assumptions can pass an adequate test, several additional questions present themselves. What characterizes 'fluidity' in group membership? How is it achieved? What happens to membership in a primary group, when a member moves into and out of the primary group, into and out of other groups? Could it mean, for example, as Thomas Green suggested regarding a related phenomenon, that 'the Jew has less identity as a Jew, the Catholic less as a Catholic, and even the Episcopalian less as Episcopalian' (Green 1966:10)?

It should also be noted in this regard that cultural pluralists are not always explicit in their discussion of the notion of freedom of association as it applies to what might be considered political groupings (or functional, as opposed to organic, groups). Research findings relating to such matters as tolerance and ethnic group attachment, and tolerance as a function of intergroup mobility, ethnic group membership, and political interest group membership, must be identified and related to cultural pluralism ideology and multiculturalism. As R.K. Merton (1950) pointed out, there is need for a close study of the processes in group life which sustain or inhibit orientations to non-membership groups, thus perhaps leading to a linking of reference group theory and current theories of social organization, including cultural pluralism ideology.

Related to the freedom of association principle is a third assumption which, as pointed out by Green (1966), holds that no one way of life can be said to be better than any other and that to be humane a society must afford room for many competing and oftentimes conflicting ways of life (1966:12). If no one way of life can without question claim superiority over any other, how does one go about resolving competing and conflicting values? What are the criteria for such judgments? If we are to live by the ideology of cultural pluralism (and multiculturalism), it is necessary to identify or create some effective principles and means for resolving conflicts in values and goals.

These questions raise fundamental problems for cultural pluralism ideology, and, thus, for multiculturalism. They suggest a need for a process to identify those aspects of a particular group's culture which should be maintained and perpetuated in a society which claims to operate on the basis of cultural pluralism ideology. Surely we can conceive of aspects of a particular culture that could be considered unworthy of perpetuation. For example, I know that my daughter is not interested in seeing the perpetuation of the kinds of male dominance and the roles for women associated with some cultural groups. How will we decide what is and what is not to be sustained? Who will make these decisions? Should they be made? If they are made, what happens to the maintenance of the society whose very existence gives a basis of the celebration of cultural diversity?

In this light, then, we must ask what elements are referred to by 'culture' in cultural pluralism and multiculturalism. Moreover, since multicultural education, at least in terms of usage, points to value differences that some would not label as cultural, it is necessary to analyze the way these differences interact with, and impact upon, those that are clearly accepted as cultural phenomena. Indeed, the interaction between cultural phenomena and other valued differences is crucial to helping decide policies and strategies for education.

A fourth assumption and attendant claim of cultural pluralism ideology and multiculturalism is that it is valuable to have many ways of life in competition, and that such competition leads to a balance or equilibrium in the social order. Yet, equilibrium in a democratic society is a question of power, specifically a question of a fair and equal distribution of power. Thus, friendly contact and open competition among and between groups can only take place when equilibrium is present, and when one or more culture(s) or cultural group(s) does not seek to destroy others. How does one reach this point, if reaching it demands intergroup contact on a fair and equal basis, and if, in turn, 'a fair and equal basis' is, *a priori*, dependent upon equilibrium?

A final assumption, at least for the purposes of this analysis, bears directly on the processes and goals of socialization. This is the assumption that loyalty to a larger society — a nation — is a function of, and dependent on, socially sanctioned loyalties rooted in a multiplicity of diverse ethnic and cultural groups. It is this assumption which leads cultural pluralists and multiculturalists to the notion that a society will be rich, unified, healthy, and nourished to a fuller life, to the extent that it is fashioned out of genuine human groupings.

In this regard, Kallen points out that a nation can be unified 'only as a union on equal terms of sovereign and independent diversities alone whose agreement could make and keep it thus one.... The oneness they turn to must ... start from plurality and can live only as the associative pattern which this plurality consent to' (p.47). In short, a healthy society must be based on a mosaic of autonomous groupings, reflecting the underlying differences in the population. Morton Grodzins presented this assumption thus:

> Groups, large and small, play a crucial, independent role in the transferences of allegiance to the nation. For one thing, they are the means through which citizens are brought to participate in civic affairs and national ceremony.... Individuals, in short, act for the nation in response to the smaller groups with which they identify themselves. ... Their loyalty to smaller groups ensures their doing it.... So it is that loyalties to smaller groups supply

the guts of national endeavor even when that endeavor has no meaning to the individual concerned.

(Cited by Wolff 1968:135-6)

From these and other assumptions, cultural pluralists are led to claim that, as an operational set of social beliefs, cultural pluralism would prevent dangerous social and personal disorganization which follow when culturally diverse individuals are pressured to reject their primary group ties. It is these assumptions, furthermore, which lead cultural pluralists to assert that a fusion of primary group loyalty with loyalty to a larger cultural entity — society at large or the nation — can only come about when the primary group is able to enjoy all those social freedoms which come to those who express basic loyalty to the larger society. In short, democracy requires the kind of freedom that not only allows, but encourages, individuals to join and maintain attachments to cultural and other groups.

We must ask, however, if loyalty to the nation does indeed follow from group loyalty? If so, how does it come about? Alternatively, could it be that in a time of mass society the assumed human need for a sense of community is so great that it gradually dissolves the bonds of some from national territory or from the common culture that unites diverse groups into a national state? In short, the bonds-that-tie at the national level may dissolve in a mass society, with the help of intensified primary group consciousness and membership need.

THE MEANING OF MULTICULTURAL EDUCATION

Finally, a few other criticisms, of a different sort, are in order. When we link multicultural with education and come up with the phrase multicultural education, we need to be clear about what we mean. An essay by Grant (1978) is enlightening in this regard. He reminds us that the word 'multicultural' is an adjective, meaning 'of,' 'relating to,' or 'designed for a combination of distinct cultures.' As an adjective, multicultural modifies education. More specifically, he suggests that when we use the phrase 'multicultural education' we are limiting or restricting the meaning of education. In this sense, multicultural education takes on a meaning function not unlike terms such as health education, special education, physical education, and the like. However, this does not appear to be what multiculturalists have intended when they use this phrase. Moreover, it may account, at least in part, for the fact

41

that multicultural education has become something that is tacked on to the curriculum at some point — added to it along the way, here and there — rather than being infused throughout.

Another issue relates to the need for a distinction between cultural pluralism or multiculturalism and structural pluralism or social stratification. Structural pluralism refers to the fact that American society is socially stratified and structured to give various groups different access to its socioeconomic resources. Theoretically, cultural pluralism, or multiculturalism, could exist without structural pluralism or social stratification. But, given social reality and US history, the former tend to coincide to some degree with the latter. In other words, some cultural groups wind up on top of the heap, others in the middle, and others at the bottom.

The past two decades have produced some rather important changes in the correlations between cultural group membership and group standing in the social stratification system, but the changes have not been as dramatic or as great as rhetoric might lead us to believe, or as great as many think they should be. The question is this: What characterized educational efforts that are designed to at once sustain or extend multiculturalism, or cultural pluralism, and at the same time promote greater opportunity or access for all?

Consider that efforts to date fall into at least two categories. The first is what we might call transitory or compensatory efforts that tend to get at the social stratification problems. The second might be called enlightenment, or enrichment efforts, that have not dealt directly with the issue of social stratification (Harrington 1978). There is some literature which suggests that the elimination of structural pluralism would lead to the elimination of cultural pluralism, or multiculturalism. Conversely, such literature also suggests that the maintenance of the latter ensures the former. These possibilities must be examined before we rush to practice whatever it is we mean by multicultural education.

Multiculturalism is too precious a societal resource to put at risk through ill-conceived public policies and practices based on limited understandings and fuzzy concepts. In turn, the laudable goals of cultural pluralists and multiculturalists are also too important to be put at risk. The educational 'rush to practice,' in the face of questionable and untested assumptions and concepts which fuel this movement, must be balanced by a large-scale, systematic effort to clarify and search out means for testing these matters.

In sum, educators should be mindful of the significance of

group affiliation, but, at the same time, recognize that group togetherness may be unthinking and unimaginative, its only purpose to maintain separateness and divisiveness. The American dilemma of finding a balance between the two ideals of 'groupism' and 'the nation' may define the next phase in the evolution of the national character.

NOTE

1. The identification and analysis of these assumptions have been influenced by Thomas Green (1966). I wish to note that I use the term 'assumption' in its fundamental sense; it refers to matters taken for granted. Horace Kallen's insights, and many of those coming from latter-day advocates of cultural pluralism and multiculturalism, emerged from an examination of personal ethnic experiences. Kallen tested these insights as hypotheses with his own and other ethnic conferees, with people who prized and acted on their own ethnicity. Long before the so-called radical or third-force historians and social scientists, he acted on the principle that the only reality was that which emerged from phenomenologically tested experience.

REFERENCES

Crèvecoeur, J. Hector St John de (1925) *Letters from an American Farmer*, New York: Albert and Charles Boni.
Gordon, Milton (1961) 'Assimilation in America: theory and reality,' *Daedalus* 90.
Grant, Carl (1978) 'Education that is multicultural: isn't that what we mean?' *Journal of Teacher Education* 29.
Green, Thomas (1966) *Education and Pluralism: Ideal and Reality*, Twenty-Sixth Annual J. Richard Street Lecture, Syracuse, NY: Syracuse University.
Handlin, Oscar (1959) *Immigration as a Factor in American History*, Englewood Cliffs, NJ: Prentice-Hall.
Harrington, Charles (1978) 'Bilingual education, social stratification and cultural pluralism,' *Equal Opportunity Review* 3.
Kallen, Horace (1956) *Cultural Pluralism and the American Idea*, Philadelphia: University of Pennsylvania Press.
Merton, Robert K. and Rossi, Alice Kitt (1950) 'Reference group theory and social mobility,' in R.K. Merton and R.L. Lazarsfeld (eds) *Continuities in Sociological Research*,

New York: The Free Press.

National Council for Accreditation of Teacher Education (1979) *Standards for the Accreditation of Teacher Education*, Washington, DC: Author.

Wolff, Robert Paul (1968) *The Poverty of Liberalism*, Boston: Beacon Press.

Chapter Three

LINGUISTIC MINORITIES AND ADULT EDUCATION IN THE UNITED STATES

C. Ray Graham and Peter S. Cookson

The number of persons in the United States who have reported that they speak a language other than English as the 'usual' language in the home has increased dramatically since 1960. Fishman, Nahirny, Hoffman, and Hayden (1966) estimated, based on census data, that almost thirteen million people in the United States spoke a non-English mother tongue in the home in 1960. This figure had increased to approximately 16.5 million by 1970 and to almost seventeen million in 1976 (Veltman 1983:6-7). While comparable figures are not available from the 1980 United States Census, because of differences in the questions asked in the interviews, the data from the Census suggest that the increases have continued. Veltman (1983) has shown that these increases have come about largely as a result of immigration, and they occurred in spite of the rapid anglicization of many linguistic minority immigrants.

COMPOSITION OF THE LINGUISTIC MINORITY POPULATION

In addition to being a time of increase in linguistic minority population over all, the two decades between 1960 and 1980 were a time of great shifting in the composition of the linguistic minority population in the United States (Fishman, Gertner, Lowy, and Milan 1985; Veltman 1983; Fishman, Nahirny, Hoffman, and Hayden 1966). This fact is made very clear in data presented by Veltman (1983) regarding the place of birth of foreign-born linguistic minority persons fourteen years of age and older, during three periods of arrival in the United States: prior to 1960, from 1960 to 1969, and from 1970 to 1976 (see Table 3.1). Notice that non-Hispanic immigration has shifted from predominantly Western Europeans, prior to 1960, to predominantly Asians in the last couple of decades. Hispanic immigration, which has witnessed

Table 3.1 Period of arrival of the foreign born by mother tongue, persons aged 14 and over, by percentage of total immigrant group in the United States in 1976

*Weighted language group**	*Before 1960*	*1960-9*	*1970-6*	*Sample*
Arab	19.6	28.7	51.7	91,664
Chinese	29.1	34.1	36.8	322,549
Filipino	25.5	27.0	47.5	308,129
French	57.2	27.5	15.3	330,838
German	81.0	15.1	3.9	932,697
Greek	50.7	27.6	21.7	231,746
Italian	72.6	19.2	8.2	894,142
Japanese	55.8	17.7	26.5	148,996
Korean	4.6	20.3	75.3	115,810
Polish	81.9	14.3	3.8	301,444
Portuguese	35.8	33.3	30.9	204,548
Russian	91.7	7.0	1.3	89,095
Scandinavian	84.1	11.7	4.2	210,432
Vietnamese	0.7	3.8	95.5	82,637
Yiddish	97.5	1.9	0.6	323,921
All other	54.8	20.9	24.3	1,124,774
All non-Spanish	61.4	19.6	19.0	5,713,422
Chicano	38.5	30.7	30.8	1,229,151
Cuban	16.6	61.3	22.1	515,408
Puerto Rican	61.3	23.7	15.0	716,916
Other Hispanic	21.5	40.4	38.1	732,775
All Spanish	27.5	36.3	36.1	3,194,250

Source: 1976 Survey of Income and Education (Veltman 1983:51)

Note: *These estimates are based on a survey conducted in 1976 in which 158,500 households were selected from participants in the 1970 US Census and re-interviewed, using much more specific questions regarding ethnicity, language use, and immigration. The estimates are weighted according to percentages of participants who were re-interviewed.

a marked increase since 1960, has shifted from Puerto Ricans and Cubans, to Mexicans and Central and South Americans.

Along with this shift in immigration patterns has come a major shift in patterns of language use among linguistic minorities. Veltman (1983) pointed out that in the 1976 Survey of Income and Education, of persons fourteen years of age and older, who reported speaking a language other than English as their mother tongue, over half of the foreign born (51 percent) and a large majority of the native born (86 percent) reported using English as their usual language of interaction. Among immigrant groups, over 85 percent of German, Scandinavian, Russian, and Yiddish speakers, choose English as their usual language of interaction, while only a fifth of Spanish speakers of Mexican origin choose English. This disparity, it would appear, is partly explainable by the fact that certain groups have immigrated to the United States more recently than others, and partly by the concentrations of certain linguistic groups within particular communities. Among native-born linguistic minorities, less than half of Native Americans and slightly less than two-thirds of Hispanics choose English as their usual language of interaction, while almost 95 percent of all other language groups choose English. Thus, we see that the groups that continue to use a language other than English as their preferred language of interaction are predominantly foreign-born Asians and Hispanics and American-born Hispanics and Native Americans.

With regard to language proficiency, the pattern also differed widely among linguistic groups. Only 17.4 percent of all non-Hispanic immigrants report having difficulty with English, while 43 percent of Hispanic immigrants report having difficulty with English. This percentage is particularly high for Hispanics of Mexican origin, 54.9 percent (Veltman 1983). Among native-born linguistic minorities, Native Americans and Hispanics are the only groups who report having large numbers of adult speakers who have difficulties with English.

These figures suggest that linguistic minorities are a very diverse group of people, and that the educational needs of some groups are quite different from those of others. While certain groups appear to adopt English as their language of normal use fairly soon after immigration, others appear to proceed much more slowly in developing proficiency in English. This fact will have implications for the types of adult education programs which might be appropriate for different linguistic minority groups.

EDUCATION AND EMPLOYMENT OF LINGUISTIC MINORITIES

The accuracy of statistics on linguistic minority participation and achievement in formal schooling is difficult to assess, given the fact that census surveys, and information collected by educational institutions, have used varied means of classifying linguistic minorities. For example, the question used in the 1970 Census for identifying linguistic minority individuals asked what languages other than English were spoken in their homes when they were children. In follow-up interviews (United States Census Bureau 1975) it was found that only a little over half of the respondents who said that a language other than English was spoken in their homes actually learned to speak that language as their first language. Over one-fourth had no proficiency at all in that language.

Likewise, educational institutions often use surname or race as an indication of language background. Many times linguistic minority individuals from Western Europe are classified as 'Anglo,' as distinct from 'Black,' 'Hispanic,' and 'Native American.'

Some of the more careful sorting out of the relationships between language proficiency and achievement in education and employment in the United States has been done by Veltman (1983). Based on estimates derived from the 1976 Survey of Income and Education by the US Census Bureau, Veltman examined the socioeconomic attainments of Hispanic and non-Hispanic linguistic minorities (i.e., those who reported that Spanish or some other foreign language was spoken in their homes when they were children) and compared them with those of white monolingual English speakers. Table 3.2 is a compilation of his data on male survey participants for each of the three groups mentioned above, broken down according to language use and competence in English. Similar statistics are presented by Veltman for female participants (pp.228-65).

Examination of Table 3.2 reveals clear patterns of achievement in education, occupation, and employment earnings, as they relate to language use and English competence. Generally, the greater the anglicization of the person, the higher the level of achievement. Competence in English is a particularly important predictor of levels of attainment in each of these areas, for both Hispanic and non-Hispanic linguistic minorities. This is, of course, as one would expect, although one should be cautious in interpreting the relationships as causal.

Table 3.2 Mean socioeconomic attainments by language group and language characteristics, full-time employed men, aged 25-64

Language characteristics	Educ-ation	Occup-ation*	Income	% Sample
Hispanic				
English Usual Language:				
English Monolingual	12.87	37.63	$14,149	9.7
English Bilingual	12.54	37.75	12,398	40.6
Spanish Usual Language:				
High English Competence	10.40	29.20	10,094	29.0
Low English Competence	7.26	17.34	7,170	20.7
Total	10.86	31.21	10,818	100.0
Non-Hispanic Linguistic Minority English Usual Language:				
English Monolingual	12.80	41.47	14,775	56.9
English Bilingual	13.52	45.44	14,801	30.7
Minority Usual Language:				
High English Competence	12.09	37.71	12,125	9.1
Low English Competence	8.23	24.14	9,476	3.3
Total	12.81	41.77	14,367	100.0
Anglo Majority				
English Monolingual	13.87	46.22	14,771	100.0

Source: 1976 Survey of Income and Education (Veltman 1983:228, 246)
Note: *Occupational achievement is measured in points on the Duncan Scale (Duncan 1961).

Additional analyses by Veltman (1983) suggest that overall differences in occupational attainment and employment earnings for Anglo monolinguals and linguistic minorities who choose English as their preferred language of interaction are not significant. Comparisons among different linguistic groups show that the Yiddish and Chinese language groups have significantly higher than expected attainment scores and earnings and the Portuguese and Native American groups have lower than expected scores.

All of the foregoing data suggest that, in considering the needs of linguistic minorities *vis-à-vis* adult education, we cannot lump them together into one group. They also suggest that language proficiency and educational level are critical variables in level of salary earned and mean level of attainment in employment. Thus, we must first look at the general needs of limited English proficient persons among the linguistic minority population and then we must consider the particular needs of individual language groups.

LINGUISTIC MINORITY NEEDS AND THE CURRENT STRUCTURE OF ADULT EDUCATION

The major emphasis of most publicly funded adult basic education programs in the United States has been the provision of learning opportunities at the elementary and secondary levels for adults who are proficient in English. These programs appear to have served English proficient linguistic minority students about as well as they have the monolingual English-speaking Anglos, although data to verify this are not kept systematically by educational agencies.

For persons with limited English proficiency, another program emphasis has developed in adult education over the last three decades, the English-as-a-Second-Language programs (ESL). Historically, these ESL programs were developed as remedial programs for those who lacked the English language skills necessary for participation in the General Education Development (GED) and Adult Basic Education (ABE) classes. The ESL classes became a prerequisite for entrance into the regular adult education program, and, as students reached the intermediate or advanced levels of ESL, they were absorbed into the regular (mainstream) ABE or GED Program.

These ESL programs were generally modeled after the foreign language education programs in colleges and universities and employed many of the same teaching methodologies and materials. As a matter of fact, many of the texts that were used in these early ESL programs were developed for teaching English as a foreign language in countries outside the United States. Generally speaking, the materials used in these programs assumed that the learners were literate and fairly well educated in their native languages.

Thus, to participate in adult basic education at the elementary level, fluency in English was a prerequisite skill. To participate in most ESL programs, literacy skills in the native language were assumed. Therefore, the adult education program was designed primarily for native English speakers and linguistic minorities with rather high levels of literacy in their native languages. It is not difficult to understand why adults who lacked both basic English fluency and basic literacy skills in the first language were unlikely to participate and why, if they did elect to participate in an ESL program, they were unlikely to succeed quickly or to participate long enough to advance to other phases of the ABE program. We will return to this matter later.

As more and more limited-English-speaking learners came into adult education programs, additional program emphases were developed. For people who did not wish to enter into the regular adult education classes, but simply wanted to upgrade their English skills, in order to be able to cope more success-fully with the everyday demands of living in the United States, survival English language materials were developed (Mackey 1972; Schurer 1979; Keltner, Howard, Lee, Kellner, Walker, Eberhardt, and Hamlin 1981; Foley, Pomann, and Dowling 1981). These materials focused on developing functional communication skills in English, by having the learner practice language related to such practical situations as going to the doctor, renting an apartment, going shopping, and opening a bank account. Even though these programs de-emphasized literacy in English, and generally met the need of many linguistic minority learners, most of the programs, none the less, made no special provisions for learners who were not literate in their native language.

During the last decade or so, other adult ESL program emphases have been developed, to meet the needs of yet other groups of learners. One of these, occupational English, is designed to help individuals with limited English language competence learn how to apply for, obtain, and keep a job (Ramirez and Spandel 1980). Occupational ESL programs generally assume literacy in the native language and focus on developing skills in locating job openings, filling out applica-tions, and participating in job-related interviews. They do not necessarily lead to preparation for, nor participation in, GED or ABE instruction.

Another major emphasis in ESL instruction, called vocational ESL, attempts to provide adult learners with English language skills relating to particular jobs or vocations

(Gage and Prince 1982; Smith 1986). The more successful of these programs not only provide the learners with language skills specific to their particular employment, but they often combine English language instruction with on-the-job training. Still, most of the materials developed for these vocational ESL programs are designed with the literate learner in mind.

The ESL programs discussed above have generally done an admirable job of attracting and serving linguistic minority adults, with minimal learning difficulties, who are literate in their native languages and whose motivation to succeed through education is relatively high and readily tapped. They have done well, in spite of the fact that most adult education ESL programs in the United States have open enrollment, classes of students with very heterogeneous language abilities and backgrounds, and poorly trained teachers.

SPECIAL NEEDS OF UNDEREDUCATED LINGUISTIC MINORITIES

Largely overlooked by most ESL programs are those linguistic minority adults who are not only non-English-speaking, but who are not literate in their own language. These include large numbers of Hispanics and other linguistic minorities who emigrated from countries with a strong literary tradition but who, themselves, received little or no formal schooling during their childhood. It also includes large numbers of Native Americans, Southeast Asians, and others from oral cultures with no strong tradition of literacy (Gee 1986).

In areas of the United States with large numbers of functionally illiterate adults, who do not speak English or have limited skills in English, such individuals are under-represented in ABE program. Nowhere in the United States is this more apparent than in the south-central part of Texas, known as South Texas. Of the five standard metropolitan statistical areas (SMSAs) in this region, Table 3.3 indicates the percentages of persons in the total population of adults of Spanish origin, twenty-five years of age and over, whose schooling in 1980 was less than high school completion. The range of percentages of this part of the population, which had received less than four years of schooling, ranged from 39 percent in the McAllen-Pharr-Edinburg SMSA to 20 percent in the San Antonio SMSA.

Table 3.3 Percentages of adults of Spanish origin (25 years and over) who had not completed high school, by grade completed and by South Texas SMSA (1980 Census*)

| SMSA | Last school grade completed | | | |
	0-4 (%)	5-8 (%)	9-11 (%)	Total (%)
Brownsville-Harlingen-San Benito	34	25	11	70
Corpus Christi	26	23	15	64
Laredo	26	26	15	67
San Antonio	20	18	21	59
McAllen-Pharr-Edinburg	39	24	9	17

Note: *United States Census of Population and Housing 1983: 104-236.

In two SMSAs, over one-third of the prospective ABE population had received less than a fifth-grade education. Not only do the vast majority of these undereducated adults lack formal schooling but they also lack basic communication skills in English, since, according to the same Census data, the percentage of those eighteen and over who spoke Spanish in the home and who lacked basic communication skills in English ranged from 18 percent in San Antonio to almost 36 percent in the McAllen-Pharr-Edinburg SMSA. Clearly a need exists for educational programming addressed to these undereducated persons of Spanish origin.

While accurate statistics on the participation of pre-literate and semi-literate adults in adult education programs do not exist, both the experience of the authors and conversations with program directors and teachers from a number of areas of the United States suggest that such learners make up a very small percentage of those being served by adult education programs. There are many factors which contribute to this lack of participation. First of all, it is generally the case that the least educated adults in the general population are also the least likely to enroll in educational programs of any sort (United States Department of Education 1983). This same tendency is apparent in the limited-English-speaking adult with little formal education, only it is exacerbated by language and cultural differences.

Second, for many linguistic minorities from pre-literate societies, there is no tradition of formal education in the sense in which we know it in this country. Therefore, in their cultures they do not see formal education as the means of upgrading their condition. Consequently, they are not likely to seek out formal education opportunities that may be available through adult programs. (See Plaister 1984, for a discussion of this, as it applies to the Hmong from Southeast Asia.)

Third, for the undereducated language minority adult there are a number of social-psychological factors which make the learning of a second language a formidable task. The life-situations of least-educated linguistic minority adults often impede language learning. To illustrate, Schumann (1977) presents a case study of Alberto, a thirty-three-year-old Costa Rican immigrant laborer who moved to the United States, and for a period of time did not enroll in an ESL class. His English-language development was monitored for a period of ten months by a group of linguists interested in studying adult second-language development in a natural setting. During this time he made little progress in his ability to speak English. Subsequently, he was given instruction over a seven-month period of time in specific areas of speech in which he had had difficulty, his performance being measured periodically. He succeeded in improving his performance immensely in an artificial test-like situation, but, when he was recorded during spontaneous speech, his performance returned to its pre-instructional level. Schumann hypothesized that Alberto's lack of progress in English was due in part to social distance, defined in terms of 'societal factors that either promote or inhibit social solidarity between two groups and, thus, affect the way a second language group acquires the language of a particular target language group' (1977:211).

These factors include such things as social position of the group, size and cohesiveness of the group, attitudes of one group toward another, amount and kind of contact the groups have with each other, the tendency within groups to assimilate or acculturate to the other group or to reject the new language and culture. Alberto was found to be in an unfavorable position with regard to each of the above variables; i.e., he was in a subordinate position politically, economically, and socially; he had a reservationist attitude toward the dominant culture, rather than a desire to assimilate or acculturate; and he was highly enclosed in a rather large Spanish-speaking community, in which he could shop, go to church, and listen to the radio in his native language. He was able to develop a rudimentary level of proficiency in English, which was sufficient to meet the demands placed on him by his surroundings and, therefore, had little need to improve his English. As with Alberto, many undereducated adults who speak little or no English are limited in their ability to learn English by this factor of social distance.

In addition to the negative effects of social distance, adults involved in second language learning may also experience a number of affective factors which make language acquisition difficult. Among these are language shock, culture shock, and lack of motivation (Schumann 1978). Language shock involves feelings of doubt as to whether one's word accurately expresses one's feelings, and concerns about making mistakes, sounding strange, or appearing child-like. A person experiencing language shock is often reluctant to try speaking the new language because of these feelings and, consequently, makes poor progress in the language.

Culture shock includes the feelings of discomfort and maladjustment that people experience when the cultural norms and role expectations to which they have been so accustomed in their native land no longer hold true in the new culture. This produces a tendency to idealize positive values in their own culture, become critical of things that are different in the new culture, and to withdraw from social contacts with people in the new culture, preferring instead to spend time with people who share their own culture and values. Such withdrawal obviously has negative consequences for learning the new language.

Motivation is a particularly important variable in language acquisition. It is often the case for adult learners, who live in a community with large numbers of people who speak their own native language, to experience low motivation to learn a second language, even though fluency in the second language would improve their prospects for economic mobility.

All of the social and psychological variables discussed here make language acquisition for the undereducated adult language minority individual a formidable task, and they necessitate special consideration in designing programs for these individuals.

A fourth factor, which works in conjunction with the three previous ones in contributing to the lack of participation of non-literate adults in adult education programs, is the kind of programming available to such individuals. As was mentioned above, most program options for limited-English-speaking adults assume that the learners are literate in their native languages. That is, in the basic ESL classes generally, there are no special classes for those who cannot read and write in their native language. They are placed in the same classes with learners who are literate, and they use texts that rely on reading abilities which they do not have. Because their progress is generally much slower than that of those who can read and write (Weinstein 1984), they often become discouraged and drop out or accommodate themselves to the lack of progress by substituting other goals in place of fluency (e.g., pleasant social interaction with the teacher and fellow students, or relief from the burden of housework and family, for at least one or two evenings weekly).

SOME SOLUTIONS

The assumption of the traditional ESL approach in ABE is that the overriding educational objective of non-English-speaking adults must be to learn English. It fails to recognize that there are other legitimate educational needs, such as those addressed in programs usually provided for English-speaking adults, which could be met concomitantly with, or independent of, the learning of English. Needs, such as vocational skills, life-coping skills, and knowledge pertaining to citizenship, and academic content areas, are now shelved for enrolled linguistic minority adults, until they reach a certain level of English fluency. Thus, individuals for whom the learning of English appears an insurmountable task, or for those for whom it is not an immediate primary objective, or for whom the all-English environment is too intimidating, are effectively foreclosed from more comprehensive and relevant learning opportunities.

In recent years, programs have been suggested which would provide the opportunity for linguistic minority learners to acquire these kinds of knowledge and skills in a more congenial environment right from the start. These programs, called bilingual education programs (Friedenberg and Bradley 1984), enable linguistic minority adults to put to use immediately what they learn in their first language. Because learning tasks are more readily understood, and can therefore be made more relevant, learners can expect to be more motivated to continue their participation in the ABE program. Concepts learned initially in the first language may be re-introduced and reviewed later in the second language. For individuals whose learning needs to go beyond fluency in the second language, bilingual adult education can provide more effective initial learning and, at the same time, prepare them for topics to be treated in subsequent ESL and ABE lessons. Because the learning of ESL may present a particularly significant obstacle for illiterate, non-English-speaking adults, it seems necessary that a great deal be done to overcome social and psychological distance factors through bilingual adult education programs. At the same time, adult learners could be developing knowledge and skills in areas important to them.

An extension of the notion of teaching language minority students basic survival skills in their native language, while developing English language skills, is the idea of developing literacy first in their native language. Not only is literacy a skill that can be easily acquired by adults in a language which they already speak, but the acquisition of literacy in the first language would likely increase the rapidity with which they could learn to read in English. There is increasing evidence that children who are taught to read first in their native language perform better in reading in the second language than those who are taught only to read in the second language (Zappert and Cruz 1977). It is likely that, for the non-literate adult, learning to read in the native language would be even more advantageous. This would apply, of course, only to those languages which use an alphabetic system of writing and for which adequate reading materials are available. Four features of such a bilingual adult education approach should be noted.

First, illiterate linguistic minority adults can be taught, either individually through tutorial or other individualized instruction, or, in the event that several learners from the same linguistic minority are enrolled, through group instruction.

Second, learning opportunities in the first language can be provided through assistance of bilingual instructors, instructional aides, or tutors. These may be paid personnel, or, in the absence of adequate funding, volunteers. Bilingual resource persons, representing various public institutions and community agencies, whose range of services includes the linguistic minority adults, may be invited to contribute to survival skills instruction in the first language.

Third, the target learners for such instruction are illiterate or barely literate linguistic minority adults. If learners already possess literacy skills in their own language, they are probably ready for regular second-language instruction. If learners already possess second-language skills, they are probably ready for the regular adult basic education (basic life skills), secondary school completion, pre-vocational education, vocational education, or job training.

Fourth, when illiterate minority adults are afforded the opportunity to acquire basic literacy and survival skills in their own language, it is assumed that the prospect of learning success and its subsequent attainment serve as powerful incentives to enroll and, once enrolled, to continue to undertake the challenging rigors of mastering the second language.

Another suggestion for improving adult education programming for non-literate linguistic minorities is to provide special classes and materials for teaching ESL, where special attention is given to developing basic literacy. This means that, either students would have to be recruited in sufficient numbers to have entire classes of students who need to develop literacy skills as well as ESL skills, or that students who need special help in this area would have to be grouped within a class and given the additional attention. In all cases, dealing adequately with the problem will necessitate special training on the part of teachers and coordinators, and the preparation of special materials for the students.

CONCLUSIONS

It is clear from the foregoing discussion that the linguistic minority population in the United States is a very diverse group and that its needs with regard to adult education vary greatly from language to language and even among persons of a particular language background. The needs of linguistic minority adults who are proficient in English generally appear to be met by currently available programs at least as well as are the needs of monolingual English-speaking adults of comparable socioeconomic and education backgrounds. Also, linguistic minority adults with high levels of formal education attainment in their native languages appear to be served by currently available programs in English as a Second Language. It is evident that administrators of adult education programs have made a number of program adjustments which meet the needs of large numbers of undereducated linguistic minority adults who seek to improve life-coping or employment skills through learning English.

The major area in which adult education programs are woefully inadequate is in meeting the needs of the least educated among the linguistic minority population: those who do not speak English proficiently and who are not literate in their native languages. This population constitutes a significant part of a number of particular linguistic minority groups, such as the Hmong from Southeast Asia; Hispanics from the Caribbean, Mexico, and Central and South America; and certain Native American groups, to mention only a few. Programs must be developed to attract and meet the needs of these adult populations, if the increasing numbers of undereducated linguistic minority populations in America are to become socially, economically, and culturally integrated into the society's mainstream.

REFERENCES

Duncan, O.D. (1961) 'A socioeconomic index for all occupations,' in A.J. Reiss, O.D. Duncan, P.K. Hatt, and C.C. North (eds) *Occupations and Social Status*, New York: Free Press.

Fishman, J., Nahirny, V., Hoffman, J., and Hayden, R. (1966) *Language Loyalty in the United States*, The Hague: Mouton.

Fishman, J., Gertner, M., Lowy, E., and Milan, W. (1985) *The Rise and Fall of the Ethnic Revival: Perspectives on Language and Ethnicity*, New York: Mouton.

Foley, B., Pomann, H., and Dowling, G. (1981) *Lifelines: Coping Skills in English*, New York: Regents Publishing Co.

Friedenberg, J. and Bradley, C. (1984) *Bilingual Vocational Information Series, No. 269*, Columbus, Ohio: National Center for Research in Vocational Education. ERIC ED240386.

Gage, J. and Prince, D. (1982) 'Vocational English: preparing for a first job,' *TESOL Quarterly* 16.

Gee, J.P. (1986) 'Orality and literacy: from the savage mind to ways with words,' *TESOL Quarterly* 20.

Keltner, A., Howard, L., Lee, F., Kellner, V., Walker, A., Eberhardt, J., and Hamlin, C. (1981) *English for Adult Competency*, Englewood Cliffs, NJ: Prentice-Hall.

Mackey, L.S. (1972) *English I: A Basic Course for Adults*, Rowley, Mass.: Newbury House.

Plaister, T. (1984) 'L2 reading for L1 illiterate adults from preliterate societies,' *Working Papers in English as a Second Language* 3, University of Hawaii at Manoa.

Ramirez, A.D. and Spandel, V.L. (1980) 'Occupational English as a second language,' *Foreign Language Annals* 13.

Schumann, J.H. (1977) 'Second language acquisition: the pidginization hypothesis,' in E.M. Hatch (ed.) *Second Language Acquisition: A Book of Readings*, Rowley, Mass.: Newbury House.

—— (1978) 'The acculturation model of second-language acquisition,' in R.C. Gingras (ed.) *Second-Language Acquisition and Foreign Language Teaching*, Arlington, Va.: Center for Applied Linguistics.

Schurer, L. (ed.) (1979) *Everyday English*, San Francisco: Alemany Press.

Smith, N.E. (1986) *Teaching Job-Related English as a Second Language*, Revised edn, Washington, DC: Office of Vocational and Adult Education.

United States Census Bureau (1975) *Accuracy of Data for*

Selected Population Characteristics as Measured by the 1970 CPS-Census Match, Washington, DC: Government Printing Office (PHC(E)-11).

—— (1983) Census of Population and Housing, *1980: Census Tracts Brownsville-Harlingen-San Benito, Corpus Christi, Laredo, McAllen-Pharr-Edinburg, San Antonio, Texas*, Washington, DC: Government Printing Office (C3.223/11:980/104-236).

—— (1983) Census of Population, *1980: Detailed Population Characteristics, Part 45, Texas* (PC89-1-D45), Washington, DC: Government Printing Office (C3.223/8:980/D-45/Sec.1).

United States Department of Education (1983) *The Condition of Education, 1983 Edition*, Washington, DC: Government Printing Office.

Veltman, C. (1983) *Language Shift in the United States*, New York: Mouton.

Weinstein, G. (1984) 'Literacy and second language acquisition: issues and perspectives,' *TESOL Quarterly* 18.

Zappert, L.T. and Cruz, B.R. (1977) *Bilingual Education: An Appraisal of Empirical Research*, Berkeley, Cal.: Bay Area Bilingual Education League/Lau Center.

Part Two

PAST AND PRESENT CONCERNS OF MAJOR ETHNIC GROUPS

Chapter Four

MORE THAN THE THREE 'R's':
THE DEVELOPMENT OF BLACK ADULT EDUCATION
IN MANHATTAN

Charlotte T. Morgan

For Black Americans equality of access to educational opportunity has been offset by disturbing questions concerning the
quality of the experience. Recent studies (US Department of
Education 1983; Werner 1986), for example, report illiteracy
among 13 percent of the general English-speaking American
population and 47 percent among Black youth. Public response
has focused on the need for instruction in the basics — the
three 'R's' of 'reading, riting, and rithmatic.' This 'back to
basics' premise, however, is as unsatisfactory for adult
education as it is for elementary schooling. The emphasis on
literacy and skills development programs overlooks the historic
struggle of Black leaders for adult education with a broader
purpose. Questions about the objectives of adult education
have been muffled by the clamor for marketable skills:
education's promise as a catalyst has been undermined by its
role as a pacifier. This dilemma is clearly evident in the
development of adult education for New York City's Black
population. The perennial issues were those of content,
control, and purpose, as the foundations of contemporary
practice were being laid.

NINETEENTH-CENTURY BEGINNINGS

New York's small Black community (7,000 in the early 1800s)
expanded rapidly, as a result of the settlement of former
slaves, emancipated by their service in the Revolutionary War,
and state legislation mandating the gradual elimination of
slavery (Ottley and Weathersby 1967). Discrimination and
segregation forced this emerging society to develop its own
institutions. Acquiring literacy, learning 'useful knowledge,'
and combating the image of Black immorality were the ends
of early adult education endeavors. Later, in the middle

decades, the abolition movement and self-help programs dominated educational efforts.

In the ante-bellum era, lyceums, or literary societies, provided the most significant community-based educational programs. Porter's 1936 study revealed at least five such organizations in existence in the 1830s. One, the Phoenix Society, provided a school, a library, reading rooms, public lectures, and employment services. Its integrated membership included Henry Highland Garnet, Patrick Reason, and Arthur Tappan — all leading figures in the anti-slavery movement. Ultimately the demands of this struggle contributed to a decline in lyceum participation.

These community-based efforts were supplemented by the charitable and religious organizations of the larger society. African Free Schools Numbers 1 and 2, operated by the Society for Promoting the Manumission of Slaves and Such of Them as Have Been and May Be Liberated (popularly known as the Manumission Society), offered evening classes to adults in the early decades of the nineteenth century. These classes ended in 1834, when the Free Schools were turned over to the Public School Society. Evening classes were resumed in the 1840s and 1850s: three schools offered classes in literacy, history, geography, and mathematics, to Blacks, at sporadic intervals, first to men and later to women (Freeman 1966). Public school education was, however, considered inferior and a sign of pauperism; consequently, Blacks were also attracted to the evening schools of the New York Association of Friends, and other religious groups serving the area.

FROM THE CIVIL WAR TO WORLD WAR I

The loosening of legal restrictions, which occurred after the Civil War, did not bring immediate improvement of the conditions under which most of New York's Blacks lived. The 1863 draft riot underscored the insecurity and vulnerability of Manhattan Blacks, and for years their numbers declined. In the 1880s, this trend was reversed and the population increased. Between 1900 and 1920, New York's black population more than doubled, primarily as a result of migration from the American South and immigration from the West Indies (Laidlow 1932).

The newcomers broke out of the confines of the older neighborhoods of City Hall and Greenwich Village and moved north to the 'Tenderloin' district, the San Juan Hill area, and finally to Harlem. In the early 1900s, however, New York

City was not a promised land. Race riots occurred in 1900 and 1906, and disease and poverty faced many. The gains made by the race — 'colored schools' had been abolished, special property qualifications for Black voters eliminated, Black jurors impaneled, and some teaching staff integrated — could not overcome social beliefs, which hampered acceptance of full African-American participation. At the turn of the twentieth century, an era characterized as the 'nadir' (Logan 1970) for Black Americans, Social Darwinism promoted belief in the backwardness of Blacks and the existence of a 'white man's burden.' This presumption of inferiority plagued Blacks who longed for a place in society. When it became clear that Blacks would not easily obtain the rights so long desired, their vision turned inward. Abolitionist William Wells Brown asserted in his 1880 memoirs that 'the final great struggle for the Negroes' rights lay with themselves.... No race ever prospered or gained respect which lacked confidence in its own "nationality"' (Meier 1964:58).

Black leadership, in turning to racial unity, race cooperation, and racial pride, upheld his contention. Educational programs were designed purposely to promote this consciousness and counter allegations of inferiority.

Between 1880 and the end of World War I, the Black churches were the dominant adult educators. Their lyceums, supported by dues paying members, offered on a weekly basis free public programs, which were a blend of instruction, entertainment, and politics. The lyceums, described by the *New York Age* (30 January 1986) as 'indispensable to the intellectual life of an improving people,' were a symbol of the gentility to which many Blacks aspired. Lyceum popularity and effectiveness coincided with the prestige of the sponsoring church, the eloquence of the pastor, the leadership of the president, and the reputation of the featured speaker. The programs of St Mark's United Methodist, St James' Presbyterian, and Abyssinia Baptist, survived changing social mores, the radio, and the popularity of movies. Adam Clayton Powell Sr, pastor of Abyssinia, then the community's wealthiest church, urged fellow ministers to provide full services for their congregations. Their operation of reading rooms, social rooms, sewing rooms, gymnasiums, and classes, he believed, would effect a 'revolution' in social conditions (*New York Age*, 21 September 1911).

The program advocated by Reverend Mr Powell was beyond the means of most churches, but well within the guidelines of voluntary agencies. The most important of these — the Young Men's Christian Association (YMCA), the Young

Women's Christian Association (YWCA), and the National Urban League — gave substantial freedom to Black leadership. The New York Colored Men's Branch of the YMCA was founded in 1905, after Black attempts to integrate existing units were rebuffed. It implemented the type of program favored by Black workers — African-American culture, general education, and job training — rather than the traditional religious interests. Their spokesman, William A. Hunton, then International Secretary for Colored Work, argued that the generally low educational attainment (80 percent left school before completing the fourth grade and almost half were illiterate) be addressed first, so that religious and spiritual development might be possible (Hunton 1905).

Affirming the integrity of Black people was the goal of John S. Brown, the branch's education director. He hoped his program of general education, secretarial training, civil service examinations preparation, and public lectures, 'would demonstrate what was best in the race' and show there were two classes, 'the worthless men and the upright, self-respecting, trustworthy, advancement desiring men' (Brown 1904:411).

The feminine counterpart of the Colored Men's Branch, organized in 1905 by Emma Ransom, Elizabeth Ross Haynes, and Mrs William A. Hunton, offered shelter and skills to the thousands of young women who flocked to New York. By the time of its move to Harlem in 1913, the Colored Women's Branch was the major provider of professional trade courses to New York's Black women. Its program expanded from dressmaking to secretarial training, and cooking. Also offered were the usual self-improvement classes in English and Bible study, as well as literary, civic, and physical culture clubs. By the outbreak of World War I, the YWCA was assuming a dominant position as the provider of job level skills training in the Black community.

The White Rose Mission, founded by journalist and club woman, Victorial Earle Matthews, also served the needs of young women. The mission rescued naive young women from both prostitution and domestic peonage. Its clients were female migrants, who were given lodging, the usual complement of classes in housework, cooking, Bible study, Black history, and a social life. After its move to Harlem in 1918, and the death of its founder, the mission served mainly as a residence hall (*New York Age*, 6 July 1905; 17 January 1920).

The social activities fostered by the White Rose Mission were the customary programs of settlement houses. The major ones chose to establish separate centers and not challenge traditional segregation. In New York City, the more popular centers were Hartley House, Hudson Guild Center, Stillman House, and the Music School Settlement for Colored People (Davis 1967). Their adult education programs were similar to those promoted by the YMCA and the YWCA: their sponsors wanted to either facilitate acculturation or demonstrate the respectability of Black people.

The National Urban League, formed in 1911 by the merger of three service agencies, stressed its ability to bring the 'best elements' of Black and white together. Originally, supporting adult education opportunities for Blacks was a primary purpose, but the demands of the World War soon led the League to concentrate on 'survival services' for the thousands of Black families migrating to northern cities (Parris and Brooks 1971). The excessive demand on League resources, and the desire to separate local needs from national priorities, resulted in the formation of a New York affiliate in Harlem in 1918, under the leadership of James Hubert. He further reduced the League's education program, by replacing those activities promoting public school adult education with projects in health care and housing.

The public school activities supported by the League were based on the efforts of William L. Bulkley, one of New York's first Black principals. Before his tenure, Black access to evening schools had been blocked by segregation and fear. There were no evening schools in the Black neighborhoods, and many were reluctant to leave their own areas. In 1906, Bulkley offered a privately funded experimental program. Classes were held in the traditional elementary school subjects and more advanced technical and professional fields. So successful was the program that its attendance exceeded all the other evening schools in Manhattan (*New York Age*, 8 April 1909).

When Blacks moved north to Harlem, evening school activities continued to be confined to one school, Public School No. 89. Moreover, a new Board of Education policy soon discouraged Black participation. The curriculum was downgraded. Traditional elementary school subjects were replaced with more eclectic offerings, hobby classes replaced professional level skills training, and admission to evening trade schools was limited to those already employed in the field (New York Department of Education, 1912).

The popular Board of Education public lecture program reached the Black community in 1905, sixteen years after the project's inception. Once again, board policy weakened Black participation. Lectures in the Black community were inferior to those presented elsewhere, the presumption being that

Blacks were of lower intellectual caliber. Lecture Superintendent Harry Leipzinger's policy, mandating the avoidance of
controversy and advocacy, meant program development
addressing African-Americans' critical understanding of
themselves or the world in which they lived would be limited
(Leipzinger 1902). Although their needs were evident, Black
people were not offered information which would help them
earn a living or improve the quality of their lives. Attendance
at the lectures never equaled the response in other
communities and interest in them floundered, until the Harlem
Renaissance gave them new life.

The public library system was also slow to respond to the
specific interests of Blacks. Official leadership promoted the
neighborhood branches as educational centers, but much
depended on local staff. The Harlem Branch had serviced a
predominantly Jewish clientele, and, as this community moved
out, library use dwindled, since Blacks did not feel welcome.
During World War I, Black library use was sporadic, despite
active promotion by the *New York Age* and the organizations
which used library facilities (New York Public Library 1918).
However, dedicated leadership and extra funding would
ultimately turn the library into Harlem's intellectual center.

In addition to the adult education programs sponsored by
the churches, civic groups, philanthropic agencies, the Board
of Education, and the library, there were numerous locally
based organizations which designed and supported educational
endeavors. Some programs were frivolous, some were commercial, and some were for racial advancement. The Lincoln
Lyceum, for example, ended its Saturday night meetings with
social dancing (*New York Globe*, 21 June 1883). Independent,
profit oriented trade schools, such as Poro College (beauty
culture), and Day's School of Pedagogy (examination preparation), created additional learning opportunities. The United
Dressmakers' Protective Association, the Colored Steno-
graphers' Association, and the Negro Business League, gave
professional development lectures to their membership and,
occasionally, to the public. The National Association for the
Advancement of Colored People held weekly forums on
political or economic issues. Adult education was an auxiliary
venture for the organizations mentioned above. For one
community organization, the Negro Historical Research
Society, organized in 1911, adult education would be the
focus. This society proposed to make New York a cultural and
intellectual center for the study of Black history. Its slogan,
'Race is the Key to Unity,' was a harbinger of the emerging
education ideals of Black leadership.

EDUCATION DURING THE HARLEM RENAISSANCE

The Harlem Renaissance, generally associated with the 1920s, was a time of rising assertiveness and optimism on the part of Black leaders. Harlem, itself, was a mecca of talent and a thriving cultural force. In a memoir, the poet Langston Hughes recalled its attraction: 'I had come to New York to enter Columbia College as a freshman, but really why I had come to New York was to see Harlem' (1969:62). He was attracted to Harlem because it had come to represent the 'new Negro,' an individual who acknowledged his racial heritage and interests with pride and self-assurance.

The racial consciousness of this 'new Negro' was intensely promoted during the years following World War I. James Weldon Johnson, contributing editor of the *New York Age*, regularly used his column to cajole, harangue, and defend the Black community. The race pride Johnson hoped to build was to be a weapon which would secure the rights of his people.

Marcus Garvey, the West Indian founder of the Universal Negro Improvement Association, made racial pride a cornerstone of his program. His Booker T. Washington Institute (in reality a meeting place) in Harlem became a powerful base. The building, designated Liberty Hall, was the site for weekly mass meetings, where portions of Garvey's paper, the *Negro World*, were read to the audience (many were illiterate), where guests and Garvey organizers delivered powerful speeches, and artists presented musical selections. 'Up ye mighty race. You can accomplish what you will,' is reported to be Garvey's most memorable exhortation to his followers (McKay 1940:154). He was extremely successful in changing the self-image of hundreds of thousands of people, but he and his organization were considered dangerously radical. His conviction for mail fraud, and his imprisonment, weakened his organization. He was deported in 1927.

Alain L. Locke, philosophy professor at Howard University, played a pivotal role in developing a rationale for race consciousness which was more acceptable to most Black educators. While a Rhodes scholar, he formulated a program to develop Black self-respect and pride through reconstructing African traditions. His objectives, elaborated on in 1925 were, first, the attainment of American ideals and institutions, and, second, the correction of a damaged group 'psychology' and reshaping of a warped social perspective. Once created, this new group psychology would lead to a more positive self-respect, self-reliance, and self-direction. Subsequently, the system of tutelage and social dependency which shackled

69

Black people would be thrown off (Locke 1938). Locke's race consciousness was not anti-American. It was, rather, a way to make known all attributes of American culture so that they could be more fully shared. Consequently, racial assertiveness was a focus of many adult education programs.

The dominance which church-related lyceums enjoyed in the late nineteenth century was lost in the twentieth. By the Renaissance era, only St Marks, St James, and Abyssinia, contained regular programs. In contrast to the relative staidness of the first two, Abyssinia's meetings became more and more controversial and disorder occasionally occurred.

The Harlem-based units of the National Urban League, the YMCA, and the YWCA, continued to follow practices developed in the early 1900s. The New York Urban League, which worked closely with the public library, sponsored community forums, book clubs, and public health lectures. In addition, its officials were frequently invited by local businesses to discuss race relations with their employees (New York Urban League 1922). The establishment of an industrial relations department in 1925 (following the lead of the national body), under Ira DeA. Reid, broadened the League's educational focus. He proposed general education classes, workers' study circles, and weekly excursions to Harlem for interested white observers (Reid 1926). The excursions were a major interracial activity, with lectures, discussion groups, and visits, co-sponsored by the Fellowship of Reconciliation and involving numerous Harlem businesses, social agencies, and churches. Reid's second objective, the formation of study circles, would not be fulfilled until the Depression. Adult education activities at the other two voluntary agencies, the YMCA and the YWCA, presented opposite scenarios. Although the YMCA had a new building, its educational program floundered. Originally, the 'Opportunity School' offered classes in commercial subjects, business English, civil service examination preparation, and the 'common branches.' A proposed curriculum included the development of courses meant to improve student earning ability, e.g., classes in sales, drawing, and services, such as programs for waiters, porters, and barbers (*New York Age*, 3 January 1920). Leadership struggles between the national office and the local created a divisive climate; within a few years, the YMCA's role as an adult education center was greatly reduced.

On the other hand, the YWCA flourished. In 1926, its new building was one of the best equipped facilities for Blacks in the nation. Under Executive Director Cecilia Cabaness Saunders, the larger educational effort was not lost to the extensive trade school program. Adults were also offered conferences, lectures, study groups, and forums, in areas as diverse as history, religion, international relations, and labor problems (YWCA 1927).

The public library's adult education role was more firmly grounded in the 1920s. Its leadership was prompted by the initiative of Ernestine Rose and funds from the Carnegie Corporation and the Rosenwald Fund. Rose saw herself as aiding a 'suffering minority' (Rose 1922). Her remedy was the development of programs to stimulate racial pride and improve race relations. Under Rose's leadership, the library became the meeting place for numerous groups. It was host to exhibitions, Black history classes, Black history clubs, and public lectures. The growing responsiveness to community needs caused conflict. The popular Harlem Forum was disbanded by Rose, who chose to follow directives from the central office, which prohibited selection of controversial or political topics (*New York Age*, 15 November 1924). Her interference prompted resentment and she failed to win community support. Attendance at library programs began to dwindle and the library lost its position as a leader in adult education until the Depression.

Public school adult education in Harlem continued to be limited in both curriculum and availability. The largest of the three centers, PS No. 89, offered the standard fare: English for the foreign born, general academic classes, arts and crafts, and shorthand. The men and women who attended this center — the only co-educational site — were typical Harlem residents. The males were elevator operators or porters, and the females were cooks, maids, seamstresses, and laundry workers (New York Department of Education 1915). No high school programs were available until 1928, when declining enrollment throughout the city led to consolidation of sites (New York Department of Education 1929).

The Board of Education lecture series flourished briefly during the Renaissance, when sessions were held at the 135th Street library — Ernestine Rose's branch. Other libraries discouraged Black participation and public school sites segregated their audiences. The lecture series ended throughout the city in 1928.

Self-supporting community based institutions continued to grow and prosper, even as older centers experienced problems. Two arts schools were founded: the Music School Settlement for Colored People, led by composer and singer, J. Rosamond Johnson, and the Mwalimu School for the Development of African Music and Creative Arts. A community of Black Jews

(Beth Hatphala No. 1) offered adults instruction in the Hebrew language and Jewish culture. The Cooper School, a private adult education venture, offered instruction to all adults who lacked formal schooling. Supplementing these schools were the less formal opportunities provided by Harlem's numerous forums, civic associations, and business leagues. By the 1930s, numerous opportunities were available to Harlem's adults for pursuit of some type of learning experience, whether informational, cultural, vocational, or political. Regardless of focus, the option for learning aspects of Black history or culture, the issues associated with the improvement of race relations, or political developments, were central to most community based education efforts.

THE DEPRESSION ERA

The Depression substantially altered adult education practice. After the 1930s, the federal government became the major provider of educational opportunities. It supplanted many private programs and determined educational content. Vocationally oriented, hobby, and general elementary courses, prevailed. Programs which touched upon the social and economic questions of the period were cautiously approached and those which caused discomfort were curbed. Few were able to address basic issues affecting Black people. In effect, going to school was simply a pastime for many of Harlem's unemployed.

Most federal programs, offered under the auspices of the Works Progress Administration (WPA), were administered by the New York City Board of Education. Free, non-credit classes were held at thirty-five centers in churches, community houses, political clubs, service agencies, libraries, and schools. WPA funds were also channeled to the more than 122 Harlem groups, which sponsored forums, until government sensitivity to criticism led to the curtailment of the entire national program. The board continued to offer city funded classes at the three sites mentioned above, with one significant curriculum change: Harlem Evening High offered a Black history course in 1938 for the first time. More than 1,000 students registered for this one class, taught by the noted lecturer, Willis N. Huggins (Morgan 1984).

Three other WPA programs, the Workers' Education Bureau, the Civilian Conservation Corps (CCC), and the National Youth Administration (NYA), offered educational opportunities with varying degrees of success. The Workers'

Bureau, distrusted by both Harlem's labor radicals and the Board of Education conservatives, set up five centers, offering economics, drama, English, and Black history. Harlem's men went to a segregated CCC camp in upstate New York, which, for a short period, offered a full liberal arts program. Other camps taught literacy and the basics of writing and civics. The NYA's basic purpose was youth control: training and service, rather than educational achievement, were clearly stressed.

Despite government priorities, Black officials pushed for the interests of their race. Ambrose Caliver, Office of Education Specialist, championed a Black history focus, 'to engender the spirit of personal and race pride' (1934:40-1). James A. Atkins (1938), WPA specialist, stressed curriculum which would help Blacks meet life's challenges, and, as department trouble-shooter, was particularly critical of the quality of Harlem programs. Leaders of private programs expressed similar feelings. Ira DeA. Reid (1936), of the New York Urban League, proposed Black folk culture as the basis of educational programs focused on racial problems. The Associates in Negro Folk Education, a committee financed by the American Association for Adult Education, chaired by Eugene Kinckle Jones, national executive director of the Urban League, promoted adult education literature focusing on race relations and Black history. The Associates' editor, Alain Locke (1938), continued his promotion of race consciousness in adult education as a tool to enhance race relations. He also urged even larger dimensions: those concerned with the broadening of human values. For all of these leaders, furthering integration was a primary goal.

The Urban League and the 135th Street library offered Harlem's major non-vocational adult education projects. The League organized a Harlem Worker's Council, originally designed to educate Black workers about union principles and push for acceptance of Blacks by organized labor. For a few years, a program funded by the Carnegie Corporation, through the auspices of the AAAE, enabled the library to regain its former prominence in adult education. An adult education committee, composed of prominent educators, designed an extensive liberal arts program with a racial focus, which operated within and beyond the confines of the library. Harlem based literary clubs, study groups, civic, cultural, and religious associations, and independent schools, also continued to provide alternatives. Enterprises, new and old, made race consciousness an important ingredient in their programming and making an impact on race relations a primary objective. However, many in the adult education movement were against such a focus. Morse Cartwright, the executive director of the American Association for Adult Education, for example, was personally against social action and he counseled that education should follow rather than lead the trends of the times (American Association for Adult Education 1940).

IMPLICATIONS FOR THE 1990s

By the eve of World War II, the foundations of contemporary practice were established and a basic question was being raised about the role of adult education in a disadvantaged community. Black leaders wanted to use adult education as a catalyst for social change. They wanted to develop racial awareness, not for chauvinistic ends, but rather for consciousness raising. The anticipated result was the emergence of a people imbued with a strong sense of self, able to challenge racism, and ready to claim a place in American society. For these educators, programs had to encompass more than the three 'R's,' more than literacy, and more than skills development. In most cases, the latter was what was most readily presented.

The organizations mentioned above continue to exist, and, for the most part, their adult education programs remain tangential. The 135th Street library is an exception: it is now the Schomburg Center for Research in Black Culture.

The newer community-based agencies have their roots in the Civil Rights Movement. First World, whose slogan is 'Free Your African Mind,' is an association which promotes the study of the history and culture of Black peoples, through seminars, forums, language instruction, and excursions to Africa. Two new arts organizations exist: The Studio Museum in Harlem and the National Black Theater (NBT). The museum offers concerts, lectures, films, symposia, and gallery talks, all with a focus on the African-American. NBT models its education programs on the church experience. Classes are given in choral singing, drama, Black history, and various dimensions of group dynamics. The Harlem Institute for Social Therapy and Research is the uptown branch of the New York Institute for Social Therapy and Research, an affiliate of the New Alliance Party. This group, which has socialist leanings, actively recruits Blacks and Hispanics for its classes, seminars, and group therapy sessions. All of the programs mentioned above have a strong cultural base, which capitalizes on the strengths of Black people.

Harlem also has its own post-secondary institution, the

Malcolm-King Harlem Extension. Most of Malcolm-King's students are non-traditional: older Black females, and many who were once high school dropouts. City College, located on Harlem's fringes, began to admit large numbers of Blacks in the late 1960s. Its continuing education division offers general interest programs, which are now widely advertised in the immediate Harlem neighborhood. Malcolm-King's program, despite its adult population, is traditional liberal arts, with a focus on earning credits for transfer to a four-year school. This Harlem college, however, has the potential to do much more.

Adult educators now have a two-fold task: first, to be aware that our educational system produces a community inadequate for the tasks of today's world; and, second, to empower that system's victims, so they might truly begin to have a life worth living. For the Black community, adult education has been an imperfect catalyst. In the hands of leaders, who seek to change the outlook of the learner and change the system, education's power is clear. However, when external forces — even those well-meaning ones — and uncritical internal forces, are in control, inevitably Blacks are offered remedies that fail to address their total situation. Adult educators must, therefore, always be conscious of the inequities of the system and the problems of the learner.

REFERENCES

American Association for Adult Education (1940) *Annual Report of the Executive Director in Behalf of the Executive Board, 1939-40*, New York: Author.

Atkins, J.A. (1938) 'The participation of Negroes in the pre-school and adult education programs,' *Journal of Negro Education* 7.

Brown, J.S. (1904) 'The New York branch of the Young Men's Christian Association,' *Colored American Magazine*, June.

Caliver, A. (1934) 'Outlook for Negro education,' *School Life*, October.

Davis, A.F. (1967) *Spearheads for Reform: The Social Settlements and the Progressive Movement, 1890-1914*, New York: Oxford University Press.

Freeman, R.G. (1966) 'The free Negro in the era before the Civil War,' Doctoral dissertation, Columbia University. *Dissertation Abstracts International* 30.

Hughes, L. (1969) 'My early days in Harlem,' in J.H. Clarke (ed.) *Harlem: A Community in Transition*, New York:

Citadel Press.

Hunton, W.A. (1905) 'Colored Men's Department of the Young Men's Christian Association,' *Voice of the Negro*, June.

Laidlow, W. (1932) *Population of the City of New York, 1890–1930*, New York: Cities Census Committee.

Leipzinger, H.M. (1902) *The Free Lecture Course of New York City: Address at the Twelfth Annual Reunion, 1 May 1902*, New York: Wynkorp Hellenbeck Crawford Co.

Locke, A.L. (1938) 'Negro needs as adult education opportunities,' *Findings of the First Annual Conference on Adult Education and the Negro*, Norfolk, Va.: Hampton Institute.

Logan, R.W. (1970) *The Negro in the United States*. Vol. 1: *A History to 1945: From Slavery to Second-Class Citizenship*, New York: Van Nostrand Reinhold.

McKay, C. (1940) *Harlem: Negro Metropolis*, New York: Dutton.

Meier, A. (1964) *Negro Thought in America, 1880–1915: Racial Ideology in the Age of Booker T. Washington*, Ann Arbor: University of Michigan Press.

Morgan, C.T. (1984) 'Finding a way out: adult education during the Great Depression,' *Afro-Americans in New York Life and History* 8.

New York Age (1905–40).

New York Department of Education (1912–35) *Annual Report of the City Superintendent of Schools: Includes Report on Evening Schools*, New York: Author.

New York Globe (1893) 21 June.

New York Public Library (1918) *Annual Report*, New York: Astor, Lenox, & Tilden Foundation.

New York Urban League (1922) *Annual Report: 1921*, New York: Author.

Ottley, R. and Weathersby, W. (eds) (1967) *The Negro in New York: An Informal Social History*, New York: Praeger.

Parris, G.E. and Brooks, L. (1971) *A History of the National Urban League*, Boston: Little, Brown.

Porter, D.B. (1936) 'The organized educational activities of Negro literary societies, 1828–1846,' *Journal of Negro Education* 5.

Reid, I. DeA. (1926) 'Steps in social progress: memorandum on the New York Urban League for 1926,' unpublished manuscript.

—— (1936) *Adult Education among Negroes*, Washington, DC: Associates in Negro Folk Education.

Rose, E. [Name misprinted in original as 'Ross'] (1922) 'Books and the color line,' *Survey*, 15 April.

United States Department of Education (1983) *On Adult*

Learning, Washington, DC: Newsletter of the Office of Vocational and Adult Education, June.

Werner, M.W. (1986) '13% of US adults are illiterate in English, a federal study finds,' *New York Times*, 21 April.

Young Women's Christian Association, West 137th Street Branch (1927) *Annual Report for 1926*, New York: Author.

Chapter Five

ADULT EDUCATION AND THE AMERICAN INDIAN

John W. Tippeconnic III

The purpose of this chapter is to discuss and analyze adult education and the American Indian.[1] The discussion will include an account of the status of the American Indian[2] in America; the education of American Indian adults; and a discussion of current leaders in Indian adult education. Projections into the future will also be made.

American Indians have a unique place in America. The uniqueness is based on a special relationship between Indian nations or tribes and the federal government. It is important to have some knowledge of this relationship, in order to understand the complex nature of the education of American Indians today and why the government plays a dominant role in the education of Indian people.

The special relationship was established during the founding of the United States of America.[3] American Indians, being indigenous to North America, were recognized as sovereign nations by the United States government. During the period 1778-1871, approximately 400 treaties were entered into between the United States government and Indian nations. In exchange for vast amounts of land, the treaties granted Indian nations specific services, like education and health. Of these treaties, 120 had conditions that specifically mentioned education (American Indian Policy Review Commission 1976). Since the end of the treaty period, presidential executive orders, Supreme Court decisions, and Acts of Congress have recognized and strengthened this special relationship.

This relationship continues to exist today and provides the legal basis for federal responsibility and involvement in the education of Indian people.

The 1980 US Census reported that there were 1,355,676 American Indians residing in the United States. An additional 56,367 Eskimos and Aleuts were counted, resulting in a total population of 1,412,043, a 72 percent increase compared to the 1970 Census.[4] The Census also revealed (Bureau of the Census 1984):

1. One-fourth (339,836) of all American Indians lived on one of the 278 Federal or State Reservations.
2. The median age of the American Indian is 22.9, compared to 30 for the total US population.
3. The unemployment rate for American Indians was 13 percent, compared to 6.5 percent for the United States.
4. The poverty rate for American Indians was 27.5 percent, compared to 12.4 percent for the total US population.
5. The percentage of families maintained by women was 23, compared to 14 for the total US population.
6. 56 percent of American Indians 25 years old and over were high school graduates, compared to 66 percent of the total population. Eight percent of the American Indian population had four or more years of college, compared to 16 percent of the total population.
7. American Indians, Eskimos, and Aleuts, represent less than 1 percent of the total US population.

The social, economic, and educational data presented by the Census clearly showed that American Indians fall behind in virtually every category. The Census represents one source of data. There are other sources, i.e., tribes, Bureau of Indian Affairs, states, and organizations, which collect similar data. Often the data are different. For example, Masterson, Cook, and Trahant (1987) recently reported a 60 percent unemployment rate for American Indians living on reservations and 26 percent for those living off reservations. There are over 290 recognized tribes in America, each with its own culture, including language differences. This diversity makes it difficult to generalize across tribes. Social, economic, and educational data can differ significantly among tribes.

From the very beginning of non-Indian contact, Indian affairs have been influenced by the federal government's policy toward Indians and by the country's political, social, and economic climate. Assimilation, either forced or through persuasion, has been the dominant policy of the federal government toward American Indians (US Senate 1969).

The resulting formal education of American Indians has not been a satisfactory one.[5] During the 1870s the federal government established the boarding school system, which separated Indian students from their families. Adults or family members were considered a negative influence, since the schools were trying to change the Indian by de-emphasizing, and forbidding, Indian languages and other aspects of their culture. One result has been a consistent concern, to this day, that parents are not involved in the education of their children.

In the 1930s there was a change from boarding schools to day schools, so children could remain home with their families. Relevant curriculum, adapted to the needs of the students, was suggested. Bilingual education and Indian cultural programs were implemented. The 1940s and 1950s saw a return to the pre-1930s approach to education. Termination of services for Indians became the official government policy, to end the Indian problem. It was believed that termination would expedite forced assimilation and make better Americans out of Indians. Again, parents or adults were separated from their children.

A special five-year program to educate Navajos was initiated in 1946. It emphasized English, academic development, and vocational training of young adult Navajos (Thompson 1975). In 1952 a relocation program was established that placed Indians in urban areas, where they would learn a skill and, it was hoped, find employment (Simpson and Yinger 1957). In 1955, the Bureau of Indian Affairs 'introduced a pilot program of adult education designed to improve adult English literacy on five reservations' (Szasz 1974:137). All these programs were a result of the termination policy and sought to assimilate the American Indian as quickly as possible.

The 1960s brought change, as the 'Great Society' programs provided opportunities for local economic and community development. Once again, parental involvement, bilingual education, and relevant curriculum were considered important in the education of Indian people. Indian-controlled schools developed during this time as alternatives to public schools and education by the Bureau of Indian Affairs (BIA).

Self-determination became the official federal government policy in the 1970s and continues to this day. The essence of self-determination is that Indian people will be in control and make the necessary decisions to determine their own destiny.

Because of the special relationship with the federal government, American Indians look primarily to Washington, DC, for funds to support programs that educate them. At times the responsibility for Indian education becomes unclear because, as American citizens, American Indians are entitled to all the rights, including education, provided by the states. Thus, the role and responsibility of the states and of the federal government in their education is not clearly defined.

During the 1980s the picture became even more complex, given President Reagan's policy of federal fiscal constraint and states' rights in education.

At the federal level, the Bureau of Indian Affairs and the Department of Education are the two main agencies that have major responsibility for the education of Indian people. Both have programs in adult education.

The BIA is located in the Department of Interior and has been involved in the education of Indian people since 1870. Currently, the BIA operates schools, provides a higher education program, supports Indian community colleges, and has an adult education program. Education is the largest expenditure in the BIA budget.

The objective of the BIA adult education program is to provide opportunities for adult Indians and Alaska natives to complete high school, acquire basic literacy skills, and gain new skills, to improve themselves as members of the community. The program is limited to individuals from federally recognized tribes, who are at least sixteen years of age, or beyond the age of compulsory school attendance under state or tribal law, and are not currently required to attend school (Jones 1985).

Typical courses offered are: Adult Basic Education (ABE); General Educational Development Test (GED) preparation; life coping skills; instructional information services from federal, state, and tribal programs; continuing education courses; and community education classes that are of personal interest. In 1984 the BIA provided $3,747,100 for eighty-eight adult education programs that provided services to 14,607 Indian adults. The type of service and number of individuals participating were: ABE, 1,958; GED, 3,480; continuing education, 3,954; life coping skills, 2,808; counseling, 2,407. In fiscal year 1987 the total adult education budget was $3,496,000 (BIA 1985). The BIA adult education budget is tied to a Tribal Priority System, which allows the tribes to determine funding levels by establishing priorities in services.

The Department of Education (DOE) is the other major governmental agency that provides funds to support Indian adult education programs. DOE administers the provisions of the Indian Education Act of 1972, Title IV, Public Law 92-318, as amended. Part C of the law authorizes adult education activities. Title IV, as the law is commonly known, also authorizes programs for public schools (Part A) and programs from childhood to higher education, primarily for Indian tribes, Indian organizations, and Indian institutions (Part B).

In budget and program support, Part C, or adult education,

is small, while Part A is the largest and receives the most attention. Part C provides activities designed to improve educational opportunities below the college level for Indian adults. Specific activities authorized are:

1. Education Services for Indian Adults which provide opportunities in basic education, to develop literacy and basic skills, and, in secondary education, preparation for the high school equivalency examination.
2. Consumer education.
3. Academic and career counseling, aptitude and vocational testing, and job referrals.
4. Planning, Pilot, and Demonstration Projects for Indian Adults, which provide opportunities to test and demonstrate innovative approaches to adult education specifically designed for Indian adults.

(Department of Education 1983:25)

Funds are distributed through a competitive grants process to Indian tribes, organizations, and institutions. Individuals are eligible for Part C adult education services if they meet the Indian Education Act definition of Indian. 'Indian' means an individual who is

1. A member of a tribe, band, or other organized group of Indians, including those tribes, bands, or groups terminated since 1940 and those recognized by the state in which they reside.
2. A descendant, in the first or second degree, of an individual described in paragraph (1) of this definition.
3. Considered by the Secretary of the Interior to be an Indian for any purpose; or
4. An Eskimo or Aleut or other Alaska Native.

(Department of Education 1984:23762)

The BIA definition of Indian is more restrictive. Their definition is an individual who is a member of a federally recognized Indian tribe; has at least one-quarter degree Indian blood quantum; and lives on or near a federal Indian reservation (Pelavin Associates, Inc. 1984:23).

Title IV, Part C, has had a difficult history. In 1979, Part C was appropriated $5,930,000, which supported sixty grants. In 1985, $2,940,000 supported twenty-eight grants in fourteen states (National Advisory Council on Indian Education 1986). A difference of approximately $3 million and a decrease of more than 50 percent in the number of grants over six years is significant.

There are other programs, beside the BIA and Title IV, Part C, that provide services to Indian adults. The Adult Education Act, PL 89-750, as amended, provides a grant program in each state. School districts and public and private nonprofit agencies, organizations, and institutions, are eligible for the funds. There is limited participation by Indian adults in these programs; it is impossible to determine the extent of participation, since accurate records are not kept (McQuiston and Brod 1981).

In 1976 the National Indian Adult Education Association (NIAEA) was established as a professional organization to promote, support, and work toward, the improvement of education for Indian adults. Although small, NIAEA has been effective in keeping attention directed toward the education of Indian adults. NIAEA meets annually to address issues and concerns and to pass resolutions, which prove to be a good source in determining issues in Indian adult education. Resolutions passed at the 1987 annual NIAEA conference addressed:

1. The creation of a 2 percent set-aside of Federal Adult Education Act funds for Indian tribes and organizations.
2. The establishment of a National Technical Assistance Center for Indian adults.
3. The support of an increased appropriation for Indian adult education.
4. Congressional testimony to support the re-authorization of Indian adult education under the Elementary and Secondary Education Act.
5. A request for funding from the US Department of Education for the annual NIAEA conference.
6. A request for a national study of Indian adult education.
   (National Indian Adult Education Association 1987)

Reva Crawford, National Co-Chairperson for NIAEA, identified two major concerns facing the education of Indian adults. First, there is no organized data gathering or research mechanism that addresses Indian adult education; and second, the education of American Indian adults has been seriously neglected, as evidenced by funding levels, lack of technical assistance, and the lack of administrative support in the Bureau of Indian Affairs.[6]

The National Indian Education Association (NIEA) and the National Congress of American Indians (NCAI) are other professional organizations that advocate quality education for

Indian people at all levels. The National Advisory Council on Indian Education (NACIE), created by the Indian Education Act of 1972, is charged with the responsibility of advising the president and Congress on the administration of Indian education programs, primarily Title IV programs, including Part C Adult Education Programs.

State departments of education have become very active in Indian education in the 1980s; however, their concerns are largely directed toward elementary and secondary school education.

There has been little systematic research and study on the nature of adult education for American Indians. Much of the work that has been done is descriptive in nature and funded by federal sources.

The following discussion will focus on two kinds of studies: those that address Indian education in general, and those that are limited specifically to Indian adult education.

The Meriam Report (1928) is recognized as the first major assessment of the economic, social, and educational conditions of the American Indian. The report was very critical of Indian education, especially boarding schools that separated students from parents. Adult education was indirectly addressed, when it was mentioned that 'a genuine education program will have to comprise the adults of the community as well as the children' (p.349). Brophy and Aberle (1966) related adult education to teaching Indian parents the value of education, especially having their children attend school regularly.

The Congressional study, *Indian Education: A National Tragedy — A National Challenge*, or the 'Kennedy Report,' was published in 1969 (US Senate). This study focused on adult education more than any other study up to that time. It found a national commitment to adult education programs for American Indians was needed, because of their low economic status, the rise in alcoholism, the lack of employment capabilities, the inability of too many Indian adults to read and write, and in the general lack of fulfillment of Indian adults on reservations. Approximately 75,000 Indian adults were reported to be functionally illiterate, or without the ability to read and write at the fifth grade level. This constituted a functional illiteracy problem more than four times the national average. High unemployment and high drop-out rates were also found.

The Kennedy Report went on to recommend national goals and objectives be established to eliminate adult illiteracy in Indian communities and to provide adult school equivalency programs for all Indian adults (p.107). The report went on specifically to recommend

> that an exemplary program of adult education be developed which would provide for the following: Basic literacy opportunities to all non-literate Indian adults, opportunities to all Indian adults to qualify for a high school equivalency certificate, surveys to define accurately the extent of the problems of illiteracy and lack of high school completion on Indian reservations, and a major research and development program to develop more innovative and effective techniques for achieving the literacy and high school equivalency goals.

> ... that the adult education program be effectively integrated with the rest of the BIA education program. The adult education program should as much as possible be placed under Indian control and contribute as well as benefit from the development of Indian controlled community schools.

> (p.129)

The Kennedy Report proved to be an influential and significant document. It was a factor in the development and passage of the Indian Education Act of 1972, which authorized Indian adult education programs.

Another general study on Indian education was the *National Study of American Indian Education*, conducted from 1967 to 1971. The primary purpose of the study was to examine the current state of Indian education. Adult education was not addressed, other than a few descriptions of programs that existed at sites selected in the study (see Fuchs and Havighurst 1972).

In 1975 Congress authorized an American Indian Policy Review Commission (AIPRC) to conduct a comprehensive study of the condition of the American Indian (1976). Like the Meriam Report in 1928, the AIPRC included a section on Indian education. The report addressed adult education briefly, and in passing, by stating:

> Throughout the history of Indian affairs, adult education has taken many forms.... Adult education like the education of Indian children has been used as an instrument of political policy periods to retrain adults to fit into the American society. The past decade has seen adult education of reservation Indians follow primarily a continuing education vein ... and the Office of

Management and Budget and the Congress do not seem to
respond to the need for literacy training or for high school
equivalency programs.

(p.128)

There have been even fewer studies that have been limited
exclusively to the education of Indian adults. The four studies
mentioned below were all conducted with federal funds,
primarily from the Indian Education Act of 1972.

The research study, *Literacy and Education Among Adult
Indians in Oklahoma* (Hall and Hackbert 1977), was released
in 1977. The purpose of the study was to survey educational
attainment and functional literacy among Indians in
Oklahoma, and to disseminate the results to tribes, state, and
national organizations. The study was the first of its kind, thus
emphasis was placed not only on the findings, but also on the
research methodology. Data were gathered that described
personal, social, tribal, and employment characteristics, and
functional literacy levels, in four knowledge and four skill
areas. The study estimated there were 63,490 adult American
Indians in Oklahoma. Major findings included:

1. Over 51 percent of the Indian adults in Oklahoma have not
   completed high school and over 22 percent have not
   completed 8th grade.
2. The illiteracy rate varies, depending on which area of
   literacy is examined. However, in total, there are an
   estimated 36,000 Indian adults living in Oklahoma who are
   functionally illiterate in one or more areas. This represents
   56.9 percent of the total Indian adult population.
3. 42.8 percent lacked the skills necessary to function as
   consumers within contemporary American society. Another
   30.4 percent were only marginally competent at consumer
   skills.
4. Over 63 percent were not able to perform daily arithmetic
   and an additional 17 percent were only marginally able to
   do so.
5. 62 percent did not fully possess the skills required to
   respond to the health problems which are of major concern
   to the American Indian community.
6. Functional literacy is highly related to income level. The
   more functionally literate a person is, the higher his/her
   income is likely to be.

(pp. xvi-xvii)

The study went on to recommend that adequate education

needs to be provided in the functional skills which are used for surviving and coping in day-to-day situations, with emphasis on reading and comprehension of materials related to health and money matters (p.196).

In 1977 the office of Indian Education, in the Department of Health, Education, and Welfare,[7] funded a national study to identify and accurately describe the extent of problems of illiteracy and the lack of high school completion among adult American Indians, Aleuts, and Eskimos. *The Status of Educational Attainment and Performance of Adult American Indians and Alaska Natives* (McQuiston and Brod 1981) was the first national study on Indian adult education. Building on the Oklahoma study previously mentioned (Hall and Hackbert 1977), the primary purpose of the study was to provide decision makers with an accurate assessment of the adult education needs of American Indians. The study focused on the levels of functional competency and educational attainment, various social indicators, and on the operations, and attainments, of federal and state supported programs as providers of adult education services to American Indians.

Data were gathered from local adult education projects, state departments of education, and 4,095 individual home interviews. The results concluded that 'Few American Indians have attended college and only 57 percent have a high school diploma or its equivalent.'

One-third of all adult Indians are dissatisfied with the education they received. Over three-quarters of them would have liked more education. In addition, two-thirds of the adult Indian populations felt that they received an inappropriate education for the kinds of occupations and lives they wanted to lead (Brod and McQuiston 1983:3-6).

> ... The performance levels of the US Indian population are far below those of non-Indians on the traditional reading, writing, computation and economic dimensions. These differences exist even though some 23 percent of the adult Indian population has attended school as recently as last year. Furthermore, the data show clear regional differences: adult Indian performance levels are consistently lower in the western states as compared to the eastern results.
>
> (McQuiston and Brod 1981:55)

Finally, surveys of state departments of education and local adult education projects, funded by the Indian Education Act (non-BIA programs), yielded the following results:

(1) Whenever numbers of Indians participating in state adult education programs and activities were requested, virtually no data were reported. Over 92 percent of the states admitted that they had never conducted a formal, documented state assessment to ascertain adult Indian education needs.

(2) The greatest difficulties states perceived in involving Indian adults as students in state operated adult education programs were: inadequate recruitment channels with Indian communities (44 percent), a lack of an identifiable community from which to recruit Indian participants (36 percent), a lack of staff trained to deal with the special problems of Indian adults (33 percent), transportation problems (28 percent), children or child care (23 percent), or a critical incompatibility between Indian adults and their educational programs (21 percent). Other problems included Indian transience (15 percent), prejudice (13 percent), program design (10 percent) and language barriers (5 percent).

(3) The five most important needs of Indian adults as identified by adult education program directors were high school preparatory (GED), basic education, vocational/technical education, life coping/consumer education, and Indian cultural activities.

(4) Although the typical Indian-operated adult education program received 95 percent of its operating budget from Title IV, Part C funding, 29 percent of these programs applied to their state agency (SAE) for direct funding. However, only 13 percent of the applications were approved for funding (Brod and McQuiston 1983:10-12).

Recommendations called for more research on Indian education, an evaluation of the delivery system in Indian education, improvement of the capabilities of teachers, provision of instruction in traditional Indian languages, provision of educational modules in the Indian and non-Indian cultures, and increase of funding for Indian education programs (Brod and McQuiston 1983:12-14).

There are two other national studies worth mentioning. They are similar, in that they both were federally funded and focused on Indian adult education programs funded by Title IV, Part C of the Indian Education Act of 1972.

The first study dealt with 'capacity building' and was conducted as a result of a direct request by the Senate and House Appropriations Conference Committees. In general, 'capacity building' referred to the ability of the grantee to develop and implement capacities for educational self-determination. The purposes of the study were to determine if adult education projects were successful in capacity building efforts, effective in providing services, and developed to the point where they can serve as replicable models (US Office of Education 1979). The findings were very positive and concluded:

> ... it is clear that projects are addressing the educational needs of Native Americans, that they are having far reaching effects on Indian children and adults, and that these results are developing Indian capacities for educational self-determination.
>
> (p.8)

An Evaluation of the Indian Education Act, Title IV, Part C: Education for Indian Adults (Pelavin Associates, Inc., 1984) is the second national study conducted by the federal government. It described and evaluated adult education programs at ten sites. The major findings of the evaluation were:

> Part C projects are doing what the law and regulations intend....

> Generally, the services delivered by Part C projects are those that seem to be the most necessary. They concentrate on providing adult education and preparation for the GED. However, in some cases adult basic education is the service that is most needed but not provided. In the few instances where the most needed service is not provided, two factors may be responsible: (1) services such as adult basic education are more difficult to provide than GED preparation; and (2) some projects seem better able to provide services that match the educational needs of their target populations.

> The grants mechanism and review process could be modified to be a more effective method for serving the target populations.

> Duplication of services, defined as instances where the same adult Indian population is served by two or more federally-funded programs offering the same or similar services, was investigated. Overall, little duplication of services was found between Part C projects and those funded by other federal programs such as state grants for adult education or adult education programs funded by the Bureau of Indian Affairs.

However, although there was little duplication of services, projects serving adult Indians have not been equally distributed throughout the nation. Some of the same grantees have been receiving awards for many years, and many of the grantees are located close to other adult education programs, particularly in urban areas.

Part C has received relatively little attention from the Office of Indian Education Programs.

(pp.iii–iv)

There have been other efforts to gather and analyze data concerning Indian adult education. Applications for funding often include data that demonstrate a need. Many local needs assessments are conducted annually to demonstrate this need.

In addition, Indian tribes, Indian organizations, and Indian institutions conduct their own studies or assessments to determine local needs. For example, the Winnebago Tribe of Wisconsin found career counseling and planning to be a need (Nelson 1982). And the Choctaw Tribe of Mississippi described their successful adult education program in an annual evaluation report (Mississippi Band of Choctaw Indians 1975).

LEADERS IN INDIAN ADULT EDUCATION

There has been a noticeable absence of leadership at the national level, both in the BIA and in the Department of Education. Rather, leadership has developed at the local program level. There are many individuals who could be mentioned; however, focus will be placed on Neel Rogers, of the Mississippi Choctaw; Reva Crawford, of the Boston Indian Council, Inc.; Mary Jo Cole, of the Cherokee Nation of Oklahoma; and Joy Hanley, of the Affiliation of Arizona Indian Centers, Inc. These individuals share an understanding of the history and needs of American Indian adults and a commitment to develop educational programs at the local level that feature respect for individual learners; respect for the culture and language of the learner; an environment that is relaxed and free from fear of failure; offer a wide variety of unstructured times; offer support services, such as transportation and child care; encourage children to see parents as learners; and clearly demonstrate that ownership of the programs are local and provide service for 'Indians, by

Indians.'

Reva Crawford is an outspoken leader in Indian adult education. She was instrumental in the founding of the American Indian Adult Education Association in 1976 and continues to be a strong advocate at the local, state, and national levels. Her program at the Boston Indian Council, Inc. has had significant success in increasing the number of GED graduates; increasing the income level of participants — thus reducing the number receiving public assistance; and increasing the formal education level of participants, many of whom go on to higher education.

Neel Rogers, Director of Adult Education for the Mississippi Choctaw, is involved in a program that has received national acclaim. Their model of providing services to American Indian adults contains the characteristics and features mentioned above and continues to be adapted by programs around the country. The impact of the program in Mississippi is such that 437 Choctaw adults have received GEDs; this represents 58 percent of all Mississippi Choctaws who ever completed high school. The program has also witnessed increased income gains and improved self-concepts on the part of participants, and more individuals going on to colleges and universities. An important part of the program is promoting the value of education to all family members.

Mary Jo Cole is the Director of the Adult Education Program for the Cherokee Nation of Oklahoma. Like Reva Crawford and Neel Rogers, Mary Jo Cole shares a very personal interest in, and commitment to, improved education for Indian people. Her program has enjoyed the same success as those in Boston and Mississippi, with over 400 individuals who have received GEDs. Mary Jo Cole is co-chairperson of the National Indian Adult Education Association, and is also active in local, state, and national educational activities for Indian people.

Joy Hanley is the Executive Director of the Affiliation of Arizona Indian Centers, Inc. in Phoenix, Arizona. She has been a leader in the development of a culture-based language arts curriculum, called 'Pathways.' The curriculum is designed for American Indian adult learners at the ABE and pre-GED levels. The curriculum was recognized by the US Department of Education and the National Indian Education Association as a showcase project which made a significant contribution to the education of American Indians.

Joy Hanley previously served as the Vice President of Navajo Community College. Her recognition of the importance of education, plus her understanding of, and respect for, the needs and culture of Indian people are undoubtedly responsible for her success.

THE FUTURE

What is the future of adult education for American Indians? As with Indian education in general, it will remain highly political. Activity will continue to center on the federal budget process, with efforts to increase the awareness and priority of adult education programs. However, increased political activity will happen at the state levels, as states become more involved in the education of Indian adults.

The future is more positive than negative. There is always the danger, or suspicion, that the federal government will return to the 'termination' policy, and do away with educational services for Indian people. This is highly unlikely for several reasons. First, there is an established and recognized legal framework that will insure continued federal government responsibility for Indian education. Second, American Indian tribes and individuals have become very knowledgeable and sophisticated in their approach to working with the federal government. Individuals like Reva Crawford, Neel Rogers, Mary Jo Cole, Joy Hanley, and others, will continue the efforts that have been successful. Any attempt to do away with services will be met with a well organized community, as well as legal, effort, which is likely to prove successful. And, third, states, faced with tight budgets, will continue to look to the federal government to fund or supplement education programs for American Indians.

It is possible the delivery system will change. In time, the education function of the Bureau of Indian Affairs may be transferred to tribes, or existing public schools, or possibly be transferred to the Department of Education. Change will not come without difficulty, since the BIA is an entrenched bureaucracy. However, more important to Indian people is the fact that the BIA is the agency that represents that 'special relationship' Indian tribes have with the federal government. Concepts like 'tribal sovereignty,' 'trust responsibility,' and 'Indian preference' are associated with the BIA more so than with any other federal agency. The delivery system will more than likely be expanded beyond the BIA and Title IV, Part C, to other federal and state public and private programs. In fact, it is already happening, as Indian people take advantage of other federal programs, or those offered at the state level. Research, and other data gathering efforts, will increase and go beyond the federally initiated studies that supported budget decisions. Rather, educational questions about adult learning will be addressed.

As mentioned earlier, the education of adult Indians is related to the larger picture of Indian education in general, to the federal policy toward Indians, and to the social, economic, and political situation in America. As these things change, so will the education of Indian adults.

NOTES

1. Emphasis will be placed on programs that are specifically labeled 'adult education.' Although other programs, i.e., vocational education and job training, are related to adult education, they will not be included in this chapter.
2. 'American Indians,' as used in this chapter, includes American Indians, Eskimos, Aleuts, and other Alaska natives.
3. A detailed account of the special relationship can be found in Deloria (1985) and the National Advisory Council on Indian Education annual report (1982:110-24).
4. The rapid growth in ten years is due to the high birthrate but also attributed to the improved methods of counting American Indians used by the Bureau of the Census. Even with this increase, many tribes feel their population figures are higher; there are some estimates of two million American Indians in America.
5. The intent here is to present a brief history. A detailed history can be found in the American Indian Policy Review Commission report (1975), Szasz (1974), and the US Senate report (1969).
6. Reva Crawford, Boston Indian Council, Inc., and Mary Jo Cole, Cherokee Nation of Oklahoma, are Co-Chairs of the National Indian Adult Education Association. The concerns were expressed in a letter from Ms Crawford.
7. In 1980 the Department of Education was established, thus eliminating the Department of Health, Education, and Welfare. When the Department of Education was organized, the Office of Indian Education became the office of Indian Education Programs.

REFERENCES

American Indian Policy Review Commission (1976) *Report on*

Indian Education, prepared as part of the Final Report to the American Indian Policy Review Commission, Washington, DC: US Government Printing Office.

Brod, R.L. and McQuiston, J.M. (1981) *Literacy and Educational Needs of American Indian Adults: Some Initial Results and Observations on Conducting the First National Study*, Washington, DC: National Institute of Education (ERIC Document Reproduction Service, No. ED 204 086).

Brod, R.L. and McQuiston, J.M. (1983) 'American Indian adult education and literacy: the first national survey,' *Journal of American Indian Education* 22.

Brophy, W.A. and Aberle, S.D. (1966) *The Indian: America's Unfinished Business*, Norman: University of Oklahoma Press.

Bureau of the Census (1984) *American Indian Areas and Alaska Native Villages: 1980*. Supplementary Report PC80-S1-13, Washington, DC: US Government Printing Office.

Bureau of Indian Affairs (1985) *United States Department of the Interior Budget Justifications, FY 1985*, Washington, DC: Author.

Deloria, V. Jr (1975) *Legislative Analysis of the Federal Role in Indian Education*, Washington, DC: US Office of Education.

Department of Education (1984) 'Indian education programs: final regulations,' *Federal Register*, 49 (111):23760–76, 7 June.

—— (1983) *Indian Education: Justifications of Appropriation Estimates for Committees on Appropriations, Fiscal Year 1984*, Washington, DC: Author.

Fuchs, E. and Havighurst, R.J. (1972) *To Live on this Earth: American Indian Education*, Garden City, NY: Doubleday.

Hall, P.R. and Hackbert, P.H. (1977) *Literacy and Education among Adult Indians in Oklahoma*, Vol. I, Norman: University of Oklahoma (ERIC Reproduction Service, No. ED 136 381).

Jones, R.S. (1985) *Federal Programs of Assistance to American Indians*. A Report prepared for the Senate Select Committee on Indian Affairs of the United States Senate, Washington, DC: Government Printing Office.

Masterson, M., Cook, C., and Trahant, M. (1987) *Fraud in Indian Country: A Billion Dollar Betrayal*. Reprint of Series in *The Arizona Republic*, 4–11 October.

McQuiston, J.M. and Brod, R.L. (1981) *The Status of Educational Attainment and Performance of Adult American Indians and Alaska Natives*, Philadelphia, Miss.:

National Indian Management Service of America (ERIC Document Reproduction Service, No. ED 237 249).

Meriam, L. (ed.) (1928) *The Problem of Indian Administration*, Baltimore, Md.: Johns Hopkins Press.

Mississippi Band of Choctaw Indians (1975) *Final Report: Choctaw Adult Education Demonstration Project*, Philadelphia, Miss.: Author (ERIC Document Reproduction Service, No. ED 115 414).

National Advisory Council on Indian Education (1982) *Indian Education: America's Unpaid Debt*, Eighth Annual Report to the Congress of the United States, Washington, DC: Government Printing Office.

National Indian Adult Education Association (1987) *Resolutions Passed at the Annual Conference of the National Indian Education Association in Washington, DC*, Tahlequah, Ok.: Author.

Nelson, O. (1982) *Winnebago Vocation Needs Assessment Study: Vocational Needs of Adults*, Madison, Wis.: Author (ERIC Document Reproduction Service, No. ED 226 157).

Pelavin Associates, Inc. (1984) *An Evaluation of the Indian Education Act, Title IV, Part C: Education for Indian Adults*, Washington, DC: Education Analysis Center for Educational Quality and Equality.

Simpson, G.E. and Yinger, J.M. (eds) (1957) *American Indians and American Life*, Millwood, NY: Kraus Reprint Co.

Szasz, M. (1974) *Education and the American Indian: The Road to Self-Determination*, Albuquerque: University of New Mexico Press.

Thompson, H. (1975) *The Navajos' Long Walk for Education: A History of Navajo Education*, Tsaile, Navajo Nation, Arizona: Navajo Community College Press.

United States Office of Education (1979) *Office of Indian Education Review of Title IV-B and Title IV-C 'Capacity Building' Projects*, Washington, DC: Author.

United States Senate (1969) *Indian Education: A National Tragedy — A National Challenge*, Committee on Labor and Public Welfare, Special Subcommittee on Indian Education.

Chapter Six

THE EDUCATION OF HISPANIC ADULTS: PEDAGOGICAL STRANDS AND CULTURAL MEANINGS

Martha Montero-Sieburth

Through the 1980s the issue of the education of Hispanics has grown more urgent, as various reports have published some disturbing information.[1]

Analysis in the Hispanic Policy Development Project (1984, vol. 2:26) indicates that, while a majority of Hispanic students enter high school with educational and career aspirations as high as any other group, over 40 percent leave before the tenth grade. Moreover, 45 percent of Mexican American and Puerto Rican students never complete high school, compared to 17 percent of Anglo students (1984, vol. 1:10). This lag restricts Hispanic entry into white-collar jobs, leaving Hispanics with 45.5 percent in blue-collar positions, compared to 31.9 percent of the total population. Further, close to 800,000 Hispanic families, or 24 percent of all American Hispanics, were classified as 'poor' by the Census Bureau, compared to 8.8 percent of non-Hispanic white families.

The combination of poverty, marginal employment, and poor public school academic performance, renders post-secondary opportunities for Hispanics all the more significant. In 1978, 21.3 percent of those persons sixteen years or older participating in federally funded Adult Basic and Secondary Education Programs were Hispanic (Cook and Quinones 1983:2), and 61 percent of those Hispanics who did finish high school, as reported in the *High School and Beyond* national survey follow-up study, attended two-year colleges (Lee 1985). Of those sixteen years and over enrolled in post-secondary school, 29 percent of the Hispanics attended non-collegiate schools, i.e., vocational and adult education programs (Census Bureau 1980). Hispanics account for 6.8 percent of the total enrollment in non-collegiate education, which is higher than their proportion of the United States population.

This chapter addresses the experience of Hispanics in

Adult Basic Education programs. It attempts to: (1) situate Hispanics within a demographic and socio-historical framework, emphasizing the diversity within the Hispanic community; (2) identify major strands in the education of Hispanic adults, namely grassroots development and Freire's pedagogy, using specific case studies and reported perspectives of particular educators and practitioners; and, (3) conclude with projections of effective adult education for Hispanics.

DEMOGRAPHY

Hispanics comprise the youngest and fastest growing population group in the United States. The 1980 Census shows that, although 14,605,880, or 6.4 percent of the population, is Hispanic, this is considered a conservative estimate, and, as of 1988, definitely out-of-date, given the influx of 'over 113,000 immigrants each year' (Cook and Quinones 1983:1).[2] More likely, according to Cook and Quinones, there are about twenty-three million Hispanics in the United States. With the high fertility rate of Hispanic women and increases in immigration, there may be as many as thirty-seven million to forty-seven million Hispanics in the United States by the year 2020, according to census projections.

Spanish is spoken at home by over eleven million persons, and close to three million are monolingual Spanish speakers (Hispanic Policy Development Project 1984, vol. 2:15). Over 70 percent of the Hispanics are clustered in five states: California, Florida, Illinois, New York, and Texas. 'Because of their geographic concentration, Hispanics over the next two decades will become the majority of the school population and the majority of the work force in many areas of the nation' (Hispanic Policy Development Project 1984, vol. 1:2-3). Hispanics tend to reside in urban areas, and are clustered in segregated inner city neighborhoods. In addition, a high rate of poverty is experienced by 38.2 percent of Hispanic youth under eighteen, compared to 17.3 percent for Anglos (Hispanic Policy Development Project 1984, vol. 1:10).

In relation to educational attainment and literacy, the picture of Hispanic adults and, in particular, Hispanic women, is desolate. 'Hispanic adults have lower educational attainment levels than Hispanic youth' (Orum 1986:35). Approximately '17.6 percent of Hispanic adults have completed only 0-4 years of school as compared to 2.8 percent for non-Hispanic adults,' (Cook and Quinones 1983:1) and many who are twenty-five years of age and over, and are parents of school-age children, are functionally illiterate. Due to limited schooling experience and illiteracy, parents cannot provide their children with the early home reading experiences that have been linked with children's later ability to read.

With regard to literacy, irrespective of the definition used — traditional measures; Adult Performance Level Study (APLS); competencies of functional, marginal, or advanced levels; English Language Proficiency Study on a sample of 3,400 adults of ages twenty and over — data indicate that 'approximately one-half of Hispanic adults cannot read and write English at a functional level, and almost nine out of ten who are illiterate in English are probably illiterate in their native language' (Orum 1986:36).[3]

Given such demographic issues, why has the education of adult Hispanics been so poorly articulated as a critical national concern? The reasons are several: (1) Adult education is not a national policy concern. (2) The problem has not been systematically researched.[4] (3) Education for Hispanic adults is often reduced to interpretations at the community level, making it visible only to participants. (4) Specific programs, such as life-long skills, are underfunded, so that the education programs are primarily considered to be English fluency or English literacy, with no concern for Spanish literacy skills. (5) There are, of course, other less tangible and overt reasons.

Among these reasons are: (1) the particular way in which Hispanics have been classified, categorized, and labeled, all tending to obscure who the adults requiring education are; (2) the series of assumptions and myths that portray all Hispanics as having a single language and culture, ignoring the heterogeneity that exists; (3) a limited understanding of the socio-historical influences on American Hispanics; and, (4) a lack of awareness regarding the contributions of Hispanics to society at large.

The term 'Hispanic,' in its American usage, is an aggregated category used by most federal agencies and includes all classifications of Hispanics, based on Spanish surname, origin, and parentage, and identifies persons of Mexican, Puerto Rican, Cuban, Central and South American, and Spanish descent, as well as other Latinos. The 1980 Census relied on self-identification, based on the question: 'Are you of Spanish/Hispanic origin or descent?'

While 'Hispanic' tends to be a 'constructed identity,'[5] it is becoming more widely used by present-day Hispanics to differentiate people of Spanish heritage from 'Anglos,' and by New Mexico Hispanos to demarcate their long-lived ancestry in the state.[6] Otherwise, the term 'Latino,' which includes all

The education of Hispanic adults

Hispanic-Americans, is used. However, among some Mexican-Americans, the concept of *La Raza* ('the race,' or 'the people') is used for the symbolic unification of Hispanic people in the New World, combining Spanish, Native American, and African heritages.

While a common language and culture is shared by all Hispanics, they are not homogeneous. The use of 'Hispanic' obscures distinctions that exist geographically (Caribbean, Meso-American, Central and South American); regionally (tropical to temperate zones, highland to lowlands); linguistically (using Spanish variations derived from Castilian, Andalusian, Creole, and slang (calo, lunfardo)); socially (upper to middle class, working class to peasant); and culturally (urban, rural, mainstream Western, rural Indian, and African).

Most federal agencies did not systematically collect data on Hispanics until 1974, when Congress required them to do so (Orum 1986). The 'invisibility' of Hispanics runs counter to their historical legacy, since Hispanic-Americans antedate the settlement of the Pilgrims in 1620. They have been particularly influential in the southwestern United States, where some families today date back to sixteenth-century Spain. The impact of Hispanic-Americans has been adversely protagonized throughout American history (El Alamo, Mexican-American War, Spanish-American war), and, in other cases, forgotten. Hispanics actively participated in the development of the mission network throughout the southwest, the extension of the railroad system, and the growth of agricultural production. 'Braceros' (Mexican hired hands who worked on farms) and 'traqueros' (migrant railroad workers) have been significant to the United States economy.

The 1980 Census shows that 59.8 percent of Hispanics in the United States are of Mexican ancestry, 13.8 percent are Puerto Ricans (excluding Puerto Ricans who live on the island), 5.5 percent are Cubans, and 20.9 percent are 'other Hispanics' (Central and South American, Spaniards, and from the Canary Islands). In terms of age, 47.7 percent of all Hispanics are twenty years of age or younger, as compared to 34.1 percent for the total US population (Hispanic Policy Development Project 1984, vol. 2:16-17, 29, 47).

The experience of Mexican-Americans in the United States is distinct from that of Puerto Rican and Cuban immigrants. Moving from a rural and agricultural background, beginning in the early 1900s, Mexican-Americans are presently more urbanized than the general US population (Hispanic Policy Development Project 1984, vol. 2:35). Their numbers and visibility in the southwestern and western states have provided them with a growing political base, as evidenced in the leadership of Mayor Federico Pena of Denver; Mayor Henry Cisneros of San Antonio; and Congressman Henry B. Gonzalez of Texas.

Mostly concentrated in metropolitan areas, particularly along the eastern seaboard, Puerto Ricans have historically migrated between the island and the mainland in search of employment, moving from unskilled to skilled labor. Distinctions are made by outsiders, such as, 'Nuyoricans, Bostoricans, Chicagoricans, LA ricans' and mainland Puerto Ricans, but insiders consider themselves Puerto Rican, whether from the US mainland or the island.[7] Puerto Ricans are characterized by their pattern of migration to and from the island, and between cities in the United States and other locations. They are also characterized by poverty. 'Socioeconomic indices for Puerto Ricans generally are the lowest of all Hispanic groups,' with 50.5 percent of mainland Puerto Rican families having annual incomes of less than $10,000 and close to half of these families with incomes under $5,000, many of which are female-headed households (Hispanic Policy Development Project 1984, vol. 2:39).

Although 85 percent of the American Cuban population is concentrated in Florida, they are characterized by the pattern of their migration to the United States: as refugees, excluding the Mariel exodus; the 'Marielitos;' those born in the United States; and those living outside Florida. Cuban refugees have fared well in social, economic, and educational arenas; their children, either US born or brought into the United States at a young age, are bilingual and in transition. The 'Marielitos' are the general exceptions. While adjusting well to America, they have not fared as well as the 1960 Cuban immigrants and their counterparts. Cubans as a group, while faring better than Mexicans and Puerto Ricans, lag behind other Hispanics and non-Hispanic Whites in socioeconomic achievements (Hispanic Policy Development Project 1984, vol. 2:43).

The category of 'other Hispanics' refers to immigrants from Central and South America, Spain, and the Canary Islands. It includes part-Hispanics (children of marriages between Hispanic and non-Hispanic) and mixed-Hispanics (children of marriages between Hispanic groupings). Hispanics in this category rank second among the major groups and are dispersed throughout the United States, with the greatest concentration in the northeast and southwest. They have fewer children, fewer working-age persons, and a higher proportion of elderly. They tend to be white-collar workers (ranging from skilled Latin American immigrants to refugee professional class, Central American economic refugees, and the part-Hispanics and mixed Hispanics) and reflect the highest education attainment (Hispanic Policy Development Project 1984, vol. 2:47).

With an understanding of Hispanic diversity, assumptions that Hispanics belong to a single monolithic language and culture can be dispelled, and a clearer picture of their needs as adult learners can be gathered. The next section deals with the conceptualization of adult education and literacy from the perspective of educators and examines its relevance to Hispanic adult learning.[8]

CURRENT EFFORTS IN HISPANIC ADULT EDUCATION

In order to make an assessment, we need to identify significant strands in Hispanic adult programs; to understand the nature of the Hispanic Adult Basic Education (ABE) programs; and to analyze representative cases drawn from research literature.

Unlike in other countries, there is 'no national program of adult education in the United States or sustained coordination or direction of adult education activities,' (Cross 1982:370) except for the enactment of the Manpower Development and Training Act of 1962, the Equal Opportunity Act of 1964, the Adult Education Act of 1966 under Title III of the Elementary and Secondary Education Act, and, more recently, the Job Training Partnerships Act. States are provided federal funding for the delivery of educational services to adults sixteen years and older who are out of school and have not completed high school. Funding may be for manpower development, training, or neighborhood services to community action programs. In some states, contributions are also derived from cities, towns, and local sources. Although approximately sixty million American adults were designated as the target population during the last decade, enrollment is estimated at only two to four million adults (Hunter and Harman 1985).

Most programs fall into the following categories: (1) those developing conventional literacy skills; (2) those addressing functional competencies; or, (3) those relying on broadcast media as delivery systems. Chall, Heron, and Hilferty (1987) describe the following categories for literacy programs: (1) volunteer programs, such as Laubach Literacy Volunteers, church and community groups which work with adults at the illiterate stage of reading; (2) competency-based programs designed for adults at the functional or advanced stages of literacy, with individualized programming; and, (3) community-based programs oriented to job placement.

Unless a program grows out of specific concerns, such as language training or skill development, the needs of Hispanic adults tend to be subsumed under a general adult basic education program. Many, if not most, of the Hispanic adult education programs develop at the community level, and are characterized by the specific context in which they operate and the population of learners they serve. Since most programs are derived from group experiences, they share certain elements: participatory decision-making, use of dialogue or group discussion, community teacher aides, and bilingualism/biculturalism.

The nature of the programs is such that, along with being dependent on local funding, many cannot be transferred to other contexts. In some cases, programs have sprung up independently, to deal with specific causes or issues; in other cases, they develop around a central community issue. The permanence of a program is contingent upon the demand for services in a community and the ability of a director to seek funding from local, state, or federal sources. Therefore, given the flux of 'older' and more 'recent' Hispanic immigrants, including those with illegal status, the actual overt demand for services and teaching personnel is in constant flux, requiring change over time.

Further complicating the delivery of services is the lack of funding, untrained staff, inappropriate and insufficient teaching materials, a significant dropout rate (50 percent on average), and teacher turnover. With limited human and material resources available, long-term effects of such programs on Hispanics are not tracked from year to year.

At another level, attempting to find a core to 'Hispanic adult education programs' is difficult, due to the dearth of research that specifically addresses Hispanic adult education. The existing literature tends to be limited to manpower development, literacy training, and courses in English as a Second Language. By emphasizing learning to read and speak English, the development of the faculty of 'learning how to learn' is eclipsed. There seems to be an over-emphasis on 'English only' fluency and proficiency, disregarding Spanish skills, thus reducing available services to Hispanics.

Although adult basic education programs differ widely, there are at least two major organizing principles that influence the development of Hispanic adult education programs: the impetus that springs from community/grassroots needs, and the theory of Paulo Freire.[9]

Community/grassroots programs

The development of some adult education programs is tied to the stability of the Hispanic groups within a community. As the membership of a community becomes solidified, through cultural activities and responses to social issues, projects are initiated with short- or longer-term goals. Many of these are of an informational, referral, or advocacy nature, but others provide adult learning opportunities, counseling, neighborhood and community development, and marketable job skills. While support from the cities and towns is provided for general programs, specific projects — Hispanic adult basic life skills, English as a second language, remedial reading — are often co-sponsored with other programs and non-profit groups, such as the United Way.

Community-initiated programs assume as their goals self-sufficiency of the low-income Hispanic population, and the provision of educational and supportive services to enhance living conditions, such as, temporary job training programs, economic revitalization, urban renewal, organized dropout prevention, and teen-age pregnancy programs. For example, Inquilinos Boricuas en Accion (IBA), in Boston's South End, provides multidisciplinary services to low-income, predominantly Puerto Rican community members. Formed as a by-product of community struggle against urban renewal, this agency gained control of the community, displacement of its members was avoided, and housing and education programs were upgraded. 'The key to the success in education for adults is invariably a high degree of community control' (Chavez 1970:115).

Literacy issues are a key concern of these community-based programs and they, in turn, are the most effective providers of literacy programs.[10] Communities are sites where the problems of illiteracy, especially for out-of-school youth and adults, can be directly addressed. The social network of the community can be accessed at different levels. When the teachers in the adult programs also teach in schools during the day, they gain a great deal of insight into the problems troubling their students. In this way, both parents and children become the beneficiaries of the program, as parents become better able to understand their children's school problems and help them with their homework and other school requirements. A broader base of communication is established, as students recruit their parents.

Yet community/grassroots programs cannot succeed

without the support of the community at large, including the school committee, various agencies, merchants, and professionals. It takes the cooperation of all to provide quality education.

Programs influenced by Paulo Freire's pedagogy

Paulo Freire, the Brazilian educator and author of *Pedagogy of the Oppressed* (1970), has been influential in the development of Hispanic adult education in the United States. His influence is sustained by 'liberation theology' — the Catholic Church's commitment to consolidation of the poor in Latin America, through creation of a popular church. Freire's pedagogy has filtered into adult education programs in the United States, through his writings and the work he has conducted in academic centers, such as Harvard, Stanford, and the University of Massachussetts, to name a few. In addition, immigrants from other countries, who have participated in Freire-like programs, have brought his ideas with them (Torres 1982; Montero-Sieburth 1985).

Freire presents an inductive model of learning that evolves from a praxis of thought and action developed in a context of continuous dialogue with a group. Freire's pedagogy stems from his literacy work with the poor and oppressed. Beginning with the peasants in northeastern Brazil, he continued his work in Chile, Cape Verde, Tanzania, Guinea Bissau, Zimbabwe, Nicaragua, and other Latin American countries (Freire and Macedo 1985). Instead of assuming that illiteracy can be equated with 'backwardness' or 'ignorance,' or described as a pathological problem of illiterate people — a disease in need of a cure — Paulo Freire cautions us that:

> Illiteracy is one of the concrete expressions of an unjust social reality. Illiteracy is not a strictly linguistic or exclusively pedagogical or methodological problem. It is political, as the very literacy through which we try to overcome illiteracy.
>
> (Freire and Macedo 1985:10)[11]

His is a humanistic approach to adult learning, involving a methodology where the teacher becomes a student and the student becomes a teacher. Through dialogue and dialectics, he identifies issues which pose problems for a group. Through these issues, the members of the group learn reading and writing, but, even more, they learn to question the *status quo*, search out reasons, and solve problems.[12] By reflecting-in-action, oppressed persons break out of what Freire calls the 'culture of silence,' as they act upon their conscious awareness of power through literacy and education, and transform their situation.

His literacy methodology uses 'generative words,' which are distilled from the analysis of issues and from the feedback from the group. These ideas about everyday values and concepts are codified in oral and visual forms (drawings, flannel board pictures, etc.). The words become the basis of literacy training and the basis of understanding the contradictions between what their lives are and what they could be. In these discussion groups, everyone participates as a teacher-learner. Themes arising from the discussion, and the level of peoples' conscientiousness, are then codified for action by being prepared for use in instructional materials.

The impact of Freire's psycho-social model of literacy and post-literacy development can be seen in many countries (Freire 1983; Freire and Macedo 1985). Some programs have developed in the United States around similar ideas and principles.[13] While in Latin American countries, the issue of oppression is always present, in the United States poverty, homelessness, illiteracy, and marginality, represent forms of oppression — taking place in an affluent and dominant Anglo mainstream society. Freire points out that, 'marginality is not by choice, marginal man has been expelled from and kept outside of the social system and is therefore the object of violence' (Freire and Macedo 1985:48).

Advocates of Hispanic adult education are concerned that issues of literacy/illiteracy and adult learning not remain at the level of isolated grassroots projects. Adult learning cannot be divorced from the wider socioeconomic dimensions of unemployment, political power, and equal opportunity. The process of acculturation, by which an individual moves from one socio-cultural setting to another and acquires the norms of the other culture, can be dysfunctional for Hispanics, if the discontinuities between their culture and the mainstream society are not effectively bridged through functional education (Olivero *et al.* 1968).[14]

Tomás Kalmar, who has developed, taught, and created adult education programs for adults over twenty years, maintains that models of adult education for Hispanics need to be analyzed critically, to measure their effect. For Kalmar, English as a Second Language (ESL) represents 'banking education' (storing up ideas by rote) and creates a serious confusion between written English and spoken Spanish. He argues that

> the learning of English in ESL is taught in halting syllables, in rhythms that people do not speak normally. ESL can't be called adult education because it only deals with the English language and you can spend much time without using much English, only ESL. Mainstream Adult Basic Education denies access to those who have accents in English, and refers them to ESL classes. The question is who decides where you get sent?
>
> (1987)

In Kalmar's opinion, adult education for Hispanics tends to be defined as an act of social welfare. There seems to be an anti-intellectual distaste for theorizing with the bilingual learners on language and cultural issues. The possibility of codeswitching between Spanish and English is forbidden in an ESL class. Yet, when codeswitching opportunities are made available through adult education, Hispanic adults can master areas of study at a relatively high academic level. Kalmar contends that,

> If you are Hispanic ... and you want to get into adult education, you can either assimilate cold turkey in an ABE class where you don't get to speak Spanish, or you can assimilate 'poco a poco' (little by little) through an ESL class, or if you don't want to assimilate you can form an adult education group in your native language, where at least you can control the flow of language ... [and] get on with the business of organizing your adult education.
>
> (1987)

In short, according to Kalmar, 'What a conscientious adult seeks in adult basic education is his or her own language. That person can study English as a subject, but can also study other subjects at a mature level' (1987).

Representative programs

In a 1969 survey of basic adult education projects across the country, the General Electric Company found only one that was targeted for Hispanics. The study included the following: the ABE Demonstration Center in Washington, DC; OIC Pupil Recruitment and Adult Armchair Education in Philadelphia;

Labor Union Participation in ABE in Columbus, Ohio; Learning Center in Fayetteville, Arkansas; Appalachian ABE Demonstration Center in Moorehead, Kentucky; the Guidance and Counseling Program in Austin, Texas; and the South-western Cooperative Education Laboratory Program in ABE for Mexican Americans in Albuquerque, New Mexico.

In the New Mexico instance, aspects of the program were found to be worthy of replication elsewhere. These were ESL television programming for Spanish-speaking adults, work-shops on teaching ESL to Mexican Americans, and dissemination of information about Mexican-American culture.

Cook and Quinones (1983) reported on the Spanish Literacy Investigation Project, which identified twenty-six agencies working in adult Spanish literacy programs through-out the country. Its purpose was to determine relevant Spanish literacy teaching methods, the relationship between Spanish literacy and English as a second language, and to describe a model for incorporating Spanish literacy into existing adult basic education programs.

In all twenty-six programs certain characteristics of the Hispanic adult student were found. Examination of Hispanics enrolled in ABE programs shows that they not only have limited English language proficiency, but they also lack literacy and basic skills in Spanish. Unlike literate Hispanics, they tend to have a higher drop-out rate, experience frustration and isolation, demand greater individual attention, have difficulty in adjusting to classroom experiences, and lack self-confidence. Over 90 percent of the participants in the literacy projects surveyed were first generation Hispanics living in the United States, with the remaining 10 percent being second generation.

Four of the programs received on-site visits for in-depth study. Three of these had developed their methodology around Paulo Freire's pedagogy, but with their own variations.

The Instituto de Progreso Latino, a community-based adult high school program, supported by community development money and foundation support, in Chicago's Pilsen area, offered not only traditional high school subjects, but also courses in human rights, housing, health, art, etc., to a clientele of mostly Mexican immigrants. With the exception of ESL, classes were given in Spanish. Spanish literacy classes were included in the program as well. The bilingual staff was representative of the community. Classes were held Monday through Thursday evenings. To establish the focus and goals of each class, facilitators made contractual agreements with the individual participants.

Universidad Internacional (formerly Universidad Abierta), in the West Town and Humble Park sections of Chicago, was a university-affiliated center, dedicated to the development of cognitive skills in the social sciences. Its courses in social cybernetics offered a methodology for individuals to identify and classify problems that prevented them and their community from changing their environment. While classes were primarily directed at survival skills, Spanish literacy classes were also created, to offer skills to participants who had never attended school. Fund raising activities provided the major support for the agency. Teachers were volunteers, and used self-made materials. Although activities tended to be teacher-centered, peer teaching occurred frequently. Cultural activities, to develop oral language abilities and thinking processes, were an important part of the program.

Universidad Popular/Centro Latino, an independent organization in Chicago that grew into an educational center, supported by federal and foundation moneys, offered adult basic education, GED preparation, classes in Spanish and ESL. In addition, through cultural activities, films, and community workshops, direct involvement with community issues was maintained. A Spanish literacy program, using small group discussions, became an important part of its course offerings.

Solidaridad Humana, in New York City, a comprehensive learning center with a basic education program, including Spanish literacy and an ESL component, was also part of the study. It is an extension program of LaGuardia Community College for degree-oriented adults. Founded in 1971, it has developed a strong track record, particularly for the active participation of student and staff members. It is presently following much of Freire's pedagogy. Among some of its notable aspects: classes are small, and students are carefully directed into appropriate ones; dialogue is promoted through group discussion; creative teachers make appropriate materials for class use and commercially produced materials are adapted to meet student needs; and paraprofessional teacher aides are available in all classes.

From the study of these four programs, a number of key components for successful Hispanic literacy programs were identified. In general, successful ones depend on a humanistic, interpersonal, and dialogic philosophy. Successful provider agencies have an open and supportive environment, visibility, strong network of community resources, and an integrated Spanish literacy program, along with other agency services. Successful programmatic elements include sensitive intake and orientation processes, flexible class schedules, small classes (7-

15 adults), fixed instruction cycles, adult involvement in their own learning, staff meetings, monitoring, and integration of Spanish literacy into the larger program.

The teachers in these programs were characterized by their role as facilitators, counselors, and managers; by their proficiency in Spanish and English; by their knowledge of the community and cultural norms; by their spirit of cooperation and goal-directedness, and their own personal development.

Instructional strategies were found to be based on group dialogue, personal interaction, active participation, appropriate materials, and an integrated curriculum, consisting of basic skills, with personal and community development, adult developmental needs, and experiences of learners (Cook and Quinones 1983:28–30).

PROJECTIONS FOR EFFECTIVE HISPANIC ADULT EDUCATION PROGRAMS

Adult education in the United States is a field growing in importance. Hispanic adults will be making up more and more of the learner ranks in years to come. Yet the field is characterized by vagueness and ill-defined concepts, obscuring rather than clarifying its purpose. Unless there are shifts in the conceptualization, there will continue to be a narrow linear model of learning which does not serve the minority adult effectively. The concept of teaching others is a critical issue; as Carl Rogers put it: 'the only learning which significantly influences behavior is self-discovered, self-appropriated learning ... which has been personally appropriated and assimilated in experience' (Christensen and Hansen 1987:135).

For whom is adult education provided, and with what intention? Undeniably, education addresses values. It is, therefore, critical that consideration be given to equity issues underlying the education of Hispanics. Is the equitable distribution of educational services in a population that suffers from poverty, homelessness, and disfranchisement, a current social goal? Is adult education addressing only specific skills and practices, or siphoning off those individuals targeted for specific jobs, e.g., factory jobs, menial work?

Brookfield's suggestion (1985) of creating a rationale for adult education will of necessity lead to uncovering the underlying assumptions in the present delivery of adult education. Unless that occurs, illiteracy will continue to be symptomatic of poverty. By exploring such assumptions, the issue of education of Hispanics will be seen as critical to the future of the United States.

Care should be exercised in judging individuals solely on the measurement of their literacy skills. Hispanic peoples have important oral traditions, which are an important part of their culture and the transmission of cultural values: folklore, the use of life histories, limericks, riddles, verses, and *corridos* (ballads). This either/or dichotomy of literacy/illiteracy obliterates many of the social and cultural values that have existed among Hispanics for centuries. In reconceptualizing literacy/illiteracy, from a deficit and normative definition toward a more social and cultural dimension, literacy can be understood in relative rather than absolute terms, and can be directed away from universal measures to more context-specific situations. We may want to heed Scribner and Cole's admonition:

> Although attempts to arrive at some overall measure of literacy competencies may be useful for certain comparative purposes, the conceptualization of literacy as a fixed inventory of skills that can be assessed outside of the contexts of application has little utility for educational policies.
>
> (1978:459)

Additionally, the special needs of adult learners must be diagnosed and addressed. Adult programs without recourse to special education services may exacerbate rather than reduce problems for the learner. Thus, attention to special needs must be part of the program of adult basic education.

Adult education must be reflective of community needs. Adult educators will need to analyze their image in and outside of the community. They will need to develop a programmatic image within the community and become linked to the socioeconomic and political issues of that community.

In teacher education, knowledge of skills, competency in subject matter, and pedagogical training, are required to become an effective teacher. In adult education, it is also necessary to know the learner personally and help the person to monitor his/her own growth realistically — important skills acquired in practice. Programs simply cannot rely on volunteers who, with the best of intentions, contribute their time. Training which is purposeful, sensitive, and emancipatory, needs to become part of the professionalization of teachers.

The curriculum of adult education for Hispanics needs to be organized around their issues, rather than on set objectives that have little to do with their lives. The bottom-up progression model of reading and grade level criteria may not be the most effective approach. The Freire-inspired model may not suit all situations, but there are other approaches. These may be based on the ethnography of the class, or the development of metalinguistic awareness. The bilingual approach has been mentioned earlier in this chapter.

Tomás Kalmar stresses the value of codeswitching and biliteracy, particularly where there is evidence of language shifts, such as that found in 'Spanglish,' and also what he and Cairns (1986) call 'transitional spelling,' where the students are induced to begin to write English phonetically, as soon as possible, before they have mastered standard spelling. By inventing spelling of words using Spanish orthography, they encounter phonemic problems which they must solve and, through the introduction of English spelling, discover the underlying logic (and lack thereof) in English writing (Cairns 1986:5-6). The importance of Kalmar's system is in identifying sources of structural difficulties and the examination of spelling errors. Thus it enables continual revision of the curriculum.

Again, each of these approaches in curriculum requires that the learner become the source of 'enacting teaching.' This concept is obviously a departure from the more traditional image of the teacher as the knowledge bearer and the curriculum as the means by which adults learn. Recognizing that Hispanics and their cultures provide rich resources for creating a 'live' curriculum is a challenge that needs to be met.

Many Hispanics, like the adult immigrants who preceded them, seek a broad education that goes beyond the teaching of English and Americanization, one that enhances rather than diminishes their adult status. Adult educators with knowledge of their native language, heritage, cultural and intellectual interests, must look to the community to help them fashion educational methods and goals.

NOTES

1. National Commission on Excellence in Education, Carnegie Forum for Education and the Economy 1988; Boyer 1983; Goodlad 1984.
2. The recent NCAS Research and Policy Report (1987) on Immigrant Students in the US Public Schools indicates that the United States has experienced an historic level of immigration, resulting in a foreign-born population which may exceed fifteen million.

111

3. Any measure of the literacy of Hispanics in English also needs to consider literacy levels in Spanish, along with acquired proficiency in English. According to *La Red/The Net* 98, July 1986, the English Language Proficiency Study mentioned here has findings which indicate that among illiterate adults who use a non-English language, 82 percent were born outside the United States, 41 percent live in neighborhoods relying on languages other than English, 14 percent are probably literate in their non-English language.

4. Even though illiteracy has received much attention since the 1960s, very little research on the illiteracy of Latinos exists. National literacy surveys have not sampled Latinos in sufficient numbers, and have not analyzed results for diverse groups within Latino communities.

    The Tomás Rivera Policy Center at Claremont, California, with support from the Ford Foundation IUP/SRCC is conducting demographic analysis of the literacy characteristics of Latinos and Latino sub-groups in the United States, under a project directed by Dr Reynaldo Macías, over a sixteen-month period. The project will carry out secondary analysis of national data sets, including: (a) Survey of Income and Education (1976); (b) National Chicano Survey (1978); and, (c) the 1980 Census. It will also gather inventories of current research, policies, and programmatic/instructional practices.

    The more recent findings on Latino reading and educational progress are derived from the National Institute of Education's *National Assessment on Education Progress* for the 1970s and 1980s, and a report from the National Council of La Raza, *Illiteracy in the Hispanic Community*, by Arturo Vargos, July 1986.

5. The notion of 'Hispanic' as an 'identity construction' comes from Tomás Kalmar, who questions the use of the term 'Hispanic,' giving the following striking example: 'An Anglo teacher tells me, "they come to my class and they don't know that they are Hispanic." (Students are Colombian, Mexican, Puerto Rican.) "They do not understand that it is my job to make them aware that they are Hispanic."'

6. In general, Hispanics tend to describe themselves in terms of the specific community they represent. For instance, for some the use of 'Mexican-American' is preferred, while for others 'Chicano' is more descriptive. In parts of the country the term 'Chicano' carries political overtones and refers to Mexican-Americans who are aware of their

political power within the mainstream. Each area of the country shows group and individual preferences for the use of 'Chicano,' 'Mexican-American,' or the simple 'Mexicano.' 'Chicano' will be more commonly heard in Denver to represent Hispanics, but an identification, such as, 'I am a Chicano from San Antonio, or Tejano from Texas,' may be preferred.

In other cases, self-identification is made in relation to the country of origin — Dominicano, Columbiano, Salvadoreno, Tico (for Costa Rican), etc. These subtle differences tend to be lost, particularly in school surveys using categories such as 'Hispanic White' or 'Hispanic Non-White' to differentiate them from 'American Indians, Asian or Pacific Islanders.' Based on the subjective perception of principals and teachers, the uniqueness of students who may consider themselves 'mestizos' (of mixed Spanish and American Indian blood), or 'mulatto' (of Black and white parentage), can easily be lost.

7. Puerto Ricans are technically migrants in the United States, since they hold US citizenship. However, because the cultural and linguistic character of the island makes their experience upon relocation to the mainland similar to that of 'immigrants' from other countries in Latin America, they are often characterized under this rubric. See *Hispanics in Massachusetts: A Demographic Analysis*, Commission on Hispanic Affairs, Commonwealth of Massachusetts, 1986. Many of the teachers with whom I work consider Puerto Rican students immigrants, based on their language and culture, irrespective of their legal standing as US citizens.

8. In 1982, the Census Bureau used the English Language Proficiency Study (ELPS) to analyze the ability levels of adults to read and understand government forms. The ELPS estimated that '17 to 21 million adults in the US were illiterate and ... 22 percent of those adults ... 3.7 to 4.6 million were Hispanic' (Orum 1986:36).

9. The emphasis on Paulo Freire does not diminish the recognition of Ivan Illich's impact throughout Latin America. However, Illich is not referred to directly, since his concern is more focused on deschooling society, and is less on methodology and theory of literacy and adult education.

10. The present definitions of literacy/illiteracy, which use as their criteria the completion of fifth grade, are being put to the test in these communities. According to Garza and Orum (1982:4, 5), when such conventional definitions of

literacy/illiteracy are applied to Hispanics, they misclassify (1) those who have left school but are literate; (2) those who complete school but are functionally illiterate; (3) those who are literate in another language, but have limited English proficiency; (4) those who are illiterate in both languages; and, (5) those who, as products of the public schools, have limited ability to read and write in English. In concentrating on oral English skills, such skills as comprehension, reading, and writing, have been neglected. Since completion rates are used to define illiteracy, Hispanics are more likely than whites to be classified as functionally illiterate, due to the fact that the school retention and completion rates are lower for Hispanics than whites. Thus, in many ways the illiteracy of Hispanics is created by the schools.

11. For an extended analysis of political consciousness in a Puerto Rican neighborhood, see Bennett and Pedraza 1984.
12. Nina Wallerstein (1983), in her *Language and Culture in Conflict*, a text for the ESL classroom, uses Freire's problem-posing approach.
13. Freire cites the work conducted at the Full Circle Institute in New York City, which is directed by Robert Fox, as being similar to his work in Brazil and Chile.
14. It will not suffice to transfer mainstream theories for adult learners to Hispanic adults. Consideration of what being an Hispanic adult implies requires concern for cultural roles more than chronological and developmental tasks. For many Hispanics, adulthood comes early. Children learn to take care of their siblings at an early age. They learn to interpret for their parents, and are often the go-betweens in financial and other important transactions. They help with adult chores, and become responsible for taking care of the group, *la familia*, rather than the individual. For some Hispanic females, the social role of becoming a mother ascribes an implicit adult status, as a woman changes from being a 'virgin' to a 'señora-wife.' One can be an adult at age thirteen or fourteen, simply on the basis of motherhood, and all the duties attached to the role are expected of the woman. Therefore, for Hispanic female-headed households, the notion of responsibility is not new, but acquiring an education at any level needs to be considered, in addition to other primary and more significant roles.

REFERENCES

Bennett, Adrian T. and Pedraza, Pedro (1984) 'Political dimensions of discourse consciousness and literacy in a Puerto Rican neighborhood in East Harlem,' in M. O'Barr, C. Kramara, and M. Schulz (eds) *Language and Power: Linguistic Resources Against Discrimination*, Beverly Hills, Cal.: Sage Publishers.

Bourchard, Don (1986) 'Cross cultural differences in adult education group settings,' in M. Brady (ed.) *Perspectives on Adult Learning*, Gorham, Maine: College of Education.

Boyer, Ernest (1983) *High School: A Report on Secondary Education in America*, New York: Harper & Row.

Brice-Heath, Shirley (1983) *Ways with Words: Language, Life and Work in Communities and Classrooms*, New York: Cambridge University Press.

Brookfield, Stephen (1985) 'A critical definition of adult education,' *Adult Education Quarterly* 36.

Cairns, Charles E. (1986) 'Prospectus for a Spanish/English bilingual literacy curriculum,' New York: Department of Linguistics and Community Language Project, Queens College of City University of New York, and Ph.D. Program in Linguistics, Graduate School and University Center, CUNY.

Carnegie Forum for Education and the Economy (1988) *Teachers for the Twenty-first Century, Report of the Task Force on Teaching as a Profession*, Washington, DC: The Forum.

Chall, Jeanne S. (1983) *Stages of Reading Development*, New York: McGraw-Hill.

Chall, Jeanne, S., Heron, Elizabeth, and Hilferty, Ann (1987) 'Adult literacy: new and enduring problems,' *Phi Delta Kappan* 69.

Chavez, Gilbert (1970) 'Adult education,' *National Elementary Principal* 50.

Christensen, Roland and Hansen, Abby T. (eds) (1987) *Teaching & the Case Method*, Boston: Harvard Business School.

Cook, Jacqueline and Quinones, Anisia (1983) *Spanish Literacy Investigation Project*, New York State Education Department, Solidaridad Humana: New York.

Cross, K. Patricia (1982) 'Adult learning opportunities in the United States,' in Richard E. Peterson, John S. Helmick, John R. Valley, Sally Shake Gaff, Robert A. Feldmesser, H. Dean Nielsen (eds) *Adult Education and Training in Industrialized Countries*, New York: Praeger.

Evans, Barbara, Franco, Jean, Cole, Mary Ellen, and D'Amore, Terry (1987-8) Personal interviews with Director and staff of Adult Education Program, Chelsea, Mass. (Steve Socha interviewed by telephone, January 1988.)

Feinberg, Lawrence (1987) 'Illiteracy crisis misread, researchers say,' *Washington Post*, 17 August.

Freire, Paulo (1970) *Pedagogy of the Oppressed*, New York: Continuum Press.

—— (1983) *Education for Critical Consciousness*, New York: Continuum Press.

Freire, Paulo and Macedo, Donaldo (1985) *The Politics of Education: Culture, Power and Liberation*, South Hadley, Mass.: Bergin & Garvey.

Garza, Francisco and Orum, Lori S. (1982) *Illiteracy in the Hispanic Community*, The National Council of La Raza and Hispanic Higher Education Coalition, Subcommittee on Post-Secondary Education of the House Education and Labor Committee, Washington, DC.

General Electric Company (1969) 'Analysis of seven special projects in adult basic education,' Final Report, Washington, DC: TEMPO.

Goodlad, John I. (1984) *A Place Called School*, New York: McGraw-Hill.

Hispanic Policy Development Project (1984) *Make Something Happen*, National Commission on Secondary Education for Hispanics, 2 vols.

Hunter, Carman St John (1987) 'Myths and realities of literacy/illiteracy,' *Convergence: International Journal of Adult Education* 20.

Hunter, Carman St John and Harman, David (1985) *Adult Illiteracy in the United States*, A Report to the Ford Foundation, New York: McGraw-Hill.

Jarvis, Peter (1983) *Adult and Continuing Education: Theory and Practice*, New York: Nichols.

Kalmar, Tomás Mario (1987) Personal interview with Adult Education Consultant, Director, Teacher.

—— (1983) *'The Voice of Fulano': Working Papers from a Bilingual Literacy Campaign*, Cambridge, Mass.: Schenkman.

Knowles, Malcolm (1970) *The Modern Practice of Adult Education*, New York: Association Press.

Kozol, Jonathan (1985) *Illiterate America*, New York: Doubleday.

Lee, Valerie (1985) *Access to Higher Education: The Experience of Blacks, Hispanics and Low Socio-Economic*

Status Whites, Washington, DC: American Council on Education.

Levine, Kenneth (1982) 'Functional literacy: fond illusions and false economics,' *Harvard Educational Review* 52.

Massachusetts Commission on Hispanic Affairs (1986) 'Hispanics in Massachusetts: a demographic analysis,' Boston: Author.

Montero-Sieburth, Martha (1985) 'A rationale for critical pedagogy,' essay review of Paulo Freire, *The Politics of Education: Culture, Power, and Liberation*, in *Harvard Educational Review* 18.

Montero-Sieburth, Martha and Perez, Marla (1987) 'Echar Pa'Lante, moving onward: the dilemmas and strategies of a bilingual teacher,' *Anthropology and Education Quarterly* 18.

National Coalition of Advocacy for Students (1988) *New Voices: Immigrant Students in US Public Schools*, Boston, Massachusetts: National Coalition for Advocates for Student Research and Policy Papers.

National Commission on Excellence in Education (1983) *A Nation at Risk: The Imperative for Educational Reform*, Washington DC: US Department of Education.

Olivero, James *et al.* (1968) 'The Chicano is coming out of Tortilla Flats ... one way or the other,' *Proceedings of the Conference on Adult Basic Education*, Albuquerque, NM: Southwestern Cooperative Educational Laboratory.

Orum, Lori S. (1986) *The Education of Hispanics: Status and Implications*, Washington, DC: National Council of La Raza.

Perez, Marla (1985) Personal interview with English as a Second Language Teacher in the Adult Education Program offered by Job Connections, Chelsea, Mass.

Rogers, Carl (1987) 'Personal thoughts on teaching and learning,' in C. Roland Christensen and Abby J. Hansen (eds) *Teaching and the Case Method*, Boston: Harvard Business School.

Scribner, Sylvia and Cole, Michael (1978) 'Literacy without schooling: testing for intellectual effects,' *Harvard Educational Review* 48.

Seller, Maxine S. (1978) 'Success and failure in adult education: the immigrant experience, 1914-1924,' *Adult Education Quarterly* 28.

Suarez-Orozco, Marcelo M. (1987) 'Becoming somebody: Central American immigrants in US inner-city schools,' *Anthropology and Education Quarterly* 18.

Time (1988) 'Magnifico: Hispanic culture breaks out of the

Barrio,' 11 July.

Torres, Carlos Alberto (1982) *Ensayos sobre la Educacion de los Adultos en America Latina*, Mexico City: Centro de Estudios Educativos, AC.

Wallerstein, Nina (1983) *Language and Culture in Conflict: Problem Posing in the ESL Classroom*, Reading, Mass.: Addison-Wesley.

Chapter Seven

ASIAN PACIFIC AMERICANS AND ADULT EDUCATION: THE SOCIAL AND POLITICAL RESOCIALIZATION OF A DIVERSE IMMIGRANT AND REFUGEE POPULATION

Don. T. Nakanishi

> In the United States it is difficult enough for a small-town New England family ... to adapt to its new home in Houston, Texas. But it is obviously far more difficult for a Latin American or Vietnamese or Korean family of rural origin to adjust to whatever US city or town it happens to end up in. Other matters may further complicate the situation. Those who began their lives under dictatorial regimes may, within a democratic haven, have learning needs that are as much political as cultural and occupational. Moreover, as a result of the chaotic national situations that uprooted them and subsequent years spent in refugee camps, some may have psychological problems in dealing with their new environments that are incorrectly diagnosed as learning disabilities. At stake here is the education of parents as well as children, as in the case of parents who fear that if they sign documents to allow their children to go on a school-sponsored trip they may never see them again.
>
> (Coombs 1985:48)

Little attention has been given to minority, immigrant, and refugee populations, in the scholarly and professional literature on adult education in the United States. A review of articles published during the ten-year period 1976-86 in the five leading journals in the field of adult education, for example, revealed that only one brief article specifically focused on an Asian Pacific group.[1] The paucity of research on Asian Pacific adult learners, of course, does not imply that Asian Pacifics do not participate in formal or non-formal adult education programs, or that adult educational issues are not of importance to this population. Numerous historical and social science works have described the activities of religious and other social institutions in providing instruction in basic

English language and other skills to different waves of Asian Pacific immigrants and refugees from the mid-nineteenth century to the present (Hosokawa 1969; Houchins and Houchins 1976; Kitano 1976; Liu and Murata 1979; Montero 1979; Kleinmann and Daniel 1981; Desbarats and Holland 1983). At the same time, Asian Pacific leaders in education, social services, and civil rights, have often expressed the need for federal and state governments, local school districts, and indeed their own ethnic community organizations, to provide more programs of organized learning for Asian Pacific adults, especially in overcoming persistent discriminatory practices and policies in the labor market, in augmenting individual-level skills, as well as in assisting immigrants and refugees in making a successful transition to a new social system (Sung 1975; Cabezas and Yee 1977; Kim 1978; United States Commission on Civil Rights 1979; United Way 1985).

This chapter, as others in this volume, seeks to provide both fresh empirical data and new analytical perspectives, on which to build a foundation of scholarly knowledge to stimulate further educational research and policy initiatives dealing with the multiethnic and multilingual composition of America's adult learner population.[2] This particular discussion will seek to contribute to the general research literature on adult education, by analyzing the rapidly growing Asian Pacific population from two distinct perspectives. First, it will provide a succinct demographic overview of the diverse ethnic, national, and linguistic groups which are encompassed by the term, 'Asian Pacific Americans.' By analyzing data from the 1980 United States Census, the National Center for Education Statistics, and other sources, this section will provide analytical and methodological guidance on special characteristics of this population that will, it is hoped, assist researchers in the field of adult education in the undertaking of comparative or cross-cultural studies in the future. Educational and quality of life indicators, such as the extent of English language fluency, educational attainment levels, immigration patterns, and participation rates in organized adult education programs, will be considered in the context of the growing scholarly literature on Asian Pacific Americans,[3] as well as adult education.[4]

Second, this chapter will focus on the contemporary Asian Pacific population to offer preliminary analytical insights for a rarely considered topic in the adult education research literature, especially in relation to the growing immigrant and refugee sectors in the United States. The discussion will address one of the issues which comparative education specialist Philip Coombs raises in the quotation above, when he writes that, 'Those who began their lives under dictatorial regimes may, within a democratic haven, have learning needs that are as much political as cultural and occupational.' In this section, I shall use and expand upon the analytical concept of political resocialization, which was most recently explored by Zvi Gittleman in his pioneering study of American and Soviet adult immigrants to Israel, *Becoming Israelis* (1982). Political resocialization will be analyzed in relation to the seemingly simple, and yet primary, act of individual-level participation in American electoral politics, namely registering to vote (Kelly, Ayres, and Bowen 1967; Verba and Nie 1972; Wolfinger and Rosenstone 1980; Erikson 1981). The brief concluding section will present and analyze data from the UCLA Asian Pacific American Voter Registration Study, the first-ever empirical investigation of patterns of voter registration and partisan affiliations among Asian Pacific Americans (Nakanishi 1986a).

DEMOGRAPHIC OVERVIEW OF THE ASIAN PACIFIC ADULT LEARNER POPULATION

Asian Pacific Americans, according to the US Bureau of the Census (1983), are the nation's fastest growing group, having increased by 128 percent during the past decade, from 1.5 million in 1970 to 3.5 million in 1980. This substantial increase can be attributed in large measure to the Immigration Act of 1965, which eliminated the discriminatory quota provisions of the Immigration Act of 1924, regarding the numbers of immigrants from particular countries, the Indochinese Refugee Resettlement Program Act of 1975, and the Refugee Act of 1980, which permitted the migration and entry of refugees from Southeast Asia.[5]

In reversing a four-decade longitudinal trend, Asian Pacifics now represent the largest group of legal immigrants to the United States. For example, between 1931 and 1960, when the provisions of the 1924 National Origins Act were in effect, 58 percent of the immigrants were from Europe, 21 percent from North America, 15 percent from Latin America, and the smallest portion, 5 percent, were from Asia. However, this situation had nearly flip-flopped by the reporting period, 1980-4. Legal immigration from Europe had decreased to 12 percent of the overall total, North America to 2 percent, while Latin America had increased to 35 percent and Asian immigration had substantially increased to 48 percent of the country's total (United Way 1985:11-15).

During the decade 1970-80, the Asian Pacific population also dramatically shifted from being largely American born to predominantly foreign born, as a result of this upsurge in international migration. For example, according to the 1980 Census, 63.1 percent of all Asian Pacifics in Los Angeles County were foreign born, with 92.9 percent of the Vietnamese, 85.9 percent of Koreans, 72.8 percent of the Filipinos, and 70.3 percent of the Chinese having been born abroad. In marked contrast, 10.4 percent of the County's white residents, 2.4 percent of the Blacks, and 45.5 percent of the Spanish-origin population were foreign born (UCLA Ethnic Studies Centers).

By 1990, it is projected that the Asian Pacific population will double again, and reach close to seven million (Muller 1984; Bouvier and Martin 1985). California, with a projected 2.5 million Asian Pacifics by 1990, will continue to be the largest population center with over 35 percent of the nation's Asian Pacific total, but there will continue to be large concentrations in Hawaii, New York, Washington, Illinois, and Texas (Gardner, Robey, and Smith 1985). By 1990, the Asian Pacific population in California is projected to eclipse the state's Black population, and become second to the rapidly growing Latino population, which will continue to be California's single largest minority group (Bouvier and Martin 1985; California Department of Finance 1985).

The Asian Pacific population, as many previous scholarly and public policy studies have demonstrated, should not be conceived as a single monolithic entity (Kim 1978; United States Commission on Civil Rights 1979; Chun 1980; Endo 1980; Endo, Sue, and Wagner 1980; Nakanishi and Hirano-Nakanishi 1983; Gardner, Robey, and Smith 1985; United Way 1985; Fawcett and Carino 1987). It is a highly heterogeneous population, with respect to ethnic or national origins, cultural values, generation, social class, religion, and other socially differentiating characteristics. For example, as Fawcett and Arnold (1987:453) describe recent Asian and Pacific immigrants:

The most evident fact about Asian and Pacific immigration is its diversity. Whether one looks at the political and economic status of the countries of origin, the characteristics of immigrants themselves, or their modes of adaptation in the host society, differences are more striking than similarities. Sending countries include socialist Vietnam, capitalist South Korea, and colonial American Samoa —

each having quite different economic resources and strategies for development. Significant groups of immigrants include Hmong hill farmers, Indian scientists and engineers, Chinese businessmen, and Filipino service workers — as well as Thai, Filipino, and Korean women immigrating as marriage partners.

Even within any particular Asian Pacific American subgroup, such as Chinese Americans, the within-group differences can be quite pronounced, reflecting different historical waves of immigration and different segments of a class hierarchical structure. Brett and Victor Nee, in their classic ethnographic study of San Francisco Chinatown, *Longtime Californ'* (1974), provide a revealing socio-historical analysis of such within-group diversity for Chinese Americans. On the other hand, Hirschman and Wong (1981) use census data to examine rigorously within-group differences in socioeconomic achievement among immigrant and American-born Chinese, Japanese, and Filipinos.

In contrast to the study of other, larger minority populations, a common technical, methodological problem facing researchers is that empirical data are not routinely collected or reported on Asian Pacifics *in toto*, or, more importantly, with respect to the different ethnic subgroups of the population. 1980 Census data tapes, for example, represent one of the few quantitative data sources that provide such ethnic breakdowns with respect to nine different Asian Pacific groups: Asian Indians, Chinese, Guamanians, Hawaiians, Japanese, Koreans, Filipinos, Samoans, and Vietnamese.[6] Census data, however, have assorted technical and substantive limitations, especially in terms of the restricted set of individual-level characteristics that are surveyed, the long periods of delay between the collection and dissemination of data, and the special sampling problems which are posed in gathering data from Asian Pacifics and other minority populations (United States Commission on Civil Rights 1979; Yu 1982).

As a result, those who are engaged in research on the Asian Pacific population must oft-times initiate and undertake specially tailored data collection activities, which are based on familiarity with or expertise about Asian Pacifics, in order to gain sufficient empirical information to investigate topics such as the extent of interracial marriages, utilization rates of mental health facilities, or levels of political involvement prior to the researcher's application of rigorous data analysis tools (Kikumura and Kitano 1973; Sue and Kirk 1973; Yu 1982; Chan 1986; Nakanishi 1986b). For example, public records on marriages and voter registration do not contain specific information on the ethnicity, national origins, generation, or racial background of the individuals who are recorded. Nor does there presently exist a computer-based dictionary of Asian Pacific surnames, although this writer is currently developing the first software package for that purpose.[7] Therefore, it is oft-times necessary to devise special data collection strategies, which are specifically geared toward identifying and analyzing those of Asian Pacific backgrounds from all the others who are listed in these public records.

For instance, in undertaking research to determine interracial marriage rates and voter registration trends among Asian Pacifics, scholars have carefully had to assemble and train panels of bilingual and bicultural researchers to identify and locate Asian Pacific surnamed individuals from others who obtained marriage licenses or registered to vote. Undertaking what some may believe to be a simple data collection exercise for Asian Pacifics in a municipality, such as Los Angeles County, involves the analysis of literally tens of thousands of marriage licenses, and the listing of millions of registered voters. The reliability of the overall identification processes in both projects were controlled through the multiple verification of names in which two, and usually three, professionally trained and linguistically or culturally knowledgeable readers examined and verified the same records. Other equally important methodological issues in undertaking research on Asian Pacifics were addressed in these two studies (Kikumura and Kitano 1973; Nakanishi 1986a, 1986b). Such added methodological attention during the initial research stage of gathering reliable and valid data is highly crucial in the examination of research topics dealing with Asian Pacific subgroups, and in the analysis of within-group differences and similarities. Future academic and policy inquiries on adult educational issues facing the Asian Pacific population should be guided by similar methodological considerations.

Differences in educational attainment levels provide a glimpse of this internal diversity, and are particularly relevant for research on Asian Pacific American adult education programs. For example, K. Patricia Cross (1979:93) who analyzed the relationship between individual-level adult characteristics and 'interests, motivations, and participation' in adult learning programs of over thirty major recent empirical studies, found that level of educational attainment was the best single explanatory variable.[8] Census data from a three-year collaborative research project on changes in quality of life indicators between 1970 and 1980 for Los Angeles County's major minority groups, which are now the numerical majority of the populace, underscore the necessity for analyzing within-group differences among Asian Pacifics in adult education research.[9] For example, Table 7.1 provides 1980 STF4 sample census data on educational attainment levels for adult males and females, 25-44 years of age, the sector most likely to be targeted for adult education programs, for six mutually exclusive[10] ethnic categories of Asian Pacifics, Blacks, American Indians, Spanish-Origin, whites, and others. Asian Pacifics and individuals of 'Spanish Origin' appear to be at polar extremes of the educational continuum, with the former having a seemingly unrivaled percentage of college graduates, and the latter exhibiting a disturbingly unmatched percentage of individuals with less than eight years of formal schooling. Indeed, on practically all educational attainment indicators, Asian Pacifics far outdistance every other population group.[11] Other studies have made similar observations (Brown *et al.* 1980; Duran 1983; Davis, Haub, and Willette 1985; Sue and Padilla 1986).

Table 7.2, which differentiates the Asian Pacific category among nine different ethnic groups, illustrates the necessity for recognizing and analyzing the internal heterogeneity of this population. Several Asian Pacific groups, for example, such as the Vietnamese, Hawaiians, Guamanians, Samoans, and other Asians, clearly do not reflect high educational attainment levels, and generally have far fewer college graduates and proportionately more non-high school graduates than Asian Pacifics as a whole, as well as Blacks and whites in the county. At the same time, other groups which appear to have stronger group-level academic profiles, such as the Chinese, Koreans, and Asian Indians, still had large numbers of individuals who were not high educational attainers. Close to one in five women of these three groups, 25-44 years of age, had not completed high school, and one in ten Chinese women had less than eight years of schooling.

Data and scholarly research on the participation of Asian Pacifics in adult educational programs is practically non-existent. The glimpses of information and insight which are available in the basic and applied bodies of literature provide fleeting suggestions on why and where Asian Pacific adult learners attend formal programs of instruction. For example, Cross (1979) reported that a small-scale, comparative survey of minority adult learners in New York City indicated that 64 percent of the Asian Pacifics were 'pursuing learning primarily for upward job mobility' in comparison with 73 percent Blacks, 73 percent Hispanic, 69 percent Native Americans, and

Table 7.1 Educational attainment levels for males and females, 25-44 years of age, in Los Angeles County, 1980

	% Eight years or less of schooling	% Non-high school graduate	% College graduate
Asian Pacifics			
Males	2.9	6.4	54.7
Females	5.1	9.7	44.5
Blacks			
Males	2.5	13.7	16.6
Females	2.0	13.3	14.7
American Indians			
Males	5.8	21.1	17.7
Females	6.6	25.3	10.3
Spanish Origin			
Males	41.7	57.2	6.6
Females	42.0	59.2	4.5
Whites			
Males	8.5	16.6	22.5
Females	8.5	17.5	22.3
Others			
Males	31.1	45.1	14.7
Females	30.1	49.0	9.8
Total Population			
Males	11.3	20.0	29.4
Females	11.0	21.1	20.9

Source: UCLA Ethnic Studies Census Project

58 percent for the overall sample. At the same time, recent reports by the National Center for Educational Statistics (US Department of Education 1981) provide information on the enrollment of Asian Pacifics in adult basic and secondary educational programs by states. California, reflecting both its status as the largest population center for Asian Pacifics in the country and the state's extensive formal adult educational system, has the largest number of Asian Pacifics enrolled in adult education programs. Of all Asian Pacifics enrolled in

Table 7.2 Educational attainment levels for Asian Pacific American males and females, 25-44 years of age, 1980

	% Eight years or less of schooling	% Non-high school graduate	% College graduate
Japanese Americans			
Males	1.9	5.1	47.4
Females	1.4	4.2	35.4
Chinese Americans			
Males	6.8	11.3	54.7
Females	10.3	16.0	40.5
Filipino Americans			
Males	2.4	6.8	51.1
Females	2.7	6.5	61.6
Korean Americans			
Males	3.6	6.8	54.2
Females	6.3	13.4	32.6
Vietnamese Americans			
Males	12.2	23.1	20.2
Females	23.8	37.4	10.6
Hawaiian Americans			
Males	3.0	16.2	18.6
Females	1.4	14.5	9.0
Asian Indians			
Males	2.1	5.0	69.6
Females	10.2	17.6	39.7
Guamanians			
Males	17.2	32.6	8.3
Females	22.2	40.0	5.9
Samoans			
Males	6.4	26.7	10.4
Females	8.0	29.6	5.8
Other Asians			
Males	7.3	13.4	38.8
Females	11.6	22.4	26.3

Source: UCLA Ethnic Studies Census Project

these programs in the nation 37.3 percent (66,129 of 177,299) are in California. Hawaii follows with 8.6 percent (15,250), New York with 7.3 percent (12,957), Florida with 4.4 percent (7,892), and Texas with 4.4 percent (7,845). Although an inventory of formal and non-formal adult educational programs for Asian Pacifics has never been undertaken, a preliminary survey by the author indicates that a range of activities has been designed to respond, albeit in an *ad hoc* and unsystematic fashion, to the internal heterogeneity and the diversity of educational needs of the Asian Pacific adult learner population. In Los Angeles, for example, these programs include basic 'survival English' courses for new immigrants and refugees, which are offered by the public school system, as well as community-based organizations, such as the Pacific Asian Consortium on Education (PACE), and the Chinatown Service Center, both long-standing, federally funded job-training and referral groups. According to the 1980 US Census, 70 percent of the Asian Pacific population in Los Angeles County spoke a language other than English in the home. Only 4 percent of the Vietnamese, 8 percent of the Koreans, 14 percent of the Chinese, and 24 percent of the Filipinos spoke only English in the home. In contrast, 87 percent of the non-Hispanic Whites, 92 percent Blacks, and 19 percent Hispanics spoke only English at home (UCLA Ethnic Studies Centers 1987). On the other hand, there are other programs which respond to other sectors of the diverse Asian Pacific adult learner population. In Los Angeles, and else-where, special assertiveness and career development programs have been founded for highly educated Asian Pacific professionals in fields such as engineering and teaching, who aspire to administrative positions in private and public institutions which traditionally have had a paucity of Asian Pacific managers, supervisors, and decision-makers. One highly successful program developed by the Asian American Educators Association of Southern California provides mentoring opportunities for Asian Pacific teachers who seek to become school principals and other administrators. And, finally, groups such as Leadership Education for Asian Pacifics (LEAP) in Los Angeles offer a variety of non-formal educational activities to enhance leadership and organizational skills, as well as knowledge of public policy issues.

The heterogeneity of the Asian Pacific population, and its corresponding diversity of adult educational needs and issues, should be more fully and rigorously explored by scholars and practitioners in the field of adult education. Careful consideration should be given to special methodological issues which previous researchers have addressed in conducting studies on Asian Pacifics. Additional applied and basic inquiries on the population should be undertaken to provide scholarly and policy insights on the nation's multicultural adult learner population.

POLITICAL RESOCIALIZATION AND ADULT EDUCATION: THE CASE OF ASIAN IMMIGRANTS AND REFUGEES

In *Becoming Israelis* (1982), Zvi Gittleman analyzes the process of political resocialization of American and Soviet adult immigrants to the Israeli political system. Although he never explicitly defines the concept, it can be conceptualized as a process by which adult immigrants and refugees, who have largely acquired their fundamental political values, attitudes, and behavioral orientations in one sociopolitical system undergo a process of 'adult political socialization, or *re*socialization' (p.170) in migrating to, and making the transition to, a newly adopted society that has its own, and usually different, political traditions, procedures, and philosophical and legal principles.[12]

> Are immigrants, in fact, resocialized politically, or do they remain outside the political arena? If they are resocialized, is it only on the level of outward behavior, while the fundamental political *Weltanschauung* remains unchanged, a product of the political culture of the 'old country'? What remains, if anything, of their former political cultures if they are resocialized into a new one? If there is, indeed, a process of resocialization going on, who are its 'agents'?
>
> (Gittleman 1982:343)

The concept of political resocialization is intended to encompass a wide range of potential political adaptation processes. They include, for example, Coombs' interest in the migration of individuals from 'a dictatorial regime' to a 'democratic haven,' as well as how other immigrants who were socialized in a political system, such as Mexico or Taiwan, which is dominated by a single political party, begin to participate in the political systems of their new host societies which are characterized as having greater competition among political parties, such as France and the United States (McDonough 1971).

Although the process of political resocialization is of both theoretical and empirical interest to political scientists and other social scientists, the specific emphasis here will be on its relationship to formal and non-formal adult education programs and policies for immigrants and refugees to the United States, especially those from Asian Pacific countries. This discussion is intended to encourage further inquiries on the process of political adaptation of immigrants and refugees to the United States and other nation states. Traditionally, in both the basic and applied bodies of research on immigrants and refugees, investigators have focused on practically all dimensions of their transition to a new host society — except for political ones — be it linguistic, cultural, occupational, or psychological. Indeed, Tomas Hammar (1978:16), after reviewing the scholarship on international migration and political socialization, wrote that, 'In the latter we find very little about migration, in the former not much about politics.'

At the same time, there appears to be a general reluctance on the part of social service providers, public school officials, and other practitioners who develop and administer adult learning programs for new immigrants and refugees, to address so-called 'political' issues. The possible exception are the customary classes in American civics and government, which are required for naturalization applications. This brief concluding section suggests that the process of political resocialization should be seriously considered, in order to further scholarship on the learning needs of adult immigrants and refugees, as well as to achieve the desired programmatic goal of making these individuals full, participatory citizens in society.

The concept of political resocialization is germane to the seemingly simple, and indeed primary, individual act of electoral participation in American politics, namely registering to vote (Kelly, Ayres, and Bowen 1967; Verba and Nie 1972; Wolfinger and Rosenstone 1980; Erikson 1981). Considerable attention has been directed by both scholars and politicians to the issue of voter registration among historically disfranchised groups, such as Blacks, Mexican Americans, and other domestic racial minorities (de la Garza 1974; Antunes and Gaitz 1975; Bullock 1981; Thompson 1982; Cain and Kiewiet 1984; Wrinkle and Miller 1984; Foster 1985; Vedlitz 1985; Abramson and Claggett 1986). However, until the mid-1980s, there were few empirical and analytical studies of voter registration patterns among post-World War II immigrants and refugees, especially from Cuba, Central America, and the Asian Pacific Basin (Brischetto and de la Garza 1983; Din

1984; Loo 1985; Portes and Mozo 1985; de la Garza and Flores 1986; Nakanishi 1986a). Massey (1981:77) in reviewing the research literature on immigrant groups to the United States, concluded that 'There is no information on patterns of Asian political participation.'

In recent years, however, a body of scholarly knowledge on Asian Pacific electoral political involvement has emerged. One of the two most consistent and puzzling findings in all empirical studies has been that Asian Pacific Americans, even after statistical manipulations have been performed to control for the high proportion of age-eligible individuals who cannot vote because they are not United States citizens, still have lower voter registration rates than whites, Blacks, and Latinos (Nakanishi 1986a, 1986b; Uhlaner, Cain, and Kiewiet 1987). The UCLA Asian Pacific American Voter Registration Study estimated that Japanese Americans, who have the largest population and the highest proportion of citizens of all the Asian Pacific groups in Los Angeles County, had a voter registration rate of 43 percent for all who were eighteen years and older. At the same time, 35.5 percent Chinese Americans, 27 percent Filipino Americans, 16.7 percent Asian Indians, 13 percent Korean Americans, 28.5 percent Samoan Americans, and an extremely low 4.1 percent Vietnamese, were estimated to be registered voters in the region. These registration rates are well below the average for Los Angeles County of 60 percent for all individuals eighteen years and older (Nakanishi 1986a, 1986b).

These findings have both practical and theoretical significance. Asian Pacific community leaders, as well as political party officials, of course, are interested in mobilizing the large increases in the numbers of Asian Pacifics, especially in major population centers, to address specific political goals (Aoki 1986; Tachibana 1986). Indeed, if the electoral representation of Asian Pacifics, who are projected by 1990 to become over 20 percent of San Francisco's population, as well as over 10 percent of the residents for both Los Angeles County and the State of California, matched their proportion of the population, then they could potentially become a critical and highly wooed 'swing vote,' as have American Jewish voters in key electoral states such as New York, California, and Illinois (Fuchs 1956; Glazer and Moynihan 1963; Isaacs 1974). On the other hand, scholarly literature on electoral participation and political behavior, the UCLA findings, along with comparative results that appear in a recently unpublished report by a team of political scientists at the California Institute of Technology (Uhlaner, Cain and Kiewiet 1987) beg further empirical testing, since they appear to challenge the long-established statistical relationship between high levels of socioeconomic and educational attainment and high levels of political participation (Verba and Nie 1972; Wolfinger and Rosenstone 1980). Asian Pacific Americans, who, like Jewish Americans, exhibit high levels of group achievement on these social indicators, would be expected to be far more politically involved, or at least to compare with other groups in the simple individual act of electoral participation, namely registering to vote.

The second of the two puzzling findings about Asian Pacific American voters concerns the pattern of their partisan affiliations, and, specifically, the extremely high number of them who declare themselves independents or of 'no party' when registering. When the UCLA Asian Pacific American Voter Registration Study conducted its first empirical analysis of voters on the official registration indexes for the June 1984 primary in Los Angeles County, it identified large numbers of 'independent' Chinese, Vietnamese, Korean, and Asian Indians. One in five declined to state a party preference at the time of registration. (For a description of the methodological strategies and issues in this project, see Nakanishi 1986a, 1986b.)

Although recent polls and studies of the American elect-orate report that a growing number of voters now consider themselves to be independents (Finkel and Scarrow 1985), the official registration indexes for the county indicated that only 10 percent of all voters — like the Japanese, Filipinos, and Samoans who were identified in the study — decline to specify a party affiliation. In our subsequent, annual follow-up studies for the UCLA project, an even greater tendency has been observed among certain Asian Pacific groups, especially the Chinese Americans, to register as independents.

Table 7.3 illustrates this movement among Chinese American voters, in contrast to other identifiable groups of registered voters, in the City of Monterey Park in Southern California between 1984 and 1987.[13] In 1984, for example, there was a plurality of Democrats among Chinese American voters, and an unusually high proportion of individuals (25.3 percent) who specified no party affiliation. By 1987, Chinese American voters, who accounted for practically all new registered voters in the City since 1984, were nearly evenly divided among Democrats (30.9 percent), Republicans (35.1 percent), and independents (32.9 percent). The 'practical' or 'political' implication of this observation is that a Chinese American candidate, who seeks the nomination of a specific

Table 7.3 Asian Pacific American registered voters, Monterey Park, 1984 and 1987

	Number registered	Democrats	Republicans	Other parties	No party
1984 Citywide	22,021 (100%)	13,657 (62%)	5,564 (25%)	368 (1.7%)	2,290 (10.4%)
1987 Citywide	23,353 (100%)	13,639 (58.4%)	6,434 (27.6%)	318 (1.4%)	2,962 (12.7%)
1984–7 Net gain/loss	+1,332	–18	+870	–50	+672
1984 Chinese Americans	3,152 (100%)	1,360 (43.1%)	972 (30.8%)	23 (0.7%)	797 (25.3%)
1987 Chinese Americans	4,430 (100%)	1,367 (30.9%)	1,554 (35.1%)	49 (1.1%)	1,460 (32.9%)
1984–7 Net gain/loss	+1,278	+7	+582	+26	+663
1984 Japanese Americans	2,586 (100%)	1,429 (55.3%)	838 (32.4%)	21 (0.8%)	298 (11.5%)
1987 Japanese Americans	2,834 (100%)	1,503 (53%)	952 (33.6%)	32 (1.1%)	337 (11.9%)
1984–7 Net gain/loss	+248	+74	+114	+11	+39
1984 Asian Pacific total	6,441 (100%)	3,265 (50.7%)	1,944 (30.2%)	54 (0.8%)	1,178 (18.3%)
1987 Asian Pacific total	7,663 (100%)	3,014 (39.3%)	2,636 (34.4%)	115 (1.5%)	1,888 (24.6%)
1984–7 Net gain/loss	+1,222	–251	+692	+61	+710

Source: UCLA Asian Pacific American Voter Registration Study

political party in a primary election, will be faced with a situation in which two-thirds of all Chinese American registered voters, who conceivably represent a sympathetic bloc of votes for the candidate, will be unable to cast ballots during the initial, 'Party members only,' primary election.[14]

When political organizers and community leaders confront these two puzzling aspects of the electoral participation of Asian Pacific Americans, their remedies tend to be short-term, action-oriented outreach efforts, such as initiating a major voter registration campaign, or organizing forums for partisan officials to speak to ethnic organizations. Generally, this is what has occurred in the Southern California area in response to the findings and analyses of the UCLA Asian Pacific American Voter Registration Project, which this writer directed for five years (Nakanishi 1986a).

Beyond such action-oriented solutions, there is a significant role which scholars and policy analysts in the field of adult learning can play in identifying and analyzing the factors leading to low electoral participation among Asian Pacific Americans — and perhaps other immigrants and refugees as well — and in proposing creative formal and non-formal adult educational programs which will serve to assist these new-comers to become full, participating citizens of American society. For example, it has been hypothesized that the low rates of voter registration and the high proportion of independent voters among certain Asian Pacific groups has to do with their political socialization in nation-states, such as Taiwan and the People's Republic of China, which have different voting procedures and far less competition among political parties than the United States. At the same time, further empirical and policy inquiries should be conducted on the extent to which traditional courses in American civics, required for naturalization application, have an impact, if any, on the political attitudes, sense of political efficacy, and knowledge of the American political process of these new-comers; and, more importantly, whether novel teaching approaches can be developed to address these issues.

As America's potential adult learner population becomes increasingly multiethnic, scholars and practitioners in the field should be encouraged to consider topics such as these, which traditionally have been beyond the paradigmatic and policy boundaries of adult education.

NOTES

1. The five journals which were reviewed included *Adult*

Education, Adult Education Quarterly, Educational Gerontology, Studies in Adult Education, and *Lifelong Learning.* The only article found on an Asian Pacific group was Howard Kleinmann (1985), 'Factors affecting second language learning in adult refugees,' which dealt with the application of the Krashen model of second language learning for Southeast Asian adult refugees.

2. Definitions of adult education vary widely. Long and Hiemstra, and Associates (1980:4) define adult education as 'any planned learning activities engaged in by and for anyone who possesses the biological, civil, and cultural characteristics of an adult.' This article, like Cross (1979:76) and Solmon and Gordon (1981:2) uses the definition of adult learners of the National Center for Education Statistics as 'persons seventeen or older, not enrolled full-time in high school or college, but engaged in one or more activities of organized instruction.' Also, for additional data on the multiethnic nature of the adult learner population in the United States, see US Department of Education, National Center for Education Statistics (1981).

3. For critical reviews of this literature, see Daniels (1976), Endo (1980), Hirata (1978), Hurh and Kim (1982), and Sue (1980).

4. An excellent up-to-date review of the research literature on adult education is provided in Huey Long (1987).

5. The Immigration Act of 1965 repealed the national origins provisions in the Immigration Act of 1924. The 1965 law created an annual Eastern Hemisphere ceiling of 170,000, with an annual per-country limit of 20,000, and an annual Western Hemisphere ceiling of 120,000, with no country limitations. On the other hand, over 200,000 Southeast Asian refugees entered the United States under the Indochinese Refugee Resettlement Program Act of 1975. See, for example, Fawcett and Carino (1987).

6. Most publications of the US Bureau of the Census, however, report data on the larger population category of Asian and Pacific Islanders, and do not provide detailed information on these nine different ethnic subgroups. For the 1970 Census, the Bureau issued PC(2)-1G, 'Subject reports: Japanese, Chinese, and Filipinos in the United States,' which provided data at the national, state, and major SMSA levels for these three Asian Pacific groups. However, the Bureau has decided not to issue a comparable report based on the 1980 Census. The category, 'Other Asians,' includes Thais, Cambodians, Burmese, Lao, Hmong, and others.

7. This software package is being developed to facilitate further research on voter registration trends among Asian Pacific American groups: the Japanese, Chinese, Korean, Filipinos, Samoans, Vietnamese, and Asian Indians. It consists of an extensive listing, or dictionary, of surnames for each of the groups, compiled from previous data collection activities for the UCLA Asian Pacific American Voter Registration Study (see Nakanishi 1986a). The program will make possible the identification mechanically of Asian Pacifics from voter registration rolls, and analysis of longitudinal trends. It should be transferable for other research purposes, in which it is necessary to identify and differentiate individuals of Asian Pacific backgrounds from others in a general list of names.

8. Cross (1979:93) writes that, 'Educational attainment is probably a better index to the interests, motivations, and participation of adult learners than any other single characteristic. This observation is consistent across a great variety of studies and is responsible for predictions that adult education will continue to rise as the educational attainment of the populace rises.' Aslanian and Brickell (1980:9) report a similar finding, when they write that, 'Learning is more common among adults who are young, white, well-educated, rich, live in the West, reside in suburbs, and work longer hours. The best single correlate of learning among all of these adults is educational attainment.'

9. The census data presented here are part of the UCLA Ethnic Studies Census Project, a collaborative endeavor of the four ethnic studies research units at the University of California, Los Angeles, and funded by the Institute of American Cultures and the California Community Foundation. (See UCLA Ethnic Studies Centers 1987.) The specific data are from the 1980 STF4 Sample and 1970 Public Use Sample for the Los Angeles-Long Beach SMSA. The tables on sex by age by years of schooling completed for persons twenty-five years and older of the different ethnic populations were derived from 1980 Table P-B48. Although educational attainment data were available on other age categories, information on individuals 25-44 years of age were selected because they would be the age group that would most likely fit the designation of adult learner in note 2 above.

10. These mutually exclusive categories were created through statistical manipulations of 1980 STF4 Sample data. Summary data tables provided in publications by the US Bureau are not mutually exclusive with respect to the

Spanish Origin population.
11. The only exception appears to be in the percentage of males and females with less than eight years of schooling for Asian Pacifics and Blacks.
12. The political socialization of children, and, to a lesser extent, of adolescents, has been the focus of much research in the field of political psychology. However, as Jack Dennis writes, 'there is extremely little in the whole area of adult political socialization' (1973:444). Researchers in political psychology have theorized about processes similar to that of political resocialization, especially in relation to what appear to be significant changes in fundamental political values and orientations as a result of experiencing major cataclysmic events. For example, Dawson, Prewitt, and Dawson (1977:86) have written: 'For most basic political orientations the social and individual pressures are for persistence of stability. However, from time to time general political or social events of significant magnitude can cause large numbers of people to alter even some of their most fundamental political outlooks. The American Civil War in the 1860s and the Great Depression of the 1930s were two such events in American history. These events caused large numbers of Americans, many of them already well into their adult years, to change basic perspectives on their relationships with the national government, their expectations of what government should or should not do, and in some instances their identification with a political party.'
13. Monterey Park has attracted substantial media and scholarly attention because of its growing Asian Pacific population, as well as its extreme racial tensions. According to the US Census, 33.7 percent of the City of Monterey Park's population in 1980 consisted of Asian Pacifics (18,312 of 54,338). By 1986, when the Bureau of the Census conducted its 'test census' of cities in central and eastern Los Angeles County, Asian Pacifics accounted for 51.4 percent of the city's total population (31,467 of 61,246). Between 1980 and 1986, the city's Asian Pacific population increased by 71.8 percent, whereas the city's white and Latino populations declined by 16.7 percent and 1.2 percent, respectively.
14. This is exactly what occurred in the November 1987 primary elections, when Lily Chen, the former Mayor of the City of Monterey Park, sought the Democratic party nomination for the United States Congress. Her campaign staff tried to persuade Chinese Americans who were

independents or Republicans to switch their party affiliations for the Democratic primary contest, but very few
did. Although she raised substantial campaign contributions from Asian Americans, she was soundly defeated.

REFERENCES

Abramson, Paul R. and Claggett, William (1986) 'Race-related
differences in self-reported and validated turnout in 1984,'
Journal of Politics 48.
Antunes, George and Gaitz, Charles M. (1975) 'Ethnicity and
participation: a study of Mexican-Americans, Blacks, and
Whites,' *American Journal of Sociology* 80.
Aoki, Elizabeth (1986) 'Which party will harvest the new
Asian votes?' *California Journal*, November.
Aslanian, Carol B. and Brickell, Henry M. (1980) *Americans
in Transition: Life Changes as Reasons for Adult Learning*,
New York: College Entrance Examination Board.
Bouvier, Leon and Martin, Philip (1985) *Population Change
and California's Future*, Washington, DC: Population
Reference Bureau.
Boyd, Robert D., Apps, Jerold W., and Associates (eds) (1980)
Redefining the Discipline of Adult Education, San
Francisco, Cal.: Jossey-Bass.
Brischetto, Robert R. and de la Garza, Rodolfo O. (1983) *The
Mexican American Electorate: Political Participation and
Ideology*, San Antonio, Texas: Southwest Voter Registra-
tion Education Project.
Brown, George, Hill, Susan T., Olivas, Michael, and Rosen,
Nan L. (1980) *The Condition of Education for Hispanic
Americans*, Washington, DC: National Center for Educa-
tional Statistics.
Bullock, Charles S. III (1981) 'Congressional voting and the
mobilization of a Black electorate in the South,' *Journal of
Politics* 43.
Cabezas, Amado Y. and Yee, Harold T. (eds) (1977) *Discrim-
inatory Employment of Asian Americans: Private Industry
in the San Francisco-Oakland SMSA*, San Francisco, Cal.:
Asian, Inc.
Cain, Bruce E. and Kiewiet, D. Roderick (1983) 'Ethnicity and
electoral choice: Mexican American voting behavior in the
California 30th Congressional District,' *Social Science
Quarterly* 65.
California Department of Finance (1985) *Projected Total
Population of California Counties*, Sacramento, Cal.:

Department of Finance.

Chan, Sucheng (1986) *The Bittersweet Soil*, Berkeley: University of California Press.

Chu-Chang, Mae (ed.) (1983) *Asian- and Pacific-American Perspectives in Bilingual Education: Comparative Research*, New York: Teachers College Press.

Chun, K.-T. (1980) 'The myth of Asian American Success and its educational ramifications,' *IRCD Bulletin* 15.

Clark, Burton (1956) *Adult Education in Transition: A Study of Institutional Insecurity*, Berkeley: University of California Press.

Cohon, J.D., Jr (1981) 'Psychological adaptation and dysfunction among refugees,' *International Migration Review* 15.

Coombs, Philip H. (1985) *The World Crisis in Education: The View From the Eighties*, New York: Oxford University Press.

Coombs, Philip H. and Ahmed, M. (1974) *Attacking Rural Poverty: How Nonformal Education Can Help*, Baltimore, Md: Johns Hopkins University Press.

Cross, K. Patricia (1979) 'Adult learners: characteristics, needs, and interests,' in Richard E. Peterson and Associates (eds) *Lifelong Learning in America*, San Francisco, Cal.: Jossey-Bass.

Daniels, Roger (1976) 'Asian historians and East Asian immigrants,' in Norris Hundley Jr (ed.) *The Asian American: The Historical Experience*, Santa Barbara, Cal.: ABC-Clio Press.

——(1978) 'Japanese Americans,' in John Higham (ed.) *Ethnic Leadership in America*, Baltimore, Md: Johns Hopkins University Press.

Darkenwald, Gordon C. and Larson, Gordon A. (eds) (1980) *Reaching Hard-to-Research Adults*, San Francisco, Cal.: Jossey-Bass.

Davis, Cary, Haub, Carl, and Willette, JoAnne (1985) 'US Hispanics: changing the face of America,' in Norman Yetman (ed.) *Majority and Minority*, Boston, Mass.: Little Brown.

Dawson, Richard E., Prewitt, Kenneth, and Dawson, Karen S. (1977) *Political Socialization*, Boston, Mass.: Little Brown.

de la Garza, Rodolfo (1974) 'Voting patterns in "Bi-cultural El Paso": a contextual analysis of Mexican American voting behavior,' in F. Chris Garcia (ed.) *La Causa Politica: A Chicano Politics Reader*, Notre Dame, Indiana: University of Notre Dame Press.

de la Garza, Rodolfo and Flores, Adela (1986) 'The impact of Mexican immigrants on the political behavior of Chicanos:

a clarification of issues and some hypotheses for further research,' in Harley L. Browning *et al.* (eds) *Mexican Immigrants and Mexican Americans: An Evolving Relation*, Austin, Texas: Center for Mexican American Studies.

Dennis, Jack (ed.) (1973) *Socialization to Politics*, New York: John Wiley.

Desbarats, Jacqueline and Holland, Linda (1983) 'Indochinese settlement patterns in Orange County,' *Amerasia Journal* 10.

Din, Grant (1984) 'An analysis of Asian/Pacific American registration and voting patterns in San Francisco,' Claremont, Cal.: MA Thesis, Claremont Graduate School.

Duran, Richard (1983) *Hispanics' Education and Background: Predictors of College Achievement*, New York: College Entrance Examination Board.

Endo, Russell (1980) 'Social science and historical materials on the Asian American experience,' in Russell Endo *et al.* (eds) *Asian Americans: Social and Psychological Perspectives*, vol. II, Palo Alto, Cal.: Science and Behavior Books.

Endo, Russell, Sue, Stanley, and Wagner, Nathaniel (eds) (1980) *Asian Americans: Social and Psychological Perspectives*, vol. II, Palo Alto, Cal.: Science and Behavior Books.

Erikson, Robert S. (1981) 'Why do people vote?: because they are registered,' *American Politics Quarterly* 9.

Fawcett, James T. and Arnold, Fred (1987) 'Explaining diversity: Asian and Pacific immigration systems,' in James T. Fawcett and Benjamin Carino (eds) *Pacific Bridges*, Staten Island, NY: Center for Migration Studies.

Fawcett, James T. and Carino, Benjamin V. (eds) (1987) *Pacific Bridges*, Staten Island, NY: Center for Migration Studies.

Finkel, Steve E. and Scarrow, Howard (1985) 'Party identification and party enrollment: the differences and the consequences,' *Journal of Politics* 47.

Foster, Lorn (ed.) (1985) *The Voting Rights Act: Consequences and Implications*, New York: Praeger.

Freire, Paulo (1981) *Pedagogy of the Oppressed*, New York: Continuum Press.

Fuchs, Lawrence (1956) *The Political Behavior of American Jews*, Glencoe, Ill.: Free Press.

Gardner, Robert W., Robey, Bryant, and Smith, Peter (1985) 'Asian Americans: growth, change, diversity,' *Population Bulletin* 4.

Gittleman, Zvi (1982) *Becoming Israelis*, New York: Praeger.

Glazer, Nathan and Moynihan, Daniel P. (1963) *Beyond the Melting Pot*, Cambridge, Mass.: Harvard University Press.

Grabowski, Stanley M. (ed.) (1972) *Paulo Freire: A Revolutionary Dilemma for the Adult Educator*, Syracuse, New York: Syracuse University Publications in Continuing Education (and ERIC Clearinghouse on Adult Education).

Hammar, Tomas (1978) 'Migration and politics: delimitation and organization of a research field,' paper presented to the Workshop on International Migration and Politics, European Consortium on Political Research, Grenoble, France.

Hiemstra, Roger (1981) 'American and Japanese adult education: a cultural comparison,' *Lifelong Learning* 4.

Hirata, Lucia Cheng (1978) 'The Chinese American in sociology,' in Emma Gee (ed.) *Counterpoint*, Los Angeles, Cal.: Asian American Studies Center, University of California, Los Angeles.

Hirschman, Charles and Wong, Morrison G. (1981) 'Trends in socioeconomic achievement among immigrant and native-born Asian-Americans, 1960-1976,' *Sociological Quarterly* 22.

Hosokawa, Bill (1969) *Nisei*, New York: William Morrow.

Houchins, Lee and Houchins, Chang-su (1976) 'The Korean experience in America, 1903-1924,' in Norris Hudley Jr (ed.) *The Asian American*, San Francisco, Cal.: ABC-Clio Press.

Hunter, Carman St John and Keehn, Martha McKee (eds) (1985) *Adult Education in China*, London: Croom Helm.

Hurh, W.M. and Kim, K.C. (1982) 'Race relations paradigms and Korean American research: a sociology of knowledge perspective,' in E.-Y. Yu, E. Phillips, and E.S. Yang (eds) *Koreans in Los Angeles*, Los Angeles, Cal.: Center for Korean-American and Korean Studies, California State University, Los Angeles.

Isaacs, Stephen (1974) *Jews and American Politics*, New York: Doubleday.

Johnstone, J.W. and Rivera, R.J. (1965) *Volunteers For Learning*, Chicago, Ill.: Aldine Publishing Company.

Kelley, Stanley, Jr, Ayres, Richard, and Bowen, William G. (1967) 'Registration and voting: putting first things first,' *American Political Science Review* 61.

Kikumura, Akemi and Kitano, Harry H.L. (1973) 'Interracial marriages,' *Journal of Social Issues* 29.

Kim, Bok-Lim C. (1978) 'Problems and service needs of Asian Americans in Chicago: an empirical study,' *Amerasian Journal* 5.

Kim, Illsoo (1981) *New Urban Immigrants: The Korean Community in New York*, Princeton, NJ: Princeton University Press.

Kitano, Harry (1976) *Japanese Americans*, Englewood Cliffs, NJ: Prentice-Hall.

Kleinmann, Howard H. (1985) 'Factors affecting second language learning in adult refugees,' *Lifelong Learning* 8.

Kleinmann, Howard H. and Daniel, J.P. (1981) 'Indochinese resettlement language education and social services,' *International Migration Review* 15.

Krashen, S.D. (1976) 'Formal and informal linguistic environments in language acquisition and language learning,' *TESOL Quarterly* 10.

Law, Michael and Sissons, Linda (1985) 'Involving adults in social change education,' in S.H. Rosenblum (ed.) *Involving Adults in the Educational Process*, New Directions for Continuing Education, No. 26, San Francisco, Cal.: Jossey-Bass.

Liu, William T., Lamanna, Maryanne, and Murata, Alice (1979) *Transition to Nowhere: Vietnamese Refugees in America*, New York: Charles Spring Publishers.

Long, Huey B. (1987) *New Perspectives on the Education of Adults in the United States*, London: Croom Helm.

Long, Huey B., Hiemstra, Roger, and Associates (eds) (1980) *Changing Approaches to Studying Adult Education*, San Francisco, Cal.: Jossey-Bass.

Loo, Chalsa (1985) 'The "biliterate" ballot controversy: language acquisition and cultural shift among immigrants,' *International Migration Review* 19.

Low, Victor (1982) *The Unimpressible Race: A Century of Educational Struggle by Chinese in San Francisco*, San Francisco, Cal.: East-West Publishers.

McDonough, Peter (1971) 'Electoral competition and participation in India: a test of Huntington's hypothesis,' *Comparative Politics* 4.

Massey, Douglas S. (1981) 'Dimensions of the new immigration to the United States and the prospects for assimilation,' *The Annual Review of Sociology* 7, Palo Alto, California.

Meinhardt, Kenneth, Tom, Soleng, Tse, Phlip, and Yu, Connie Young (1985) 'Southeast Asian refugees in the "Silicon Valley": the Asian Health Assessment Project,' *Amerasia Journal* 12.

Montero, Darrell (1979) *Vietnamese Americans: Patterns of Resettlement and Socioeconomic Adaptation in the United States*, Boulder, Colorado: Westview Press.

Muller, Thomas (1964) *The Fourth Wave: California's Newest Immigrants*, Washington, DC: The Urban Institute.

Nakanishi, Don T. (1986a) *The UCLA Asian Pacific American*

Voter Registration Study, Los Angeles, Cal.: Southern California Asian Pacific American Legal Center.

——(1986b) 'Asian American politics: an agenda for research,' *Amerasia Journal* 12.

Nakanishi, Don T. and Hirano-Nakanishi, Marsha (eds) (1983) *The Education of Asian and Pacific Americans*, Phoenix, Arizona: Oryx Press.

Nee, Brett and Nee, Victor (1974) *Longtime Californ': A Documentary Study of an American Chinatown*, Boston: Houghton Mifflin.

Piven, Frances Fox and Cloward, Richard (1988) *Why Americans Don't Vote*, New York: Pantheon Books.

Portes, Alejandro and Mozo, Rafael (1985) 'The political adaptation process of Cubans and other ethnic minorities in the United States: a preliminary analysis,' *International Migration Review* 19.

Robinson, C. (1980) *Special Report: Physical and Emotional Health Care Needs of Indochinese Refugees*, Washington, DC: Indochinese Refugee Action Center.

Shu, Ramsay Leung-Hay (1985) 'Kinship system and migrant adaptation: Samoans in the United States,' *Amerasia Journal* 12.

Solmon, Lewis C. and Gordon, Joanne J. (1981) *The Characteristics and Needs of Adults in Postsecondary Education*, Lexington, Mass.: Lexington Books.

Strand, Paul J. and Jones Jr, Woodrow (1985) *Indochinese Refugees in America: Problems of Adaptation and Assimilation*, Durham, NC: Duke University Press.

Sue, Derek and Kirk, B. (1973) 'Differential characteristics of Japanese and Chinese American college students,' *Journal of Counseling Psychology* 20.

Sue, Stanley (1980) 'Psychological theory and implications for Asian Americans,' in Russell Endo *et al.* (eds) *Asian Americans: Social and Psychological Perspectives*, vol. II.

Sue, Stanley and Padilla, Amado (1986) 'Ethnic minority issues in the United States: challenges for the educational system,' in Bilingual Education Office, California State Department of Education, *Beyond Language: Social and Cultural Factors in Schooling Language Minority Students*, Sacramento: California Department of Education.

Sung, Betty Lee (1975) *Chinese Americans and Manpower Employment*, Washington, DC: United States Department of Labor.

Suzuki, Bob (1977) 'Education and the socialization of Asian Americans: a revisionist analysis of the "model minority" thesis,' *Amerasia Journal* 4.

143

Tachibana, Judy (1986) 'California's Asians: power from a growing population,' *California Journal*, November.

Thompson, Kenneth H. (1982) *The Voting Rights Act and Black Electoral Participation*, Washington, DC: Joint Center for Political Studies.

UCLA Ethnic Studies Centers (1987) *Ethnic Groups in Los Angeles: Quality of Life Indicators*, Los Angeles, Cal.: UCLA Ethnic Studies Centers.

Uhlaner, Carole, Cain, Bruce E., and Kiewiet, D. Roderick (1987) 'Political participation of ethnic minorities in the 1980s,' Social Science Working Paper, No. 647, Division of Humanities and Social Sciences, California Institute of Technology, Pasadena, California.

United States Bureau of the Census (1983) 'Population profile of the United States: 1982,' Series P-23, No. 130, Washington, DC: Author.

United States Commission on Civil Rights (1979) *Civil Rights Issues of Asian and Pacific Americans: Myths and Realities*, Washington, DC: Author.

United States Department of Education, National Center for Education Statistics (1981) 'Women and minority groups make up largest segment of adult basic and secondary education programs,' Bulletin, 17 August.

United Way, Asian Pacific Research and Development Council (1985) *Pacific Rim Profiles: A Demographic Study of the Asian Pacific Profile in Los Angeles County*, Los Angeles, Cal.: United Way.

Vedlitz, Arnold (1985) 'Voter registration drives and Black voting in the south,' *Journal of Politics* 47.

Verba, Sidney and Nie, Norman (1972) *Participation in America: Political Democracy and Social Equality*, New York: Harper & Row.

Verhine, Robert E. and Lehmann, Rainer H. (1982) 'Non-formal education and occupational obtainment: a study of job seekers in northeastern Brazil,' *Comparative Educational Review* 26.

Wolfinger, Raymond E. and Rosenstone, Steven J. (1980) *Who Votes?*, New Haven, Conn.: Yale University Press.

Wrinkle, Robert D. and Miller, Lawrence W. (1984) 'A note on Mexican American voter registration and turnout,' *Social Science Quarterly* 65.

Yu, Eui-Young (1982) 'Koreans in Los Angeles: size, distribution, and composition,' in Eui-Young Yu *et al.* (eds) *Koreans in Los Angeles*, Los Angeles, Cal.: Korean and Korean American Studies Program, California State University, Los Angeles.

Part Three

INNOVATIVE APPROACHES TO PRACTICE AND RESEARCH

Chapter Eight

EDUCATION AS A SOCIAL AGENT:
ONE UNIVERSITY'S ANSWER TO A MULTIETHNIC
GRADUATE ADULT POPULATION

Philip T.K. Daniel and Vesta A.H. Daniel

The current state of adult education may be characterized by the presence of varying, often disparate goals, objectives, methodologies, and delivery systems. Nevertheless, it has the potential for enhancing the quality of life of its clientele. To do this, it must make adjustments to meet the varying specific needs, such as the acquisition of literacy and job training, but also it can affect local and world communities on a broader plane, which includes the identification, analysis, interpretation, and adjustment, of social realities.

Current thinking among socially oriented adult educators makes obvious that the discipline is no longer constrained to the traditional academic exercises performed in campus classrooms and laboratories. Its domain has been expanded to include the objectives of: (1) responding to social change; (2) constructing problem-centered educational programs; (3) educating for the social and cultural consciousness of its clientele; (4) training and further educating the educationally disadvantaged; (5) developing the understanding of adult educators to include the needs of disfranchised and culturally diverse adult learners; and, (6) clarifying methodologies, to support educational programs at the community level.

Because these complex objectives have not been attained generally, further discussion of the theoretical and contextual components undergirding an expanded view of adult education will be the subject of this chapter. Central to this position is the premise that education is not neutral, and, therefore, that it must incorporate and respond to contextual demands, in order to serve its clientele effectively.

This chapter will also focus on the question of whether the educationally disadvantaged should be dismissed as 'failures,' and thus the cause of their own lack of employment and of poverty; and whether the system (i.e., public schools, universities) actually establishes 'official knowledge' in such a way

147

that it can neither be obtained nor utilized by the educationally disfranchised. The position espoused here is that the
modern university has the responsibility to make education
available to the adult minority population. In order to function
effectively in their domain, adult educators must determine
where the individual fits into the system, where biography
meets structure, what the role of the university is in clarifying
this relationship, and how to develop methods of delivery
which benefit the adult learner's needs outside of, as well as
within, the mainstream population.

To explore these issues two conceptual approaches to
learning will be presented: reproduction theory, and experiential learning theory and its relation to cognitive theory and to
empowerment theory. In the process, the involvement of the
Northern Illinois University community-based Adult
Education Service Center in addressing these issues will be
described.

REPRODUCTION THEORY

Fundamental to reproduction theory is the concept that the
dispensing of knowledge can be used to enforce conformity
and to maintain the *status quo*, by means of the school's
reproduction of the social division of labor. In a Marxist-
oriented study of American education, Bowles and Gintes
(1976) contend that the nature of the economic base
'corresponds' to the structure of the school, i.e., wages,
advancements, hierarchical relationships, efficiency of
production, time control, etc. This structure, they contend, is
similar to grades, promotion, authority of teacher over student,
scholastic assignments vs play, and the structure of the school
day. Moreover, students are consciously and unconsciously
'prepared' for the 'natural' roles in the work force, both
mentally and physically. Like the population most in need of
adult education programs in general, and community-based
programs specifically, the adult recipients of this social
engineering, or cultural hegemony related to educational
practices, are likely to be those people not of the dominant
culture (Thompson 1980).

Illich (1983) suggests that education is repressive and that
the traditional school leaves individuals with a consciousness
that confuses teaching with learning, grade advancement with
education, a diploma with competence, and fluency with
creativity and intelligence. Illich and Jencks (1972) view
formal education as an essential instrument for repression and

as a barrier to progress and equality.

Nasow (1979) criticizes American schools and their role in preserving a hierarchical social order. His thesis is that 'the common school, the high school, the colleges and universities, maintain social order and increase material productivity' (p.4).

Cunningham (1983a) specifies that graduate programs are instruments of cultural and social control and suggests that 'critical analysis of graduate programs' curricula and conference programming might support the argument that no education is neutral — it either domesticates or liberates' (p.5).

Thus, according to these concepts, the type and delivery of educational service by adult educators is a function of their understanding of the purpose of education in social, political, and economic contexts. The challenge to adult educators is to extend the traditional goals of education, by permitting the adult individuals to assume some responsibility for determining the kind of educational services they think will suit their real needs.

EXPERIENTIAL LEARNING THEORY

Non-traditional adult educators, concerned with a sociological orientation, believe that some adults are not well served by the traditional approach to education. For them, the process of experiential learning, that is, learning which occurs through experience, may be a valid approach, in contrast to learning which is dependent only on 'communication by abstractions codified through written or spoken language' (Cunningham 1983b:57).

With a growing population of adult learners, who relate directly to the concrete experiences of daily life and to a philosophy advocating 'maximum control of the education experience by the learner' (Cunningham 1983b:59), experiential learning is viewed as a method of facilitating collaborative, self-directed, and community education.

Three groups of educators have articulated issues related to experiential learning: (1) non-traditional continuing educators concerned with assessment, legitimization, and information assimilation; (2) continuing educators concerned with techniques and technology; and, (3) empowerment educators, focusing on the acquisition of power by groups subordinate to the mainstream population. The third group more logically can be considered separately, due to their prevalent sociological and political philosophy.

The primary concerns of non-traditional adult educators,

working with secondary or higher education, are the problems of assessment and legitimization. They usually have a narrow definition of experiential learning, which limits it to those activities of the student, either prior to, or after enrollment, which can be substituted for course work in qualifying for credit. The assessment issue is joined by the second issue of the question of legitimization of experiential learning, since the practice is sometimes viewed as the acquisition of 'cheap credit.' Tumin (1976), a strong advocate of the role of experiential learning in formal education, nevertheless cautions that institutional certification depends on acceptance by professionals with traditional degrees themselves, who may be reluctant to accept changes which might endanger their status.

Coleman (1976), who strongly supports experiential learning, augments this view of the process by suggesting that it be mixed with more symbolic abstract learning, or information assimilation.

The virtue of the information assimilation process, as compared to experiential learning, lies in its efficiency and usefulness in transmitting knowledge of the fact. It is problematic, however, in that it can be critically dependent on academic language, that moving from symbolic learning into the field of action may be difficult, and that students will need artificial motivation. By contrast, the strengths of experiential learning are intrinsic motivation, direct relationship to further action, and less tendency to forget learning gained from action. However, the time-consuming nature of extracting general principles from particular experiences is a weakness. Since, according to Coleman (1976), subordinate groups within the culture may lack elaborated language codes, they can start with experiential learning, but must eventually learn language codes necessary to succeed in the traditional systems.

A second group of continuing educators (focusing on facilitating adults in collaboration and self-directed education) seems mainly concerned with techniques and technology. They prefer to implement andragogy, which, in contrast to pedagogy, builds on the experiences adults bring to learning and recognizes their responsibility for their self-education.

Rather than focusing on assessment of experience and legitimization (that is, playing the game of translating experience into credit), non-traditional adult educators at Northern Illinois University (NIU) consider the experiential learning process as a foundation for approaching symbolic or information assimilation. This program will be described in a later section of this chapter.

Cognitive theory

Experiential learning has been variously approached by cognitive psychologists relative to development and preferred learning style (Bruner 1968). In cognitive style, Witkin (1975) categorizes learners as either 'field dependent' (including the symbolic or informational assimilation learning method) or 'field independent' (tending toward experiential learning).

Kolb (1981) applies cognitive theory to experiential learning and identifies four learning styles and their strengths: for convergers — the practical application of their ideas; for divergers — their imaginative ability; for assimilators — the ability to create theoretical models; and for accommodators — the ability to take risks and the practical ability to do things. The extent to which an individual displays a predominance of type (although all are needed) indicates the strengths of that individual's approach to learning.

Cognitive theorists suggest that experiential learners can improve their reasoning skills by, (1) using a 'rehearsal strategy,' to systematically classify experiences and generate principles characterizing them, and (2) using concept formation or concept attainment, which enables them to move from classifying events to inferring the rules that bind the category together.

Recognition of how these theoretical bases affect educational strategies is fundamental to the development of curricula which incorporate the cognitive contexts in which students learn.

Empowerment theory

Another approach to learning to be considered here is that espoused by empowerment educators. These theorists concentrate on the sociological and political analysis of structures. They submit that individuals develop within a social and cultural context and that recognition of the power relationships within societies fosters the best analysis of differences among individuals.

Among the empowerment researchers, Reed (1981) constructs the framework for his 'empowerment learning process.' Its basic premise states that problems for individual learners

may have their source in the structures of society which

have developed in close accord with the logic and interests of the social classes which dominate the given society.... Thus, a learner ... of a given race, gender and cultural origin is dealt with in predetermined ways which are far beyond the mere will of the individual to change.

(Cited in Cunningham 1983b:6-7)

The learning process is valid, in his view, if learners understand how to change their oppressive situation and how to participate 'critically, creatively in the defense of their social interests' (cited in Tumin 1976:7).

Moreover, Mezirow (1978), in his discussion of 'perspective transformation' points out that traditionalists question the ability of subordinate groups to extract unique or special meaning from their experiences, since the only value they see is reflected in the existing or 'official' knowledge of the dominant culture. Consequently, the goal of empowerment education is to legitimize the experiences of subordinate groups and to allow the knowledge created by these groups to be recognized as at least competitive with 'official knowledge.'

The question of what one learns from experience, and who judges its worth, is central to empowerment educators, although it may be considered irrelevant by cognitive psychologists. Empowerment educators intend to help the learner to analyze power in social relationships through experience. If a new view of social reality regarding schools, teachers, subject matter, and pupils, results, the learner will have undergone the 'perspective transformation' referred to by Mezirow. Just as the learner's ability to analyze social structure will depend upon his understanding of power and how it works, the educator's approach to improving adult learning through an experiential process is also dependent upon an understanding of these social realities.

In summary, Reed's empowerment learning process and Bruner's cognitive theory argue convincingly for the importance of experiential learning, but for different reasons. Bruner maintains that an inability to utilize the information assimilation process is, indeed, the deficiency of the student. Because the student has not developed the capacity for 'abstract symbolic learning,' he prefers the more primitive enactive mode. In contrast, Reed places the problem in the structures of society, which encourage the dominant cultural system to reproduce itself to the detriment of learners outside the dominant culture. Thus, a learner not from the dominant culture is likely to receive very different definitions of experience, meaning, learning, and education, from continuing educators representing the dominant culture.

The fundamental principle supported by the present research is that empowerment of groups outside of the mainstream of dominant culture is a supportable and necessary education strategy. It includes the premise that the threshold for curriculum development and the educational process is experience and its relationship to learning. Moreover, the educational process is inextricably linked to cultural contexts, thus requiring that one begin with the concrete experiences of the learner within the subordinate culture. Tasks inherent in this process involve helping learners elicit generative themes from their experience, facilitating their ability to code and decode experiences, linking up critical reflection about experience with knowledge systems, and learning to analyze social realities.

FROM THEORY TO PRACTICE

Turning to practice and the application of the aforementioned theories, the strategies and successes of a midwestern public university in the United States are now examined.

In the state of Illinois, federal funding was combined with state funding to develop a delivery system for a literacy program, beginning in 1964. The maximum amount of special set-aside money for staff development (15 percent) was utilized to do two things: provide each local program with staff development money, and to develop a state-wide network of Adult Education Service Centers, staffed with professionals, to provide technical assistance to these local programs. Currently, the state is divided into three tiers, with a service center in each tier.

The Northern tier of Illinois contains most of its 11.5 million population, including six million persons in the four-county area surrounding the city of Chicago. Northern Illinois University lies sixty-five miles west of the city and, at the time the service centers were being developed in 1972, had just started a graduate program in adult education. In 1976, the NIU graduate program in adult education won the contract to develop the service centers for the Northern tier, and has held the contract for twelve years. NIU is a university located in the rural 'bread basket' area of Illinois, and its graduate student population, with the exception of international students, is almost entirely white and Anglo. Consequently, a decision was made by the new faculty to place one of their centers in Chicago, on the south side of the city, in the heart of the Black community.

The responsibility of the Service Center is to serve all program personnel who are funded through public literacy funds, which in Chicago means large numbers of Asians, Blacks, and Hispanics. Illinois has the fourth largest Hispanic population in the United States, following New Mexico, Arizona, and Colorado. The majority of this Illinois population lives in Chicago and was characterized by a 1970 National Census as having the lowest level of education among race/ethnic groups and, in 1976, as having the second highest unemployment rate nationwide. In comparison to this relatively new population, Blacks have a long history in Chicago, but are still denied full access to education, employment, political power, and material acquisitions.

It is reasonable to assume that barriers built into the educational system may have prohibited the delivery of adult education to the educationally disfranchised, such as members of the Black community. However, following the political upheavals and protests of the 1960s, universities were forced to serve a previously excluded population of low income and minority individuals. This gave rise to the notion of university extension centers and community service, employing an expanded definition of adult education in formal settings and in informal groups, to encourage the involvement of Blacks and other minorities.

Since the relevant experience of many adult learners (Black or other) was likely to be in their own communities, emphasis was placed on community-based education oriented to empowerment. The issue then arose as to whether community-based empowerment programs should be supported by public funds. To date, Illinois will fund projects with tangible results, but will not support theoretical research. Private sources will not fund social action, but will fund research.

The Northern Illinois University Adult Education Service Center is a response to the need for diversity. Because it is housed in a university which contributes three administrative salaries, as well as a number of support services, the Service Center is not limited to serving those programs funded by the state. Anyone teaching in adult literacy programs is eligible to use the services of the Center free of charge. Accordingly, it has become the mechanism for channeling university resources into the development of services to practitioners working directly with those 'most in need,' both in publicly supported and community-based programs. While there are graduate courses available, which constitute 10 percent or less of the services available, the remaining 90 percent include teacher assistance in the form of workshops, on-site visits, and telephone advisement.

THE NIU SERVICE CENTER IN CHICAGO

The Chicago Center, which started in 1976, supported by a $100,000 annual budget, now operates with a $270,000 annual budget, and is one of three centers operated by the University. It is unique in its provision of an operational base for the University directly in the city of Chicago. The Service Center, which physically is a moderately sized office/library, houses a collection of 5,000 materials, and is staffed by three urban-based, full-time field consultants (who also hold rank as instructors in the faculty, while concurrently doing advanced doctoral work in the graduate program). They make visits to local adult education programs, advise in the techniques of adult instruction, diagnose adult learner abilities, and help with program planning techniques and materials usage. Also, an associate professor, assigned as a field consultant, gives graduate advisement in Chicago at the Center.

In addition to the services mentioned above, the Center holds workshops and annual conferences, publishes a newsletter, and provides networking opportunities with local agencies, students, and community groups. Round tables and forums are arranged, to make adult education programs more inclusive of new ideas generated under both formal and informal educational situations.

Other staff members include one to three part-time graduate assistants, one full-time office manager, and a secretary. The primary duty of the graduate assistants is to immerse themselves in this special learning experience. Their routine duties include assisting with workshops, evaluating educational materials, preparing the material for the newsletter, and responding to telephone requests for assistance. They also conduct special projects designed to integrate their objectives as doctoral students with their responsibilities at the Center, such as using their experiences at the Center as a laboratory for understanding and fostering human resource development. The responsibilities of the office manager are to organize and regulate the work loads of the graduate assistants and the secretary. The latter orders supplies, materials, and subscriptions, and keeps the schedules of the professional staff, in addition to providing support services to the group, running the office, and serving as an information gate-keeper.

Most important to the operation of the Center are the

services of two senior faculty members from the campus, who, as part of their assignment, manage the project and spend much of their time in Chicago. While the same two faculty members, Dr Phyllis Cunningham, Director, and Dr Paul Ilsley, the Associate Director, stay with the project on a continuing basis, junior faculty members change often, due to graduation and promotion to other positions, or because they have reached their saturation level, in terms of their learning experiences at the Center.

Over a twelve-year period, approximately twenty junior faculty members were employed at the Center, providing them the opportunity to do their doctoral work there. A notable exception to this pattern is Dr Paul Ilsley, who was a graduate assistant in training at the Center for five years. After working for six years in adult education administration in another state, he returned to the position of Associate Director of the Center. The several purposes of the Center are: to support research leading to national participation and leadership in enhancing adult literacy and to find the funding necessary to an expanding program; to recruit and graduate ethnically and culturally diverse graduate students; to strengthen the links between NIU and the city of Chicago; and to do all this for the purpose of fostering social change, to enable persons educationally disfranchised to help shape the system of education to meet their real needs.

In carrying out its responsibilities, the Center conducts conferences and workshops for adult learners and some 3,000 teachers of adults. The majority of these are part-time ABE and GED teachers, but others are full-time teachers, counselors, or administrators. Courses available to this population are related to the understanding of the needs of community education and are conducted as workshops. The topics include: needs assessment, instructional design and processes, and the unique characteristics of adult learners, vs those of children, as learners. Many teachers request 'hands-on' and 'ready-to-use' materials as well. One of the objectives of these courses is to expand the models and definition of literacy beyond those commonly used by the teachers. As a consequence of the process of definition building, educational 'radicalism' has resulted, based on the notion of literacy as a political problem, not a technical or individual problem, and the need to analyze the roots and causes of illiteracy.

Minority participation and research in the graduate program

The NIU graduate program in adult education has maintained a minority enrollment of about 12 percent, as it has grown to be one of the largest programs in the country, with 250 students divided equally between the masters and doctoral degree candidates. Beginning in the winter of 1977, 75 percent of the students at the Chicago Service Center were Black. There was no Hispanic enrollment. By 1981, 50 percent of the students (including those in non-credit classes) were Black, with still only a few Hispanic students enrolled. By 1987 the enrollment was almost equally divided into Black, Hispanic, and white students. The ratio of female to male students as of spring 1988 was as follows:

	Female (%)	Male (%)
Black	65	35
Hispanic	50	50
White	60	40

These figures are fairly consistent with national ratios. Beginning in 1984, NIU increased the effort to recruit and support Hispanic graduate students, resulting in the current doctoral program, which includes thirty-four Hispanic students.

The ability to enroll minorities in the program was dependent on externalizing the master's degree as well as assigning a portion of doctoral study to Chicago. Fifteen to twenty courses are offered on extension in the city by regular faculty members from the NIU campus.

Research emanating from the Service Center, and conducted by minorities, results in publications and occasional papers by the Center staff, as well as dissertations, and papers presented at meetings and national conventions. Among the topics addressed have been issues related to GED programs for Latinos; staff development; instruction and curriculum; recruitment and retention of ABE students; community-based education; steel workers' culture in south Chicago; bilingual education; Governor's Council on Literacy; adult education in Ecuador; and participatory research in the Chicago Housing Authority (CHA). Graduate students, ABE students, Service Center staff, and other adult educators, have also published articles in the *Adult Educator*, the newsletter of the Northern Area Adult Education Service Center (NAAESC).

Other research has been directed towards redefining the

purpose of the Center. Two special subjects of research have concerned the needs of single Black women and unemployed steel workers, with an emphasis on the services required by these groups. Actually, a few members of these two focus groups pursued graduate study, as a consequence of their involvement with the Center. However their primary objectives were to complete the GED program, acquire job skills, and learn to participate in community decisions by identifying and exerting their personal power. It is hoped that a deeper understanding of these realities will help to shape the direction of the Service Center and will lead to participatory research between students and professors. The effect of social activism on one's lifelong history is being researched; also research is being carried out on issues related to public offenders; and the value, skill, and belief developed in nurses' education. Recent research on phenomenology has been included in a book written by a NIU professor.

Several courses have been developed, including 'The Pedagogy of the Oppressed,' 'Adult Education and African Development,' 'Participatory Research,' 'Community Based Program Administration,' 'Education in a Cultural Context,' and 'Adult Education in Asia, South America and Africa.' Notable international colloquium speakers were brought to campus to address cultural diversity, participatory research, and Third World perspectives and basic literacy.

Consistent throughout these research areas is education toward social criticism and awareness, encouragement toward participatory research, and applying experiential learning to formal research analysis, skill building, and the recognition of knowledge.

Service to, and outcomes for, minorities

Several kinds of actions demanded, or developed, by minority students have helped to maintain a cultural and ideological diversity in the graduate program. Among these are the establishment of a student advisory committee; minority tuition waivers from the Graduate School; availability of contract courses of study, predominantly for Black community colleges; increased minority involvement in the political leadership of the Illinois Association for Adult and Continuing Education (IAACE), which focuses on adult literacy and encompasses various types of adult educators; minority involvement in appointed councils, such as the Governor's

Council on Literacy; and the creation of formal and informal alliances with community members, agencies, and other community-based organizations.

The outcomes for students at the Service Center are varied. Successes are often based on the validation that accompanies receiving an adult education degree. Among the doctoral students completing degrees, 80 percent received their first or second job choice. Students completing master's degrees received their first or second job choice at the level of 40-60 percent. Involvement in research has resulted in the specific instances of a $60,000 dissertation grant to an Hispanic student, and appointment to a nurses' training standards board by a nurse whose adult education dissertation research addressed this topic. Among these adult learners, whose average age is 35.5 years, jobs have frequently resulted from internships. Students have also opted to remain involved in community and political organizations, because of their newly developed awareness of empowerment on a local as well as an international level. Whether or not they complete degrees, students often continue to do research, publish, and to support other adult learners. Typically, students matriculating through the Service Center value this experience.

The problems engendered in developing an outreach to minorities are several. They include recruitment, retention in, and graduation from, graduate degree programs. Students facing a dissertation, while attending school part-time, are often discouraged by the lack of a consistent support system. Several minority students could not find the courage to take the Graduate Record Exam (GRE), for admission to a graduate program. Other students found the campus atmosphere unreceptive to them, and others failed their comprehensive examinations. In addition, to date, there are no senior minority faculty members in the graduate program.

Recommendations for augmenting services

The Service Center is a dynamic agency which views its profile as temporary, from one period to the next, dependent on its ability to recognize and facilitate social change through the medium of adult education. The following recommendations for enriching the services are made, based on that perspective, and are gleaned from interviews with Dr Phyllis Cunningham, Project Director of the Northern Area Adult Education Service Center, Dr Paul Ilsley, Associate Director, and NIU faculty members who work in the Chicago Center. The recommendations also reflect reviews of written project proposals, reports, and an evaluation of the project, completed in June 1988, by Dr Jeri Nowakowski. He is not connected with the Northern Area Adult Education Service Center, but is Director of the Office of Education Evaluation and Policy Studies, Northern Illinois University.

1. Survey the needs and interests of its population through community contacts reflecting disparate community preferences. Incorporate periodic assessment and re-interpretations of the results.

2. Provide orientation and follow-up strategies for adult learners new to the on-campus graduate student experience, including mentoring from previous successful students from the same or similar circumstances.

3. Translate the assessment of learning needs ascribed to Black adult learners into educational programs and specific practices that appeal to Blacks in both content and format, avoiding isolation from existing programs serving the larger community.

4. Continue emphasis on providing atypical formats and opportunities for students to conduct participatory research that is personally relevant.

5. Increase opportunities for on-campus adult education students to learn about non-traditional approaches to research and learning by interacting with the Service Center students and instructors.

6. Analyze the current systems of delivery to identify barriers to minority utilization of resources.

7. Continue to use the newsletters as a forum for exploring social, cultural, and political issues applicable to the empowerment of adult learners.

8. Continue to develop curricula which point out the legitimacy of experiential learning and self-training as creditable processes at the level of traditional academics, to encourage participation of more adults in adult education.

CONCLUSION

At the outset of this chapter, it was suggested that all education has the potential for maintaining the *status quo*, or initiating social change. Adult educators are in a precarious position. They may either function as translators of cultural conditions as they presently exist, or help counteract those which effectively victimize adult learners.

The existence of community-based adult education centers is fundamental to the development of informed, self-motivated, action-oriented adult learners. The function of adult education can be to maintain a healthy and lively tension between cultural and intellectual conviction and the potential radicalism motivated by a new sense of responsibility. This is not to suggest that the varied and complex components characterizing adult education should or can reach stasis. Rather, adult education is bound by context and therefore must remain dynamic to be relevant.

Activities within the universities, which do not fault the under-educated adult for his/her dilemma, but recognize the repressive potential of educational systems, must be encouraged. Community-based service centers can develop politically and culturally relevant training programs and graduate courses and create structures for recognizing and responding to social change.

The adult educators at Northern Illinois University recognize that education for liberation from predetermined destinies, and the empowerment of the individual and community, are not traditionally part of the curriculum which prepares adult educators for their professional service. However, due to a strong commitment to the democratization of education, they have opted to implement adult education programs and services that provide a forum for responding to, and facilitating, social change for the education of individuals within, and outside of, the mainstream, majority population.

REFERENCES

Bowles, S. and Gintes, H. (1976) *Schooling in Capitalist America*, New York: Basic Books.

Bruner, J.S. (1968) *Toward a Theory of Instruction*, Cambridge, Mass.: Harvard University Press.

Coleman, J.C. (1976) 'Difference between experiential and classroom learning,' in M. Keeton (ed.) *Experiential Learning: Rationale, Characteristics, and Assessment*, San Francisco: Jossey-Bass.

Cunningham, P. (1979) Testimony on 'Regulations,' Adult Education Act, United States Office of Education (USOE), Region V, presented at Roosevelt University, Chicago, Illinois, 7 August.

——(1983a) Review of *Adult Education for a Change*, ed. June L. Thompson (London: Hutchinson & Co.), in *Adult Education Quarterly* 33.

—— (1983b) 'Helping students extract meaning from experience,' in R.M. Smith (ed.) *Helping Adults Learn How to Learn*, New Directions for Continuing Education, No. 19, San Francisco: Jossey-Bass.

Dobb, M. (1947) *Studies in the Development of Capitalism*, New York: International Publishers.

Illich, I. (1983) *Deschooling Society*, New York: Harper & Row.

Jencks, C. (1972) *In Equality*, New York: Harper & Row.

Kay, E.R. (1982) *Participation in Adult Education, 1981*, Washington, DC: Center for Educational Statistics.

Kolb, D.A. (1981) 'Learning styles and disciplinary differences,' in A.W. Chickering and Associates (eds) *The Modern American College: Responding to the New Realities of Diverse Students and a Changing Society*, San Francisco: Jossey-Bass.

Mezirow, J. (1978) *Education for Perspective Transformation: Women's Reentry Program in Community Colleges*, New York: Center for Adult Education, Columbia University.

Nasow, D. (1979) *Schooled to Order: A Social History of Public Schooling in the United States*, New York: Oxford University Press.

Reed, D. (1981) *Education for a People's Movement*, Boston: South End Press.

Ross, J.M (1986) 'Adult education: are Black Americans participating?,' *Black Issues in Higher Education* 2.

Thompson, J. (ed.) (1980) *Adult Education for Change*, London: Hutchinson & Co.

Tumin, J. (1976) 'Valid and invalid rationale,' in M. Keeton (ed.) *Experiential Learning: Rationale, Characteristics, and Assessment*, San Francisco: Jossey-Bass.

Witkin, H.A (1975) *Field-Dependent and Field-Independent Cognitive Style and Their Educational Implications*, Princeton, NJ: Educational Testing Services.

Chapter Nine

EXPERIENCING THE UNFAMILIAR: MATRIX FOR LEARNING

Thelma Barer-Stein

Phenomenological research sometimes provides a jolt to the reader, because so much about it is unfamiliar. However, the very experience of experiencing the unfamiliar here may validate that it can be a matrix for learning.

A differing approach to research can only be necessitated by a differing research question. I had no hypothesis, nor did I seek to prove cause and effect. Because of my own lifelong interests in ways and things that differed from the usual, I did not want to be an objective observer, nor even a 'primary conduit for data collection and analysis' (Merriam and Simpson 1984:89).

I wanted to share my experiences and collaborate in dialogue with others and to do so in a celebration of subjectivity that openly depicted 'the primacy of human existence' and the 'consciousness of ourselves' (Lawrence and O'Connor 1967:32). I wanted to find a way of comprehending human culture itself and the paradox of familiarity and difference that it represents.

For example, there are some things that each of us knows, but we do not know how it is that we know them. We know what is familiar and what is not. Familiar people, things, places, and ways, have already been worn smooth with well-acquainted use and contribute to our sense of comfort, identity, and belonging. Familiar things represent relevancy and provide meaning in our everyday life. They are the basis of that everyday life; and perhaps some of the comfort in familiarity that we feel may result from the minimal effort required for the habitual. No effort is needed to learn what we already know. There seems no need to study one's own culture.[1]

That which appears to be different jars us from this everyday complacency. Even the smallest flicker of awareness of the unfamiliar disturbs the usual routine and elicits a brief and superficial reflective pause: we skim some surface information, we question it and compare it with what we already know, and decide whether to find out more or return to the familiar.[2] However, familiar things have become so because of some previous effort to make them so.

The great difficulty in understanding culture is that of making explicit what is already familiar, implicit, and assumed to be universal.

> The class was basic English for foreign students, and an Arab student ... was describing a tradition of his home country. Something he said embarrassed a Japanese student in the front row, who reacted in the proper Japanese way: he smiled. The Arab saw the smile and demanded to know what was so funny about Arab customs. The Japanese, who was now publicly humiliated as well as embarrassed, could only reply with a smile and, to his misfortune, he giggled to mask his shame. The Arab, who now likewise felt shamed, furiously hit the Japanese student before the teacher could intervene. Shame and anger erupted in a flash, as each student dutifully obeyed the rules of his culture. Neither could imagine, of course, that his rules might not be universal.
>
> (Tavris 1982:62)

Understanding culture, one's own and that of others, must begin with an understanding of ordinary everyday life. The simplest routines, gestures, and behaviors are often the most confounding and serve to set us apart one from the other (Barer-Stein 1988a).

While there are many ways of defining and thus constraining the meaning of culture, in my own work I have come to speak of culture as 'expressing the many unique ways in which individuals group together, compose, understand and live their daily lives and in so doing, transmit a way of daily living to others' (Barer-Stein 1985:2). This view of culture helps to suggest something of its dynamism and the centrality of the individual. It suggests a sense of communal effort, sharing, and concern, a rootedness in the past and a commitment to the future. It may be helpful in grasping the notion of 'multiculturalism' as representing multiple ways of daily living within a particular context. Understanding culture as 'the learned part of the environment' (Montagu 1968:v) is intriguing. Just how is culture learned and transmitted within a cultural group, and how do exchanges occur between individuals of markedly different cultural backgrounds?

The study of difference itself had long been of passionate

interest to me. As a child, I imitated accents, gestures, and other body language, of people from different lands. Years later I studied food traditions (Barer-Stein 1979, 1980) and I gradually realized how this notion of difference had dominated both my work and my studies. Probing food differences drew me into a deepening appreciation of the cultural differences that were the source of those diverse food ways. More recently I carried this interest into educational studies, which have resulted in this particular research effort.

Seeking an everyday experience in which the confronting of obvious cultural differences forms a central part, I chose to study English Second Language teachers (ESL), whose task is to teach English to Canadian newcomers for whom English and Canadian ways are all but unknown. Daily, these teachers face, and are immersed in, the unfamiliar, even as their students are. Yet, eventually, the differences between them are somehow bridged and they come to understand each other. What is happening in these classrooms? How do these teachers learn to teach adults from different cultures?

Five ESL teachers readily agreed to share their experiences with me. I had no agenda, no list of questions, only my singular query, 'How did you learn to teach adults from different cultures?'

We conversed like friends, intermittently sharing the tasks of speaker, listener, questioner, appraiser, and analyst. They showed me their classrooms, introduced me to their students, and provided class materials. They spoke of their students: 'When my class was predominantly elderly Chinese ...,' 'The first Hungarian immigrant students ...,' or, 'When several Muslim students brought their prayer mats to class....' They spoke of how class ideas came to them out of their own daily activities, yet in the next breath they would relate how one person's problem, haltingly stated, suddenly became the class topic. However, despite our enthusiastic conversations, the mutuality of our interests, and cross-cultural experience, there was no direct response to my initial question: 'How did you learn to teach adults from different cultures?'

As I pored over the many pages of transcripts of our dialogues, I became increasingly aware of one teacher, Elizabeth. While I studied the words of others, in her case I would hear (feel?) the urgency in her voice, as she struggled to depict her experiences and explore an understanding of them with me. Her words and phrases became like a third presence over my shoulder,[3] reaching out and touching everything I did. Her interests and experiences reverberated deeply with my own, and our dialogue consumed my attention.

It was in this way that the articulate recollections of cross-cultural experiences in Elizabeth's everyday life became the focus of my phenomenological work.

The intent of my research was to comprehend culture in a deeper way than I already had, and to grasp something of the bridging of familiarity and difference that somehow takes place. The issue is not one of looking for obvious cultural differences, but, rather, it is the understanding of this tension of difference that I seek. Perhaps I was drawn to Elizabeth because her passion to understand this matched my own.

The fact that my research focuses on the experiences of one person may lead some to conclude that this is a 'case study.' It differs from a case study in two important ways: I, the researcher, am not 'the primary conduit for data collection and analysis,' (Merriam and Simpson 1984:89) nor does the work end with conclusions drawn from analysis of the collected data. Instead, I, the researcher, am included in both the collection and analysis; this work offers possibilities of understanding, derived from interpretation as well as analysis of the collaborative data.

Throughout, Elizabeth and I thought we were exploring an understanding of culture grounded in our own cross-cultural experiences. It was only much later, after intensive phenomenological work of 'scraping away the surface details,' in order to reveal the underlying structures of our experiences, that a concept of a process of learning emerged. It can be argued that all human experiences and activities hold an inherent aspect of learning. The real problem is to understand just how the learning appears, develops, to what end it progresses, and by whom this end is determined.

Understanding difference itself was the purpose of this work, with cross-cultural experiences being merely a vehicle. To this end, that is, the understanding of a human experience, the ensuing pages will explain this phenomenological approach more fully. Brief highlights from our dialogue will be quoted, together with enough of the analytic interpretation to give the reader the flavor of the work's progression. Finally, the model of the emergent learning process will be shown, together with references to other writings that have extended the implications of these findings.

Since such a work is intended to offer possibilities of meanings emerging from the essences exhumed, the sense of incompleteness is intentional. It reaches out and provides a connecting link of attention to readers to become involved in these possibilities by asking, 'How might this possibility have a relevant meaning for me?'

EXAMINATION OF A PHENOMENOLOGICAL APPROACH[4]

The term 'phenomenology' appears in the literature of diverse disciplines, as well as in many approaches to qualitative research. Close examination often reveals that the intent is to study a particular phenomenon, or as Silvers (1982:11) expresses it, ' a phenomenon as objectified knowledge,' and thus really just another topic to be researched by any one of many methodologies.

Further confusion exists when some writers interchange the terms 'qualitative' and 'phenomenological,' (Bogdan and Taylor 1975) perhaps because many aspects of qualitative research methodology have emerged from Husserlian phenomenology (Husserl 1913), such as, its emphasis on observing/studying real-life experience, unmanipulated or constrained; an emphasis on understanding rather than predicting; and care in describing what has been observed (Merriam and Simpson 1984).

I interpret phenomenology as a process of thinking, rather than a body of knowledge to be learned or a method to be followed.

In a phenomenological work, rather than assuming a stance outside of the thing to be studied, the researcher becomes as one with the thing or person researched. The profundity of concentrated reflection temporarily suspends one from the real world, in the same way that intensive reading of an exciting book does. Gradually, I developed my own way of expressing this personal understanding of phenomenology: 'To think phenomenologically is to force aside the natural reluctance of thinking about what is not exposed and of what has not been said. It is to reflect on that which is known and visible (Surface Knowings) as well as what is not (Submerged Knowings).'[5] It is to call forth an assembly of all possible facets of Surface and Submerged Knowings for concentrated reflection. It is to encompass within each act of reflecting an analytical separating, and then an interpretive reunion, into new possibilities of meaning 'that makes no sense to doubt' (Wittgenstein, quoted by Blum 1970). 'Phenomenological research lifts this process from the private to the public sphere within its meticulously written display of each moment' (Barer-Stein 1985:44-5).

This brief examination of the phenomenological approach will help the reader understand the intensity of effort shared by the researcher and Elizabeth, in the analysis and interpretive reflections, and in the effort to describe in writing how each subsequent unfolding of meaning proceeded out of the one before through the posing of specific questions: What is the meaning here? How is it that this is possible? What is it that could have made this possible? What other possibilities make this possible?

Phenomenological writing strives to record, not only what has entered the researcher's probing reflections, but also to show how these reflections shift and what it is that has gradually transformed their meaning. 'It is a manner of recording at once the process and the content of reflection' (Barer-Stein 1985:46). 'The specifically deliberate process by which Submerged Knowledge is repeatedly exhumed, analyzed and interpreted becomes part of the hermeneutical process within a phenomenological work' (Barer-Stein 1987a:92).

While a condensation of the original work necessarily omits the depiction of this process, such a condensation is presented here because the emphasis is on what emerged.

HIGHLIGHTS OF ELIZABETH'S CROSS-CULTURAL EXPERIENCES

The hesitancy of the other ESL teachers to discuss their experiences before they actually came to be ESL teachers, stood out in distinct contrast when I juxtaposed Elizabeth's transcripts with theirs. Her opening response to my question asking how she learned to teach adults from different cultures, came slowly and thoughtfully:

> Maybe some awareness started in my family. My mother is Irish Catholic from Quebec City and my father is old Ontario WASP [White, Anglo-Saxon, Protestant] and there were cultural conflicts between them. I don't think they ever described the problem as cultural conflict. I guess I just grew up hearing the descriptions from my mother — certain things she may say or do, things she was struck by, or surprised by, that was different living in Ontario. Maybe that was the beginning of my cultural awareness.

I wanted to understand how it was that Elizabeth opened our dialogue with this assumption regarding the beginning of her cultural awareness. For her, awareness of culture itself was a necessary prerequisite to the understanding of cultural differences. She had come to equate culture itself with ways of living. The ongoing conflict in her home over differing ways had long puzzled her, for she could not understand what it was that was held so deeply, yet seemed to defy reasonable explanation.

Elizabeth was also expressing something in what she had not stated. She never mentioned engaging in these conflicts, asking questions, or even taking sides. Her observations of these incidents early in her life set her apart as an outsider, the neutral observer.[6] Yet, within this early awareness, a small seed of curiosity would continue its insistent stirring over the years. She went on to say:

> I grew up wanting to travel. It was the only goal I had at university: to get through and to travel. I never thought of anything else.

She lived and worked for a time in England, and she was able to relate those experiences as vividly as if they had just occurred.

> Oh, living in England, I observed the natives, but I never had to deal with them in any way, in anything too deep ... in any way that would cause me serious conflict. I just observed that they did things differently.

Intent on distancing herself from the 'natives' (and avoiding the type of conflict that had so frequently embroiled her parents), she seemed quite unaware that there was a shift in her behavior, from passively observing as a Spectator, to deliberately seeking out just how things were done differently. She had now adopted the behavior of a Sightseer — one who deliberately seeks out points or things of particular interest.

In the many humorous anecdotes that she related subsequently, despite her protestations that she had not become involved in any way at all with the 'natives,' she described working at Harrod's department store near Christmas time:

> People were most anxious that their turkeys get to their homes before Christmas and that their gifts be delivered on time. Well, I worried more about this than anyone else in the store, as far as I could tell. After the third complaint about a turkey, I went right down to the loading dock and, I can remember, I was practically stamping my feet in frustration and anger, insisting on getting that turkey out, and the man who was head of the loading dock told me why didn't I just relax and have a cup of tea?
>
> Well, it was after that, I started to notice that they were far more relaxed over that sort of thing than I was.

I was the one all keen on efficiency, not the British! Not the store!

Elizabeth's former Observer stance now shifts to her actually becoming a part of the scene she is observing and, further, she is beginning to be aware of Appraising what she is Witnessing. In describing other incidents, she depicts her own growing ability to make comparisons with Canadian ways by collecting (albeit brief and superficial) information about these different ways. Each of these successive Reflective Pauses[7] provides a deepening grasp of her ways, as well as the ways of others. Increasingly, through her keen attentiveness to these experiences, she became aware of the daily ways of living that she had previously taken for granted. Her discovery that 'the natives' seemed to have one view and way of doing, and she had another, brought her to a stage of Passive Confrontation.[8]

In stating that she had 'started to notice,' she had made a shift in her stance from Sightseer to a Witness-Appraiser. That is, her narration had an added awareness of her own watchfulness. She was now fully present in the scene and reflectively reacting to her own presence. In my own reflections I had noted that 'this *Acting-in-the-Scene* actually represents a type of experiencing that lacks present commitment, ongoing concern, and that does not require any rootedness in the past. It provides a means to appear to be participating/experiencing (to oneself and usually to others) without actually becoming involved' (Barer-Stein 1985:77).

What seems central here is that the cumulative learnings from each aspect of the experience together shape the present experience. The cumulation seems to incite the Curiosity (desire/need to know) and it is this intertwining of Curiosity and Seduction which serves to push the learning forward. Increasingly, Elizabeth's movement indicated depth and progression, as she distinguished between two ways of life: hers and theirs.

This retrieval process, encompassing the recently-learned, as well as the exhuming of what one already knows but has submerged, helps to explain how each deepening grasp of the unfamiliar drives us to a more profound knowledge of what lays embedded within ourselves. Seeking to discern the unfamiliar external to oneself results in a correspondingly deeper renewal of familiarity with the submerged knowledge within. Interest begets interest, understanding begets understanding, and learning begets learning.

Shortly after her travels abroad, Elizabeth returned to

Canada and a new job with the Children's Aid Society, where she became a liaison worker between troubled teenagers (whom she referred to as children), their families, and the community. She described them:

> Their lives seemed so chaotic, I don't know how else to describe it. They'd move every month or two to a new place and get a new job. They didn't eat regularly. They didn't know how to eat. They had no skills. Women who didn't know how to cook, so they'd feed their kids corn flakes all the time. And there's none of this sort of hard-core working class pride or anything. These are people with really nothing. No education, no skills, no adherence to any kind of values.

Previously, Elizabeth's observations of persons in other countries seemed aptly summed up in her own phrase: '... which I can't imagine any Canadian doing!' But now she was back in Canada. Her previous sharply-drawn images of Canadians began to falter. Now this 'they' that she was observing were Canadian, too. Compared to the lives of other Canadians, it was not difficult to see how she could describe them as having nothing. For the first time, she had felt moved to do something about this imbalance:

> I wanted the children that were in my care to get a good reputation. The way they dressed, the way they behaved themselves. I wanted them to have my manners. I don't see anything wrong with that. They'll do better with middle-class manners than with none at all. If they ever wanted to gain mobility in our society, they would have to acquire them. So that's not bad.

Elizabeth now felt propelled to participate in their world. I call this new behavior shift 'Cultural-Missionary,' which carries the following attributes: a clear sense of differentiation between her culture and that of others; a conviction of the rightness of her culture; the twofold capacity which enabled her to see no fault with her own and, thus, its appropriateness for all others, and at the same time her unquestioned assumption that others need, or want, this right way; her charitable desire to share this culture with others less fortunate than herself.

But her efforts were to no avail. In conversing with her supervisor, she began to see how the children considered all the social workers as 'creatures from Mars.' 'We're so

171

different, [but] they just think we are all alike,' was her
supervisor's comment. Both Elizabeth and her supervisor had
failed to see that they too, were party to this same sort of
Cluster-judgment, the inability, or unwillingness, to differentiate among individuals within a group. Elizabeth left the
Children's Aid, never really understanding the reason for her
lack of impact. The children had not really changed with her
presence and efforts, neither had she.

Now our talk took an abrupt turn. We were wondering if
she consciously drew on any of her experiences in her present
ESL teaching. She said:

> No, not consciously. In fact, I went to Mexico first as a
> tourist and then returned to marry a Mexican. And, until
> I married a Mexican and until I lived the life of a Mexican
> housewife, I guess I didn't really think there was such a
> thing as cultural differences. I would never have. I would
> have said, oh yes, the Germans have their beer and the
> Italians have their spaghetti. I knew, oh I knew all that. I
> had traveled. And, because I had traveled, I was deluded,
> or I deluded myself into thinking that I knew something
> of foreign places. [long pause] In fact, I knew nothing at
> all.

With what had seemed to me at the time like a surprising
leap, Elizabeth had responded to my original query by
discussing her early awareness of culture. Now I sensed this
same kind of leap: that it was not cultural awareness *per se*
that had helped her with ESL, but rather comprehending the
reality of culture. What did this mean?

So intent was Elizabeth, that I seemed to disappear from
the room, as she vividly re-enacted the episodes that brought
the reality of culture to her. I asked her if she was saying that
something in her Mexican experience gave her a different
perspective. Her answer:

> Oh, yes. Completely. Since that ... that ... battering of my
> head against the differences in culture, that I finally
> learned that there really was such a thing. That it was real.
> I had thought such things were just kind of stupid. Stupid.

There followed an emotional recollection of how she had
wanted to take on an evening volunteer job, manning hot-line
telephones for English-speaking kids involved in drugs in
Mexico City. She had arranged a ride there and back and had
even secured her mother-in-law to baby-sit. Her husband said

no.

But that wasn't it! It was that I as a woman should not be alone at midnight! That was the problem. It was not anything a Canadian would think of! It was me, alone, at midnight.

The jagged rush of words had now been repeated over and over; they held within them the full force of what must have been her original incredulity. It seemed as though it was all happening now, this moment. Feeling myself swept up in her torrent of tears and dismay, it struck me that her husband's sole concern had been for the shame this act would bring upon his name. 'It was not anything a Canadian would think of!'

She had quite literally believed that, in 'Living-the-Life' of a Mexican housewife, she really was a Mexican housewife. Now her Canadian rationality had been confronted with the ways of daily Mexican living and she found herself battering against a wall she had not known existed. Watching her, as she held herself and rocked in the chair, I recalled an episode from my early life, when I realized a customer in our delicatessen store was buying a tin of rattlesnake meat to *eat*. The customer was shocked at my disgust. Our shock was instant and mutual; almost like hitting a brick wall with my bike. Until then, I had thought everyone was like me, and my family. Now I saw her and all the customers in the store as being very different.

All along, Elizabeth and I had shared similar experiences of travel and interest. Only now did I see that we each had come up against a wall that we had not known existed, a submerged wall that everyone assumes is understood and so needs no explanation. 'It was only when the familiar became unfamiliar, when the comfortable became uncomfortable, and when it all suddenly refused to work, then the bedrock quaked' (Barer-Stein 1985:103).

Such recognition of difference/unfamiliarity, requires the closeness of coming face to face with the thing. Although 'confronting,' in common usage, is often taken to infer conflict, I have chosen to use it in its essential meaning, that of literally coming face to face. Previous to this particular experience, she had faced the unfamiliar with some passive interest, but in this incident she faced it with anger, argument, and conflict. These ways had seemed sufficient in the past encounters; they did not work now. Stunned by this, Elizabeth withdrew into herself:

And I stopped cooking Mexican food and I stopped speaking Spanish unless it was absolutely necessary and I stopped going to language school and talking to Mexican friends. I had a kind of paranoia and hostility towards all Mexicans. I just didn't advance or progress any more. I refused to learn anymore.

While all of the phases she had progressed through thus far had been sequential and voluntary, the choice of remaining in a phase, regressing or progressing, did not seem an issue; she had always been spurred forward by the intensity of her Curiosity. Until now, her deeply-held interest had propelled her forward to learn more; now she spent more than three months wavering between Passivity, Conflict, and Withdrawal. Finally, she returned to Canada with her child, believing that she had left her confusions behind.

Elizabeth could offer no explanation for being drawn to teaching ESL classes, nor even what drew her to ask strangers, who appeared to be newcomers, how they were adjusting to life in Canada. It was difficult for her to realize that her work and these encounters were all part of her personal quest to understand cultural differences and how they might become satisfactorily resolved. It was also difficult for her to grasp that with her own endless questioning of 'How ...?,' she herself was Involving herself. I had asked her how she thought it might be possible for one to surmount the superficiality of participating in another's culture merely by 'Living-the-Life of,' and she nodded thoughtfully, and answered: 'I think that if you want to learn more about other places in a more profound way, you have to involve yourself somehow.'

Later, in my own reflections on our cross-cultural experiences, I came to see that 'involvement was not something that was done to you, nor even something that someone could do for you ... it was representative of a deliberately willful movement not just towards, but actually within, something, connoting almost inextricable connectedness' (Barer-Stein 1985:98). Adding my own thoughts to what I had heard about Elizabeth from her peers and her students, I realized that she had progressed into a profound involvement in the lives of these newcomers to Canada, such that their concerns and dreams literally became her own. This new behavioral shift into Involving was expressed by her in this way:

I think there is a quality about the mind, a willingness to move into a different way of seeing, a willingness to understand a differing point of view, at least to entertain it, to listen....

Elizabeth herself was scarcely aware that, in fact, she had not left her confusions behind in Mexico, but had brought them back with her to Canada, continuously asking herself and others, 'How is it that cultural differences come to some kind of resolution?' I could find no word in English that embodied the complexity of such an ongoing questioning, and the intensive hearing and listening, as well as heeding what was being expressed and enacted. The profoundly concentrated reflection and the meaningful action that results from the intense desire to understand and appreciate the 'how' of something, catapulting one from merely coming face-to-face into actually involving oneself, could not be depicted in any English word or expression. Recalling the Hebrew word *shemah*, which commonly means 'to hear' (but implies also that, having heard, one can thereafter not plead ignorance and therefore is bound to 'heed'), seemed the closest to signifying the openness and obligation inherent in Involving.

I began to see also that the *Sh'ma* (as the essential aspect of Involving) was, in fact, the process by which Submerged Knowledge may be disclosed, to make possible the discovery of personally relevant meaning. Like phenomenology itself, I saw the Sh'ma not as a body of knowledge to be learned, nor as a method that could be memorized (for this would be akin to Acting-in-the-Scene). I saw it as a way of reflective thinking that could open unpredicted knowings, and as Montagu had noted, 'transcend what is learned; a potentiality for innovation, creativity, reorganization and change' (Montagu 1968:239). Eventually, I was able to encompass the essence of the Sh'ma in this way as hearing/listening, reflecting/heeding:

1. The *hearing*[9] represents immediate awareness and recognition of what is heard, pressed forward by the intensity of the need to know more (Curiosity as the need/desire to know).

2. The *listening* represents the concentrated attentiveness of dialogue with the thing or person: deeply absorbing all that is proffered.

3. The *reflecting* explores the parts of that which has been collected (analysis as separating into parts), and places the possibilities of meanings in a display (through imagination, inferences) to determine:
— How did this come to be?
— What are the possibilities here?
— Which possibilities make sense?

— Which is the relevant meaning for me in this context?

4. The *heeding* represents the now effortless movement to embrace and enclose the newly-discovered thing in a oneness with the self, precisely because of its meaningful place in the enhancing the self (Barer-Stein 1987a:100-1; 1987b:40).

The Sh'ma not only represented phenomenological thinking, it could also be delineated into what had already emerged as Phases — and their essential themes within — of a process of experiencing the unfamiliar. Hearing was like Being Aware, Listening like Observing, while Reflecting was a non-threatening way of trying out possibilities. Instead of Confronting the unfamiliar with either Passivity, Conflict, or Withdrawal (usually resulting in a regression to the previous phase), it was possible to move directly to the Sh'ma by asking, 'How ...?' and, in this way, moving within Involving oneself.[10]

The Paradox of Involvement is not another phase, but an aspect of being involved that is only escapable by a vigilant desire to retain a continuous Awareness-of-Interest. 'The more profound the Involving, the more deeply the interest has become internalized and an inextricable part of oneself, the more it threads its way with the common, habitual daily activities of the individual.... This is like saying, *the better you know something, the less you are aware of knowing it*' (Barer-Stein 1987a:101).

Great tolerance must be shown to any attempt to express the complexity of any human experience within the constraints of a simplistic, two-dimensional drawing. Figure 9.1 is no exception. Some points deserve emphasis: (1) The main phases and their essential themes are named by the experiencing individuals. (2) 'Essential' is used here in the Husserlian sense: that without which the thing could not be what it is. (3) The arrows attempt to indicate movement; the confusion of arrows under Confronting is meant to depict the possibility of movement in any direction, while the large arrows moving to the right indicate the deflection out of a phase and a movement towards another Awareness-of-Interest. The reader is referred to more detailed discussion in other writings (Barer-Stein 1987a, 1987b, 1987f, and 1988c).

It was by scraping away the surface details of the cross-cultural experiences, to reveal their underlying essential structures, that this process began to appear, develop, and eventually progress, to both Elizabeth's and my own Involving understanding and appreciating. There was no doubt that each phase was propelled forward by our 'urge to understand.'[11] It also became clear that, no matter how fleetingly one rested in any phase or the essential theme within, the phases and

Figure 9.1 Model of the emergent learning process

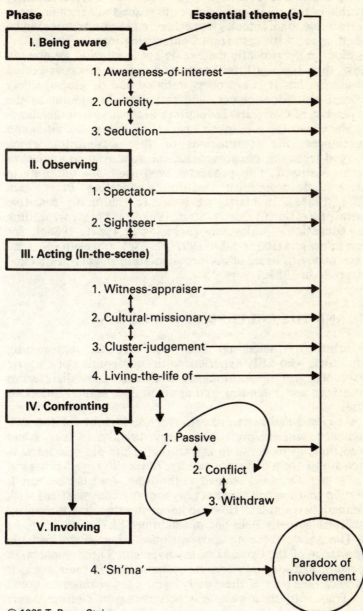

© 1985 T. Barer-Stein

Source: Studies in the Education of Adults, 19 October 1978:93

their essential themes were sequential; it was impossible to progress without their order. It was, however, frequently possible to remain in one place, or to regress to a former, more comfortable, one. It took great effort (and some practice) to be able to move with ease from Confronting into Involving.

Since it is axiomatic that we do not learn what we already know, then learning itself must be a process of experiencing the unfamiliar. It is a process initiated and developed solely through individual choice, and sustained throughout by the persistence of Curiosity/Seduction and the urge to understand.

Since learning is so much a part of all human activities and experiences, the implications of the possibilities which emerged from this phenomenological work seem as endless as experience itself. This process proved itself in attempting to define home economists as cultural educators (Barer-Stein 1987c, 1988a), in clarifying issues for culturally-sensitive health professionals (Barer-Stein 1987d, 1987e), for probing into educational philosophy (Barer-Stein 1987f, 1988c), for adult educators (Barer-Stein 1987f, 1988c), and even for those concerned with issues of culture adaptation and culture 'shock' (Barer-Stein 1988c).

ESL AND THE CULTURE/LEARNING LINK

In arbitrarily selecting ESL teachers, as representing individuals who daily experienced the confronting of cultural differences, yet somehow managed to bridge those differences and effect understanding and appreciation, several questions arose.

At first I had been puzzled over the inability of the ESL teachers to answer my initial query directly. In fact, I had noted that, in response to my asking, 'How did you learn to teach adults from different cultures?,' they did everything but answer me. Or, so it seemed at the time. And the persistent question that nagged at me throughout my conversations with Elizabeth was similar: 'How did her comprehending the reality of culture actually help her in teaching ESL?'

The answer became apparent once I myself grasped the importance of the Paradox of Involvement. These teachers, to a person, had long ago become so immersed in their work, it had become a part of their daily lives. They themselves noted how frequently their own daily activities provided the theme for a class, and how often a student's problem or decision became the topic for discussion. The classes reflected the flow of the daily lives of the participants. Teachers and students alike participated and learned from each other.

Their devotion and enthusiasm for their ESL work attested also to the need for centrality of individuals to make their teaching relevant. They did not see a mass of people, they saw different cultural groups: Chinese, Hungarian, Muslim. They did not think in terms of lessons only, they were ready to turn individual needs into individual sharing within the group. Where did this sensitivity come from?

I thought of how vivid my conversations with Elizabeth had been. Throughout, we shared the sense that everything we talked about was happening here and now. Elizabeth had frequently relived these past cross-cultural experiences in her own reflections, to understand herself more fully. She had kept the initial impact of the reality of culture as vividly in her mind as I had. Through this framework of her own experiences she was able to recognize others moving through a similar process and was stirred to help them and, in turn, learn more about what was taking place in this necessary behavioral change so much a part of any adaptation.

I had wondered what was really happening in these exemplary ESL sessions and now I understood how language facility was the foundation of cultural understanding, of discovering a level of tolerable comfort in everyday living.

I had asked, 'How did you learn to teach adults from different cultures?' As the research progressed, the importance of different cultures, and even adults, gave way. What remained as the essence of my own question was, 'How did you learn?' That is what eventually emerged as the underlying structure — the how of learning.

EXPERIENCING THE UNFAMILIAR: MATRIX FOR LEARNING

My original intent in this work was to 'comprehend culture in a deeper way.' That is, not just to give recognition to the obviously different individuals and ways of living as a tourist meandering through an exotic scene, but to grasp something of how such uniqueness happened. In my own musing over ordinary things in this way, I began to realize that doing so requires a disengagement from what would have been the ordinary flow of thinking, leaping over the taken-for-granted. This very act of stepping aside, or disengagement from the ordinary, is to the act of questioning as reflection is to experience: it made it possible for me to see the question itself as something to be questioned, to see flickers of the unfamiliar in the habitual.

Elizabeth's progress in understanding herself as a Canadian, and as a unique individual, rested on her ability increasingly to make comparisons between what she believed herself to be and what she really was. In our dialogue, we were each not only Confronting the unfamiliar in our daily world, but also discovering unknowns within ourselves. As each Awareness-of-Interest progressed in the process of learning, some even to the point of slipping into Submerged Knowledge, the persistence of our questioning, 'But how is it that this is possible?' sent us each burrowing to the very center of our 'beings of learning' (Barer-Stein 1985:56).

If it is true that 'culture is learned,' then the learning of it must represent daily living itself, and the accumulation of that learning must form the richly textured matrix from which we draw, in order to find understanding. We are always surrounded by the unknown and the unfamiliar, and are continuously selecting what is relevant for our lives. There are already some universals that we know about learning: (1) It is a voluntary activity. Imposition, or coercion, results in an appearance of knowing, and the ability to repeat by rote, words and phrases to satisfy an external authority; authentic understanding and involvement demands the personally driven curiosity to engage in the Sh'ma. (2) Learning, the ability and the need/desire, are an inherent part of each human at any age. (3) Learning is cumulative; but the effort of the Sh'ma is necessary to exhume Submerged Knowings and to make sense of both Surface and Submerged Knowings in any setting. (4) While learning is a part of most human activities, we must distinguish between Being Aware, Observing, Acting, Confronting, and Involving, both from the viewpoint of individual learning — so that we understand learning as the process that it is and can see where we are in each of the countless learning processes that any one individual may be engaged in at any particular time — and from the viewpoint of one concerned that teaching become truly as Dewey had insisted 'a guiding of the learning.' (5) The most important task of teachers, whether they be parents, friends, lovers, co-workers, siblings, or our own selves, is to recognize that Confronting the unfamiliar, by asking 'How?' and thus engaging in the Sh'ma, is always an extension of learning and an enhancement of the self. (6) Achieving the goal of understanding the unfamiliar is not always that which is external to ourselves. It may well begin with the unfamiliar (what we thought ourselves to be, as opposed to who/what we really are) within ourselves.

Asking myself, 'What is really happening in these exemplary ESL classrooms?' proved to be important. The teachers' own curiosity about cultural differences and ways of living were continually renewed through their well-practiced openness 'to seeing differently.' The only thing that had become habitual and therefore taken-for-granted was this very openness. For these teachers, the language of English was merely a vehicle to deepen their own understanding of unique individual experiences which formed unique individual matrices for learning, helping each of the students to be open to each other, and to guide their experiences towards a comfortable understanding of their own place in Canadian ways of daily living.

Prepared lessons represented what the teachers assumed students needed or wanted to know. But creating an atmosphere conducive to the unrestrained expression of personal needs required a teacher, not only to be open and flexible, but authentically and visibly so. Their descriptions of their work reverberated with the excitement evident in any collaboration of learning.

In phenomenological thinking and research, and within the experiencing of the Sh'ma, reflecting on experience becomes an intensive re-enacting of the past, with the intent of displaying it as clearly as possible for analysis and interpretation into possibilities, until finally one possibility seems to emerge from all the others and shimmers with sense. Understanding emerges only with effort. It presses forward to be grasped, but only if we are willing to extend ourselves to reach that which forever dangles just beyond easy grasp.

Understanding the unfamiliar and that which differs from what we already know and, more especially, understanding that it is always an enhancement of the self, will be crucial, but only for as long as one individual differs from another, and one mind wants to ask, 'How is it that this is possible?'

NOTES

1. 'Studying our own culture' is seen as the foundation for any understanding of the concepts of culture. See Landes (1965), regarding a successful experiment in sensitizing teachers to culture. Also see Barer-Stein (1988a and 1988c).

2. Expressed here so casually, the familiar details of the Reflective Pause (explained later in the text) may well elicit a 'Well, of course' from the reader. It is this very

expression that confirms its familiarity in everyday life.

3. Others who have expressed this phenomenon are Betti (1984:30): '... in the sense that another mind different from ours and nonetheless intimately linked with ours makes itself recognizable to us through this form and calling upon our sensibility and intelligence,' and Gadamer (1979): 'The experience of the "Thou" also manifests the paradoxical element that something standing over against me asserts its own rights and requires absolute recognition: and in that very process is understood.'

4. The discussion here focuses on what phenomenology is, with a view to showing how it was used as a process for research. The author intends to expand on this in future writings.

5. The notions of Surface and Submerged Knowings is discussed more fully in Barer-Stein (1985:10-17, and 1987a: 90-2).

6. From my work (1985:66): 'I wondered how really neutral one is in any scene that one is merely observing. Surely the fact of attentiveness to that which is being observed, in itself depicts some latent interest that moves one beyond neutral emotionless seeing. (And is this possible?)'

7. From Gadamer (1975:237): 'How do we discover that there is a difference between our own customary usage and the text (or anything else) ... generally it is the *experience of being pulled up short*.... Either it does not yield any meaning or its meaning is not compatible with what we had expected.' (Emphasis is mine.) Also, Mezirow's 'discordant Experience' (1981) relates to this.

8. Re 'confronting': I am fully aware of the usually negative connotation popularly evidenced, but the actual meaning is 'to come face to face,' and it suggests the closeness of really seeing something. The commonly held connotation of confrontation as 'conflict' might be worthy of interesting reflection.

9. There are many who speak of the notion of 'hearing,' but I am especially drawn to Palmer (1969), who says, '... there is nothing that is not accessible to *hearing* through language,' and, 'Because through *hearing*, through language, one gains access to the world to which we belong.'

10. This taken from (1985:55-6): 'I take for granted that we live our daily lives on the topmost layer of our many levels of sedimented accumulated learning and that only now and then, does something occur in our lives to give us cause to reverse our usual pursuits and deliberately direct them *to*

an inward reflection that burrows to the very essence of our beings of learning.'

11. From Polanyi and Prosch (1975:42): 'The characteristic structure of all our personal knowledge comes out even more vividly when we realize that all knowing is action — that it is *our urge to understand* and control our experience....'

REFERENCES

Barer-Stein, Thelma (1979) *You Eat What You Are: A Study of Ethnic Food Traditions*, Toronto: McClelland & Stewart (distributed by Culture Concepts, Toronto).

—— (1980) *Glossaries of Foods and Food Terms*, Toronto: Culture Concepts.

—— (1985) 'Learning as a process of experiencing difference,' Ph.D. Thesis, University of Toronto, Ontario Institute for Studies in Education, 1985; Microfiche edition, Thesis Division, National Archives of Canada, Ottawa.

—— (1987a) 'Learning as a process of experiencing the unfamiliar,' *Studies in the Education of Adults* 19.

—— (1987b) 'On the meaning of learning: reflections with Dewey,' *Canadian Journal for the Study of Adult Education* 1.

—— (1987c) 'The home economist as cultural educator,' *Canadian Home Economics Journal* 37. (Also, 'Author's Response to Professor McCleave,' ibid.)

—— (1987d) 'Reflections on diabetes and culture,' *Diabetes Educator* 13.

—— (1987e) 'Why can't they just all be Canadians?,' *Multicultural Health Coalition Bulletin* (Toronto) 2.

—— (1987e) 'Whose body is it anyway?,' *Multicultural Health Coalition Bulletin* 3.

—— (1987f) 'Who needs teachers?,' *Australian Journal of Adult Education* 27.

—— (1988a) 'Eating what you are,' in Keith McLeod (ed.) *Multiculturalism for Family Studies Teachers*, Toronto: Kagan & Woo.

—— (1988b) 'John Dewey dialogues with an adult educator in 1987,' a play reading, *Proceedings 1987 Canadian Association for the Study of Adult Education*, Hamilton, Ontario: Canadian Adult Education Association.

—— (1988c) 'Experiencing the unfamiliar: culture adaptation and culture shock as aspects of a learning process,' *Canadian Ethnic Studies* 22.

——(1989) 'Reflections on literacy and the universal learning process,' in Maurice Taylor and James Draper (eds) *Adult Literacy Perspectives*, Toronto, Canada: Culture Concepts.

Betti, Emilio (1984) 'The epistemological problem of understanding as an aspect of the general problem of knowing,' in Gary Schapiro and Alan Sica (eds) *Hermeneutics: Questions and Prospects*, Amherst: University of Massachusetts Press.

Blum, Alan F. (1970) 'Theorizing,' in Jack Douglas (ed.) *Understanding Everyday Life: Towards the Reconstruction of Sociological Knowledge*, San Diego, California: University of California Press.

Bogdan, Robert and Taylor, Charles (1975) *Introduction to Qualitative Research Methods: A Phenomenological Approach to the Social Sciences*, New York: Wiley & Sons.

Darroch, Vivian and Silvers, Ronald (1982) *Interpretive Human Studies: An Introduction to Phenomenological Research*, Washington, DC: University Press of America.

Gadamer, Hans-George (1975) *Truth and Method*, New York: Seabury Press.

——(1985) *Philosophical Apprenticeships*, Cambridge, Mass.: MIT Press.

Husserl, Edmund (1962) *Ideas: General Introduction to Pure Phenomenology*, trans. W.R. Boyce Gibson, New York: Collier Books (first published 1913).

Landes, Ruth (1965) *Culture in American Education*, New York: Wiley & Son.

Lawrence, Nathaniel and O'Connor, Daniel (1967) *Readings in Existential Phenomenology*, Englewood Cliffs, NJ: Prentice-Hall.

Merriam, Sharan B. and Simpson, Edwin L. (1984) *A Guide to Research for Educators & Trainers of Adults*, Malabar, Florida: Robert E. Krieger.

Mezirow, Jack (1981) 'A critical theory of adult learning and education,' *Studies in the Education of Adults* 32.

Montagu, Ashley (1968) *Culture: Man's Adaptive Dimension*, London: Oxford University Press.

Palmer, Richard E. (1969) *Hermeneutics: Interpretive Theory in Schleiermacher, Dilthey, Heidegger, Gadamer*, Evanston, Ill.: Northwest University Press.

Polanyi, Michael and Prosch, Harry (1975) *Meaning*, Chicago: University of Chicago Press.

Silvers, Ronald (1982) 'Teaching Phenomenology,' prepared for the Annual Meeting of Phenomenology and Existential Philosophy, Pennsylvania State University.

Tavris, Carol (1982) *Anger: The Misunderstood Emotion*, New York: Simon & Schuster.

Chapter Ten

THE USE OF A NEGOTIATED APPROACH IN HEALTH CARE:
UNIVERSITY-COMMUNITY GROUP INTERACTION

Joan S. Reeves

Primary Health Care, as defined by the World Health Organization (1978), is a comprehensive concept encompassing far more than the availability of a doctor for a patient in time of need. Rather, it speaks to a variety of human activities which affect health, including: (1) food production and preparation; (2) prevention of diseases through sanitary practices, such as safe water and immunization; (3) health promotion activities, such as breast feeding and child spacing; and, (4) basic decision-making. However, in the case of disadvantaged or under-educated groups, knowledge and training are needed for responsible decision-making. Nevertheless, this knowledge and training must not be imposed, but, rather, be developed with the members of a community in the way that best suits their needs and interests.

In this chapter a case study is presented to describe the Negotiated Process Approach used with Latina women in an inner-city community in Chicago. Subsequently this same approach has been used successfully with Korean women during two summers in the same city. The Negotiated Process Approach (NPA) is a practice model which was designed for the use of a university health care team and a community group while they worked together to solve community health problems (Reeves 1987).

In the summer of 1984, a faculty group from the University of Illinois-Chicago developed a course to train professionals from related health disciplines to use a Primary Health Care (PHC) approach in developing a practice model to meet health needs of urban women in industrialized countries. Since women carry the major responsibility for health care of families and communities, the faculty wanted to find a practice model that would be supportive of community women working with a group of health professionals. The exploratory work in 1984 led to the empirical development of the Negotiated Process Approach, which was put to use in summer 1985 in the Women's Health course field experience.

This type of practice model, as explained by Reid and Epstein (1972), is descriptive and prescriptive, rather than analytic and is used to guide the participants. While the model will be described here, the course is more fully described in another paper (Dan, Keys, Reeves, Hennein, Holden, Petty 1985).

Utilizing accepted theory about group and intergroup dynamics, the Negotiated Process Approach is designed to foster shared control, to the satisfaction of both professional health teams and community groups in direct interaction, and to promote community involvement.

COMPONENTS OF THE MODEL

The Negotiated Process Approach model has the following ten components: overall goal, negotiated agreements, collaboration, joint decisions, education, joint participation, structured intergroup interactions, health activities, process consultation, and joint evaluation. In this case study, these components will be treated in the context of a specific situation.

The NPA begins when the health care team and the community group agree to collaborate on a general goal of working together to define community health needs and to carry out a health activity, with the help of a process consultant who provides information to all involved. However, it is important that the process consultant maintain a role independent of the two groups, but be available to each group throughout the process. Members of both groups need to develop a common understanding of group dynamics, primary health care, and principled negotiation. They particularly need to understand four basic concepts.

1. *Community Participation.* The NPA promotes influential participation, which is defined as shared influence between the groups in determining the content of a decision, plan, or solution. This definition rests on participants being both offered, and provided with, opportunities to influence the process and the decision. In research on community participation, the key point is that participants have the feeling of influence (Appleby 1980).

2. *Negotiation.* The primary approach in managing conflict is not based on initial conflict resolution, but seeks to recognize differences which enhance interactions, before

negotiating solutions to conflicts. In this process there is the promotion of knowledge exchange and a tendency to progress toward agreement.

With NPA, the differences in the two groups are emphasized and, then, as the groups move toward an outcome, these differences narrow. This is accomplished in each stage of the process by the two groups meeting separately and then together. Both groups are taught to use the method of principled negotiation (Fisher and Ury 1981).

3. *Process Stages.* Five process stages begin after there is an initial decision for the two groups to collaborate. Separate education sessions are held for each group. The process stages are assessment, planning, strategy development, implementation, and evaluation. It is important that the planning for these stages be carried out in sequence, because the results from one stage provide the basis of thought for the next stage, although this does not preclude the group from questioning later their decisions in earlier stages.

4. *Lay Knowledge and Professional Knowledge.* The knowledge of the health professional will obviously be very different from that of the lay person. It will be deeper, more highly concentrated, and perhaps narrowly focused (Hayes-Bautista 1978). The lay person, however, has a more intimate knowledge of the context (Friedman 1976). For example, the professional is more likely to use statistical data, like mortality rates, whereas the lay person knows about the people who have died in the community. Discrepancies in knowledge are recognized through interactions between the professional group and lay group and are managed through the process of negotiation. Through this exchange of knowledge, the participating community group learns more about the special knowledge of the professional group, and the professional group learns more about the perceived needs and knowledge of the community group.

The separate development of plans gives each group the opportunity to develop its own best thinking. This is particularly important for the community group. If they had worked together with the professional group from the beginning, it is more than likely that they may not only have deferred to the professional persons, but that they may never have developed their own ideas in any systematic way. Eventually both groups together agree upon a health activity, which is then implemented. Finally, the two groups jointly evaluate the results of their work and the process itself.

APPLICATION OF THE NEGOTIATED PROCESS APPROACH

The first application of the Negotiated Process Approach took place in the summer of 1985. Organized as a field experience course for graduate student health professionals in their credit program, this first trial case had to be completed in a matter of ten weeks. While this imposed certain limitations on. the project, nevertheless, it proved an instructive example of this innovative approach.

For the students, the field experience required six hours per week during the quarter. Three hours of this time was devoted to face-to-face work with the community women, and the rest was used for seminars, training, and research. Seminars with the psychologist, who was the process consultant, concentrated on helping the students to understand the basic philosophy and planning team activities for each stage of the process.

The student health team included two men, one a physician from Korea and the other an American medical student; a nurse from Korea and one from Bahrain; and two American public health students, one with expertise in nutrition and both with a background of health education. This was not a full-time project for them, since they were carrying other classes and some had families and jobs.

A small grassroots urban Latina women's agency indicated interest in working with the student team, and agreed to organize the team of community women. This agency was well known and was part of a network of small non-profit agencies serving the Hispanic community. Persons in these agencies helped each other with grant proposals, shared some resources, and maintained close contact with each other. This was helpful to the student team, which received easy access to the network of agencies in the course of their research on the health problems of the community.

Unfortunately, this agency also had a funding problem, which resulted in the termination of positions of two women who were working with the community team. While this situation was not optimal, it did not sidetrack the project. However, it did point out one of the endemic realities of working with community groups, i.e., that one cannot expect faithful commitment of members under all circumstances.

The psychologist, who served as process consultant, also met with the community group on a regular basis, to help them understand the philosophy of this participatory project and the various phases of the work to be accomplished. It should be stressed that the basis of this interactive group project was the importance of the development of the community group as an authentic entity which might continue when this particular project was completed. The team of health professionals was to work with them as resource persons and to learn from them but not to dominate them.

Five of the women in the community group were Hispanic, from Colombia, Peru, and Mexico. One woman was not Hispanic but had been working with Hispanic community agencies. The women ranged in age from fifteen to fifty years and their educational backgrounds ranged from two years of high school to graduate education. They were all connected to agencies. While it would have been optimal to have 'grassroots' women (the term used by the director of the agency), this was not possible for several reasons, which are worth mentioning for the lessons they teach. In the first place, many families return to Mexico during the summer months, when children are not in school. These community women are usually interested in a one-time educational program, not in working on community problems over a period of time. Also the agency person, who was delegated to do recruitment, was new and perhaps not sufficiently acquainted with the members of the community.

ASSESSMENT AND PLANNING

Prior to interacting with the women's group, the students prepared themselves by reading materials about Hispanic culture and the role of Hispanic women. They paid particular attention to their beliefs and practices in health care. A walking tour of the community, along with a tour of community agencies, helped the students to understand the health problems. In addition, community leaders were interviewed.

The community group did not make this kind of effort, because they chose to rely on their experiences and knowledge of the community.

A three-hour block of time was set aside each Wednesday morning, which included time for each group to meet separately and then together. The field experience coordinator from the university and the process consultant met with the groups, to share information about the concepts of primary health care, the Negotiated Process Approach, group dynamics, and special principles of negotiation, based on the work, *Getting to Yes: Negotiating Agreement Without Giving In*, by Roger Fisher and William Ury (1981). Their concept, 'principled negotiation,' alludes to a process of expanding understanding of all differences.

In this process, misunderstandings and even some differences disappear, and this leads to a simplification of the negotiation process. Therefore, at each stage of the process, the two groups needed to work separately, in order to allow the differences between them to be developed as much as possible before they worked together. This allowed each group time to become aware of its own members' ideas, to sort them out, and to come to its own perspective.

Techniques used were brain-storming, role-playing, polling each member, to bring out personal ideas, and then reducing these to writing, to share them with the other group. Two levels of negotiation occurred as groups came to agreement among themselves and later with the other group. Agreement was to be sought at each stage, before moving ahead to the next. However, when necessary, the groups could return to an earlier stage. During the first two weeks, the main tasks were for the members of the two groups to become acquainted with each other, developing an atmosphere of trust and understanding about the project, so that both the community group and the student team would have a common and shared understanding of how the Negotiated Process Approach could be applied in this situation.

The amount of time consumed, and the order of the meetings of separate and combined groups, varied to meet 'felt needs.' To choose the health activity, the two groups first met together, and, through a process of brain-storming, came up with a list of problems. As a second step, they discussed criteria for choosing items from that list. At that point, they preferred to meet separately. Each group was encouraged to think about standards, or guidelines, which could be used to judge each health problem, before investing energy on it. For example, each group had time constraints and each had different amounts of time available for the health activity.

The items that appeared on the first list of possible health activities were the following: (a) teen-age pregnancy; (b) alcoholism and drug abuse; (c) gang violence; (d) language barriers; (e) battered women; (f) sexually transmitted diseases (some members were uncertain about this one); (g) teen runaways; (h) unemployment; (i) rape; (j) depression/frustration; and, (k) domestic violence (wife and child abuse).

The process of choosing criteria, and finally selecting a single health activity, required several weeks, during which time both teams added additional topics. Addressing the problem of criteria for selecting the final topic also required negotiating sessions, both within groups and between groups. Eventually, the community team decided that some of the topics mentioned by the students should be dropped, because they were not relevant in their community. Progress came when a student suggested that the complete list of remaining problems should be ranked by all the members as to priority: high, medium, or low. In this manner, the list of topics was finally reduced to seven: (a) teen-age pregnancy; (b) language barriers; (c) unemployment; (d) parenting skill; (e) battered women; (f) sanitation; and, (g) gangs. Five of these problems had been suggested by the women in their first meeting with the students.

Out of many criteria discussed, the possibility of making a contribution to the solution of the problem became an important consideration, which helped the groups reduce the list to three: (a) battered women; (b) teen-age pregnancy; and, (c) parenting skills.

Encouraged by the progress the community women were making in examining community problems and defining priorities, the student group wanted to continue the discussion. However, the women's group became upset. They wanted to get into action. For a while, it seemed that the final three topics could be lumped together under domestic problems. However, it was at this point that the two members of the community team were laid off from the agency and left the group. This was a bit discouraging to the student group, which thought the agency looked forward to a bleak future. There was some discussion about working on the agency's funding problem by writing a grant proposal, but it was decided to consider the three problems in relation to this new information on agency funds and personnel.

In an effort to narrow the subject of interest to meet the constraints of time and personnel, the topics of battered women and teen-age pregnancy were selected for action. However, an interesting study was cited that indicated that a high percentage of teen-age mothers had been abused and had alcoholic fathers. This led the group to decide to focus on the basic problem of battered women.

When discussing the problem, there was general agreement that the focus should be on prevention; therefore, the goal of the two groups was to work on a health activity which would decrease the number of battered women. Education programs, speakers, fliers, forums, work with churches, writing grants, and a health fair were all considered. The groups realized that no person in either group had the actual knowledge needed to support many of these activities.

STRATEGY DEVELOPMENT

To gain more understanding about battered women and services available, the student team did more assessment in the community. They visited agencies and talked with community people about the problem of domestic violence. At the next meeting, persons knowledgeable about the problem were brought in to share information. This discussion led to a more realistic view about a health activity which could be implemented within the final three weeks. The activities engendering the most interest were education (a forum), developing a flier, working on a grant proposal for a new shelter, and an education program for the police department. Discussion of the difficulties in carrying out these activities finally reduced the options to some type of forum and, possibly, a flier. The purpose of the forum was to: (a) educate people about the problem; (b) explain the legal rights of battered women; and, (c) tell people where to go for help.

IMPLEMENTATION

Student team members went out into the community to discuss this program and were pleased to find general interest in the forum. To promote continued work in the development of the program, the names of contacts with other agencies were shared. One agency actually agreed to host the forum during the last week of August. This agency, which provided adult education classes for Latino people, suggested that twenty-five to fifty persons could be expected to attend. However, the program would need to be presented entirely in Spanish, since a complete bilingual presentation would take too much time.

The members of the two groups previewed a film, *Women: Love and Fear*, in Spanish, with English subtitles. It became clear that the film needed to be used in conjunction with a speaker who would discuss rights and resources in the local community. An agency staff member involved in the domestic violence program agreed to speak (in Spanish). The length of the program, the number of speakers, involvement of group members, refreshments, plans for equipment, and other details, were all items included in the planning meeting. It was agreed that information about employment opportunities would be available, since one team member worked in this area. Further, the group decided that all the members of the student team should be presented and thanked for their work in the community.

On the day of the program, the groups were pleased, and perhaps a little surprised, to experience a warm reception by the people of the community, who even brought refreshments, including many special traditional dishes, and helped in arranging the room for the program. Of the approximately thirty-five persons who attended, there were equal numbers of men and women. The program was carried out as planned, and most participants showed interest in the topic by actively participating in the discussion, and suggesting further programming on the subject.

EVALUATION

To evaluate the program, the groups met separately in the morning, and then joined together for lunch, during which opinions were shared. One of the community women said that the process had focused on group goals and group process and she wondered how the personal goals of members had meshed with group goals. She continued, 'Personally, this has been a good experience. I feel that I have been able to help this agency and also do networking for my organization. I have led groups [in the past], but this was a good experience — to be part of a group working with another group.'

Another woman shared her views: 'I learned a lot about working with groups.... I felt that [some of us] did not know enough about this community and I was sorry that some of our more knowledgeable women had to drop out.'

Part of the discussion centered on the issue of professional knowledge versus the community's 'felt needs.' The community women expressed the opinion that the student team should do more research ahead of time, so that they would not have to ask so many questions. The process consultant explained that the students needed to ask questions, that this was the only way they could learn from the community women what their ideas were.

All regretted the fact that the sponsoring agency had financial difficulties, which had caused some knowledgeable persons to leave the group.

When the university coordinator of field experience later met with one of the community leaders, she mentioned that she had already used the ideas from her experience with the group to plan future programs.

CONCLUSION

Research findings from the case study and the Negotiated Process Approach evaluation demonstrated that the health care team and the community group were able to use the NPA to work together on a community health activity, so that the community would gain some enduring benefits. Differences of ideas, both in the separate groups and the combined group, were managed through shared leadership, in which the women believed they had played an influential role. Knowledge was exchanged between the two groups, as they worked toward these agreements in each stage of the NPA. This was a very important aspect of the success of the project for the students who, as future professional health workers, need to know about community health problems from the point of view of the community itself.

REFERENCES

Appleby, M. (1980) 'Organizing for participatory decision making in public affairs,' *Volunteer Administration* 13.

Dan, A., Keys, E., Reeves, J., Hennein, S., Holden, J., and Petty, J. (1985) 'An experimental course in the application of primary health care concepts to women's health in an urban setting,' *Proceedings of the Seventh Annual Conference on Interdisciplinary Health Team Care*, Chicago: University of Illinois, Interprofessional Education Committee.

Fisher, R. and Ury, W. (1981) *Getting to Yes: Negotiating Agreement Without Giving In*, Boston: Houghton Mifflin.

Friedman, J. (1976) 'Retracking America: a theory of trans-active planning,' in W. Bennis, K. Benne, R. Chin, and K. Corey (eds) *The Planning of Change*, 3rd edn, New York: Holt, Rinehart & Winston.

Hayes-Bautista, D.E. (1978) 'Chicano patients and medical practitioners: a sociology of knowledge paradigm of lay-professional interaction,' *Social Science & Medicine* 12.

Reeves, J.S. (1987) *Use of a Negotiated Process Approach in Health Care Team-Community Group Interactions*, Ann Arbor: University Microfilms International.

Reid, W., and Epstein, L. (1972) *Task-Centered Casework*, New York: Columbia University Press.

World Health Organization and UNICEF (1978) *Primary Health Care*, Geneva: World Health Organization.

Chapter Eleven

THE DYNAMICS OF HOSTING AN INTERNATIONAL EXCHANGE STUDENT

Kimerly Miller, Cornelius Grove, and Bettina Hansel

AFS Intercultural Programs, of American Field Service, is one of the oldest and largest of the world's numerous exchange organizations. It maintains a full-time research staff that is constantly probing the nature and impact of the intercultural experiences of AFS program participants. Although the focus has most often been on the teen-age exchange student, the research staff has also studied the exchange experience from the point of view of host families. A 'Study of the dynamics of hosting' began in early 1980 and has been, for AFS, the major effort directed at understanding hosts.

Prior to this study, conducted over a period of four years by the AFS research staff, associates, and volunteers, only one major study of international host families had been carried out. In the mid-1970s, Raymond Gordon studied families in Bogotá, Colombia, who were hosting young American Peace Corps volunteers and university students. His study, *Living in Latin America* (1974), illustrated the seemingly trivial cross-cultural misunderstandings that, in a surprisingly high percentage of cases, seriously undermined relationships between the young American adults and their Bogotano hosts.

The current AFS study, 'The dynamics of hosting,' was not conceived as a replication of Gordon's study. Rather, the AFS research team hoped to clear its head of all preconceived notions about the nature of the student-host relationship. There was a very practical reason for this study. As with many exchange organizations, about twenty-five percent of all students placed in AFS programs encounter problems serious enough to warrant a change of family. Staff working on these problem cases necessarily focus on the specific issues, or misunderstandings, that have created the feeling that student-host separation is necessary.

As fascinating as these cases may be in their depiction of cross-cultural *faux pas* and interpersonal miscommunication, they nevertheless represent only those hosting experiences which run into trouble. Since many hosting experiences never come to the attention of AFS staff members, the research team had to assume that numerous families have entirely successful experiences, or are able to resolve problems without the intervention of the national staff. Consequently, the research team wanted to study the general nature of the host family experience, in hopes of contributing to the body of knowledge, small as it is, on why families choose to host a student from another culture and how the experience influences their lives.

Fifteen families were selected to represent the kinds of families that typically volunteer to host AFS students. All of them were White, but they were drawn from lower, middle, and upper-middle class social strata. Among them were families headed by a laborer, a dairy farmer, a truck driver, a widowed bank teller, a college librarian, a minister, an engineer, an orthodontist, and a vice president of one of the world's best known corporations. One family consisted of a couple without their own children; another was a single parent; most were families with teen-age and/or young children. They lived in medium-sized cities, affluent suburbs, small towns, and isolated rural areas. Due to financial constraints, most of the families studied were located within several hundred miles of AFS headquarters in New York City: in Pennsylvania, New Jersey, New York, and Connecticut. However, three of them resided in the vicinity of St Louis, Missouri. The families were selected in such a way that their exchange students would be representative of the students AFS brings into the United States: six from Europe, three from South America, two from Africa, two from Asia, one from the Middle East, and one from Oceania.

The study was a descriptive, longitudinal documentation of the experiences and feelings of the fifteen host families before, during, and following the ten months they were hosts to an adolescent exchange student under the auspices of AFS. The sole method of gathering data consisted of semi-structured, open-ended, audio-taped interviews. Each family was visited by the same investigator several times during the ten-month period. Interviews lasted from one to three hours. The occasions on which interviews were conducted were the following: (a) just prior to the student's arrival; (b) just following the student's arrival; (c) three or four times during the year; (d) immediately following the student's departure; and, (e) one year later. The purpose of the interviews was to document the process of adjustment that each family was undergoing, from the initial period of anticipation to the post-departure reflection on the quality of the hosting experience. Occasionally the exchange student was interviewed separately, at the time of the family interview, but his or her views were only taken into consideration to the extent that they shed light on the experiences that the family was relating. The interviewers made a deliberate effort to refrain from counseling those families who were experiencing problems with the hosting arrangement. Nevertheless, in some cases a move may have been prevented simply because the family had the unusual opportunity of unburdening themselves to a patient, knowledgeable, and sympathetic listener (Grove 1984).

Each family's pattern of adjustment was plotted on a graph, indicating its relative satisfaction with the experience at any point during the year. On the graph, the horizontal midline indicates emotional neutrality. Increasing distance above the line indicates increasing contentment, satisfaction, and positive affect. In the same way, the distance below the midline illustrates increasing conflict, dissatisfaction, and negative affect. While the plotted distance above or below the line for any given family is subjectively meaningful to members of the research team, it is impossible to specify this objectively or in terms of any recognized unit of measurement. However, great pains were taken to insure that all fifteen graphs are consistent and meaningful in relation to each other.

In other words, if Family A's graph is higher for the month of December than Family B's, this indicates the interviewer's conviction that A's experience was proceeding more positively than B's. Moreover, the linear distance between the two graphs at that point is directly proportional to the degree of difference between the relational and emotional states of the two families at that time. It is particularly worth noting that each graph was drawn by the interviewer in consultation with the family involved. The drawing was first agreed upon at the interview immediately following the exchange student's departure, and was reviewed at the interview one year later.

At the end of four years of interviewing, when the graphs of the fifteen families were compared, three patterns emerged which represented the kinds of experiences the families had had:

1. The experience was uniformly positive, from beginning to end (5 families).
2. The experience ended more or less positively, after periods of significant conflict and dissatisfaction (6 families).

Figure 11.1 A type 1 hosting experience — family E (Quinn) graph

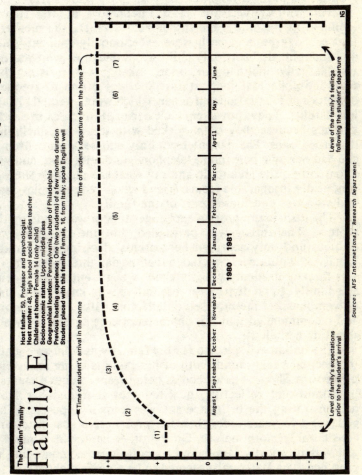

The 'Quinn' family

Family E

Host father: 50, Professor and psychologist
Host mother: 48, High school social studies teacher
Children at home: Female 14 (only child)
Socioeconomic status: Upper middle class
Geographical location: Pennsylvania, suburb of Philadelphia
Previous hosting experience: One (two students) of a few months duration
Student placed with this family: Female, 16, from Italy; spoke English well

Time of student's arrival in the home

Time of student's departure from the home

(1) (2) (3) (4) (5) (6) (7)

1980   1981

August September October November December January February March April May June

Level of family's expectations prior to the student's arrival

Level of the family's feelings following the student's departure

Source: AFS International, Research Department

3. The experience ended negatively (4 families), if not prematurely, with the student being removed before the end of the year (2 of the 4).

HOSTING EXPERIENCE TYPE 1

Those families which experienced a uniformly positive year can be best represented by the family in the study that most closely achieved the ideal student exchange experience. In this family, the student made a very positive impression on the family from the first day, developed a close relationship with the host sister, and the feelings of satisfaction increased from month to month throughout the year (see Figure 11.1).

This family was the most intellectual of the fifteen included in the study: the father held a Ph.D., the mother a Master's degree, and both were exceptionally well informed and thoughtful. Their only child was a daughter who was not intellectually inclined, or, more likely, was resisting her natural intellectual inclinations. She was prone to frequent outbursts of frustration and anger, which were directed toward her parents. They, however, took her explosiveness in stride, perhaps because they both worked with teenagers, including disturbed ones. The daughter not only had her own bedroom, she had her own bathroom, telephone, and television, and was apparently quite free to do and say what she pleased. She was practically inseparable from a friend who lived two miles away and who was considered part of the family.

The decision to host an exchange student was made by the mother. The father was persuaded, but the daughter was dubious and only accepted her parents' decision reluctantly. Local AFS volunteers concluded that the daughter's personality was the key to identifying an exchange student to place with this family, but a district representative who knew the family also emphasized the intensely intellectual nature of the family and recommended that this characteristic be considered when selecting a student.

The Italian girl selected for the family was from an equally intellectual background, both of her parents being university professors. She was described as being respectful and mature, but timid and reflective, qualities that inhibited her from demonstrating the brilliance she was known to possess. This girl was two years older than her prospective host sister and considerably more mature. On the other hand, the American girl was physically larger and socially more commanding in presence. The Italian girl seemed to be a perfect choice, from the point of view of the parents, but perhaps not so from the point of view of the daughter.

The exchange student made a good impression on the family from the very start, due in large part to her delightful and charming personality. Immediately, she and the host sister began to develop an unexpectedly close friendship, which never seriously wavered throughout the year. The mercurial daughter readily accepted the reserved European as a model for behavior, as well as an older sister, and indicated that she was grateful for her parents' reduced level of attention to herself. The host parents were delighted with the student and with the improvements they began to see in their own daughter, in her interest in studying and her general behavior. The daughter's long-standing friendship with the girl nearby was not damaged; the three girls sometimes did things together. Equally important, the host parents began communicating with the Italian girl's parents by letter and, occasionally, by telephone, and a very positive relationship began to bloom. They all found it difficult to part company at the end of the year. By this time, the American family was planning a trip to Italy to visit their AFS daughter and her family.

This family's uniformly positive experience with their exchange student appeared to rest on the following factors:

1. The Italian girl had a delightful personality and was sensitive to others.
2. The host parents had a great deal of experience with adolescents and were committed to a child-centered family.
3. The host family and the natural family of the exchange student shared a common intellectual level.
4. The AFSer's natural parents remained open to the development of feeling between their daughter and her host parents, without their own closeness to her being threatened.
5. The host daughter readily accepted the exchange student as a role model and older sister, a reaction that no one could have predicted.

HOSTING EXPERIENCE TYPE 2

The second type of hosting experience, that which ends quite successfully, following a year of roller coaster adjustment, can best be represented by a family that deliberately chose to host a student from a very different cultural background. The

Figure 11.2 A type 2 hosting experience — family M (Beckmann) graph

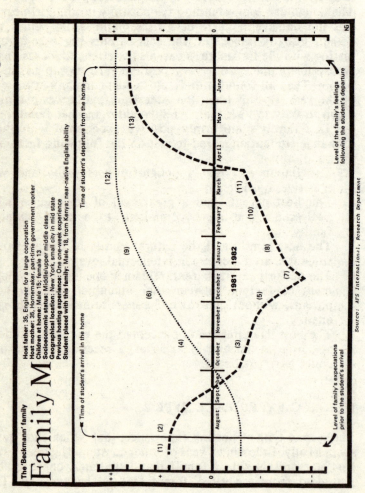

The 'Beckmann' family

Family M

Host father: 35, Engineer for a large corporation
Host mother: 35, Homemaker, part-time government worker
Children at home: Male 15; female 13
Socioeconomic status: Middle/upper middle class
Geographical location: New York, small city in mid state
Previous hosting experience: One-week experience
Student placed with this family: Male, 18, from Kenya: near-native English ability

Time of student's arrival in the home

Time of student's departure from the home

Level of the family's feelings following the student's departure

Level of family's expectations prior to the student's arrival

1981   1982

August September October November December January February March April May June

(1) (2) (3) (4) (5) (6) (7) (8) (9) (10) (11) (12) (13)

Source: AFS International, Research Department

student came to the United States with expectations for the year which conflicted with the family's expectations. Following intensive counseling with an AFS volunteer and, then, a short separation, the family and their exchange student discovered some common ground and proceeded to develop a warm relationship, which grew stronger up to the time of his departure (see Figure 11.2).

This family, with two teenagers, was flexible and spontaneous in their dealings with one another and in their extra-familial relationships. The parents were open-minded and non-authoritarian. The children, a boy and a girl, were good students and active community citizens, although they were frequently in conflict with one another. The boy, who was to be the exchange student's principal host sibling, was not terribly enthusiastic about the hosting idea. The daughter and parents looked forward to it as a learning experience and as fun. The student placed with this family was from a village in Kenya; he had never even been to Nairobi, before traveling there for the AFS orientation. As was the custom in his tribe, he lived apart from his parents and younger siblings in a house nearby. He was an excellent student and a concerned, respectful, and helpful young adult in his community. His extracurricular activities included visiting the sick and raising money for the disabled.

The prospects for this placement looked as good as they could, given the large cultural gap. The family recognized the potential adjustment problems for themselves, as well as for the student. Later, the daughter admitted to thinking that he might be 'primitive.'

As soon as the student arrived, he announced that he intended to take a job and earn as much money as possible while in the United States. (Although AFS students frequently take small jobs to supplement their pocket money, no student is allowed to hold down a full-time job. This AFS policy is in accordance with immigration and visa regulations.) His intention was clearly in conflict with the expectations of the host parents for the year to come. They were disappointed that AFS had allowed one of its students to come to the country with such a goal. Nevertheless, the student took a full-time job and subsequently began having trouble in school. With the aid of an AFS volunteer, an easier school schedule was arranged.

At home, the situation was not much better. The host brother still did not like the idea of hosting; he often left the house in order to avoid the student. The host sister took to criticizing the exchange student's behavior, which precipitated some heated arguments between the two. The host parents found the student to be lacking in warmth and responsiveness. Intellectually, they were able to rationalize this problem as stemming from the student's living arrangements in Kenya, but they were disappointed that he seemed more a stranger than a family member.

During the winter, the tension in the household increased. The host sister criticized the student so freely that he began to avoid doing things with the family. He even left the room when other family members entered. Seeing the student so distant and discontented, the host parents believed that they were failing in their roles. Moreover, they felt burdened by the student's transportation needs to and from his place of employment.

One small change was taking place, however. As the exchange student and his host brother spent time chopping wood for a stove, their relationship began to warm. The host brother found that the Kenyan never violated his confidences (unlike his American friends) and, so, the two began to share intimate secrets.

Despite this turn for the better, the overall situation remained so bad that the parents seriously considered having the student placed in another family. About this time, an AFS volunteer entered the picture. She worked intensively with both the family and the student, then gave the family a respite by arranging for the student to spend a short period with a Kenyan in another state. After the student returned, she held individual counseling sessions with him and with each family member. Everyone was encouraged to try again on the basis of better mutual understanding.

Although the situation remained far from satisfactory, it definitely showed signs of improvement during the first three months of the new year. Near the end of March, the Kenyan went on a senior class trip with forty or fifty peers. Because he shared a room with three other boys, and generally became well acquainted with several other classmates, he established himself as part of a large circle of friends. Upon returning home, he was obviously happier, which proved a great relief to the host parents. The journey also provided a break in the tension-filled relationship between the AFSer and the host sister; when he returned, their relationship improved rapidly and soon they actually were 'joking around' with each other.

In the final months of the home stay, everything fell into place. The Kenyan remained happy, because of the good times he was having with his schoolmates. The host sister lost all animosity toward him. The student began riding a bicycle to work, relieving the parents of the burden of transportation. The host brother continued to view the student as his closest and most trusted friend. The host parents were pleased, because the AFSer had finally gained what they had hoped he would gain: he had become a member of an American family.

This family's experience focuses on the following factors:

1. The Kenyan's initial goals were at odds with the expectations of the host family.
2. The Kenyan and the host sister had very different personal styles.
3. Extreme cultural differences separated the exchange student from his host family.
4. The host parents were open-minded, flexible, and non-authoritarian.
5. The short separation mid-year appeared to have a salutary effect on a very tense situation.
6. The AFS volunteer, who counseled the student and family, was skillful and, ultimately, successful in enabling the hosting experience to end positively.

HOSTING EXPERIENCE TYPE 3

The third type of hosting experience identified by the AFS research team ends negatively, and, in some cases with the student being removed from the home and given another placement. The most thought-provoking example of this type of hosting experience involved a family with two teen-age girls, which played host to a female exchange student from Jordan. In this case, communication between the host family and the student never developed fully. It was, in fact, practically nonexistent, a phenomenon which was not questioned by the family at first, for they suspected cultural or personal reasons for the student's lack of communication. The student herself was concerned about her inability to communicate with her hosts, but, in a Catch-22 fashion, was unable to discuss her concerns with them. By the time those involved realized how poorly things were going, it was too late to repair the damage. The student moved into a new home, and, to the consternation of the original host family, carried stories about them into the community (see Figure 11.3).

Ironically, this placement had looked promising. The family was close-knit and committed to family life. Three married children kept in close touch, grandparents lived nearby, or were frequently in touch by telephone, and family

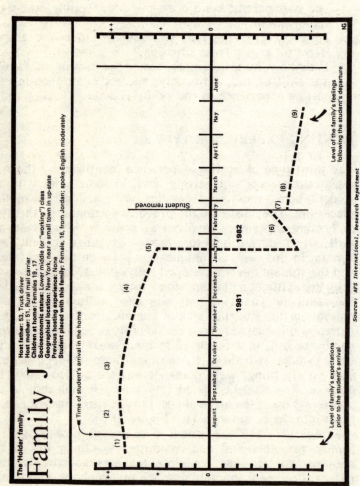

Figure 11.3 A type 3 hosting experience — family J (Holder) graph

Family J

The 'Holder' family

Host father: 53, Truck driver
Host mother: 51, Rural mail carrier
Children at home: Females 19, 17
Socioeconomic status: Lower middle (or "working") class
Geographical location: New York, near a small town in up-state
Previous hosting experience: None
Student placed with this family: Female, 16, from Jordan; spoke English moderately

Time of student's arrival in the home

Level of family's expectations prior to the student's arrival

Student removed

Level of the family's feelings following the student's departure

1981

1982

Source: AFS International, Research Department

gatherings occurred with regularity. The host family, taking the responsibilities of parenting seriously, had established household rules which their children perceived as arising out of concern and warmth. The family had decided to play host because they enjoyed having teenagers around the house, and because they previously had come to know two exchange students befriended by the older daughter during her senior year in high school.

The Jordanian girl placed with the family was young (barely sixteen years old) and had lived a rather sheltered life ('spoiled,' according to her older brother) with her mother, a widow. Supposing that her daughter would be homesick in the United States, the mother had asked that she be placed in a friendly home. Moreover, because of her mother's traditional Middle Eastern values with regard to mixing non-sibling boys and girls, she had requested a home with girls only as host siblings. The host family was eager to learn something of Middle Eastern culture and assumed that a student from a socially conservative background would not object to the house rules that governed their own daughters' behavior.

The student arrived and, as expected, accepted the host parents' rules without a murmur. The seventeen-year-old host sister helped her to become acquainted at school, but stopped short of accompanying her during every available moment. The Jordanian was distressed by this, but said nothing. At home, she spent a great deal of time studying behind the closed door of her bedroom. The host parents admired her determination to succeed academically, but were disappointed that she did not interact more frequently with family members. They rationalized their disappointment, believing that the AFSer's self-isolation was a feature of her personality, or her culture, and they noted that there were no outright conflicts involving her and other family members. Besides, they were unsure whether they had authority to compel her to join in family activities.

Meanwhile, the Jordanian was feeling very 'uncomfortable.' Although it is difficult to determine what exactly caused her anxiety, several reasons may be surmised. First, the host parents did not doubt their authority in all respects. If they were concerned about her physical well-being, or concerned that she was showing interest in the wrong crowd, they were sure to let her know. Their over-protectiveness may have had an inhibiting effect on the student. Second, they seemed to assume that she was more self-reliant than she actually was. No one in the family gave her the kind of attention to which she had become accustomed at home, and she was apparently incapable of taking the initiative to seek it. Third, there appeared to be some misunderstanding, based on the parents' non-verbal behavior, which made her believe they were upset with her. Finally, she did not like the family's habit of holding conversations in her presence in which she was not explicitly included.

Within the first few months, there were many signs that all was not well. The student spent most of her time alone in her bedroom, consuming large quantities of candy. She gained weight rapidly. She spoke more and more frequently to her brother, who was studying in California. At first the family thought that this contact with her own family member would be beneficial, but it later became clear that she was relying on him rather than on them for advice and support. They found it hard to restrict the number of calls made, since the brother paid for them and thus eliminated the one rationale they would have had for such a restriction. They simply continued to assume that the student's behavior was an expression of her culture or personality. However, by this time communication between the family and her was practically nonexistent.

One day in school, during the month of January, the student burst into tears in the middle of a class. Her guidance counselor contacted the AFS volunteers. She asked them to remove her from the family because they were unwilling to share themselves with her. The family was stunned and hurt by this pronouncement and noted that they had made requests for her to join them, which had been ignored.

Local AFS volunteers counseled the student and the family, and certain problems were pinpointed at this time. One concerned a misunderstanding involving the Jordanian's wording and intonation of requests which made them sound to American ears like demands. Another concerned the sharp difference in the expectations of the AFSer and the host sister, regarding their relationship: the AFSer had expected an extremely close and dependent relationship, whereas the reticent and more self-reliant host sister had never been prepared for this level of commitment. Following the counseling, both the student and the host family made an effort to improve the situation. But the host parents were confused about the exact role they should be playing, and the student was now suspicious of their motives. At the end of a trial reconciliation period, an AFS volunteer came to the house to help the student pack her bags and move to another home. Only later did the family learn that she had used the reconciliation period to ask around the community for another family with whom to live.

The AFSer's departure, however, did not end the experience for the family. They learned that she was spreading stories about them in the community, which made them even more confused and upset than they had been when she left. They continued to wonder why the student had been unhappy living with them, and they speculated about what they might have done to make her feel more comfortable and accepted.

An analysis of this family's experience focuses on the following factors:

1. The student had unrealistic expectations regarding the kind of relationship that she would have with the host sister, and, perhaps, also with the host mother.
2. The parents assumed that the student would need direction concerning issues of physical safety and moral behavior, but would otherwise be self-reliant.
3. The student relied increasingly on her own brother for advice and support.
4. The parents, for whatever reason, failed to notice and act upon the signs that indicated the student was becoming unhappy and maladjusted; the student, on the other hand was unable to express her disappointment with the quality of the exchange experience.
5. The student had her own bedroom, which allowed her to retreat into isolation.
6. Misunderstandings involving facial expressions, conversational practices, and other subtle cultural differences surfaced and went untreated.

CONCLUSION

These case studies represent the three types of exchange experiences that were identified by the AFS research team. Using findings from all fifteen study samples, the research team has concluded that several factors contribute to feelings of relative satisfaction for families regarding their hosting responsibilities.

1. If the exchange student participates wholeheartedly in family activities, the family is more positively disposed toward the hosting arrangement. In other words, those students who wish to demonstrate their independence from the restrictions of family life are less likely to appreciate the exchange experience with an AFS family, which is expected to treat exchange students as family members rather than as guests.

2. When students rely on their host families for advice and support, rather than on their natural families, the host

families generally find the relationship more satisfactory. Students who are in frequent telephone contact with their own families often receive advice that is erroneous and counter-productive, thus undermining the quality of the experience with the host family.

3. A satisfactory experience frequently depends more on student-host sibling relationships than on student-host parent relationships. This calls into question the expectation that a successful exchange experience is likely to be judged by the student-host parent relationship.

4. Although sibling relationships may have more impact on the hosting experience than commonly believed, student-host parent relationships may prove pivotal in the overall success of the experience if the parents are highly authoritarian. Such parents may be unable, or unwilling, to make the adjustments necessary to maintain harmonious relations with students from different cultures and family backgrounds. Students who are accustomed to living with authoritarian natural parents have a better chance of tolerating authoritarian hosts, but most exchange students find it difficult to fit into the highly structured environment that such host parents create.

(5) The final conclusion drawn from the chief findings of this study is that personality factors are of crucial importance in bridging the cultural gaps that naturally occur between exchange students and their host families. Although the research team uncovered subtle cross-cultural differences that were undermining student-host relationships, they were equally impressed with the extent to which interpersonal difficulties seem to be grounded in individual styles and temperaments. The team concluded that no exchange student or host family member is going to fail or succeed in the exchange experience on the basis of his or her cultural background. Rather, cultural differences will determine the nature and extent of the challenge, and personal differences will determine how the challenges are to be met.

REFERENCES

Gorden, Raymond L. (1974) *Living in Latin America: A Case Study in Cross-Cultural Communication*, Lincolnwood, Illinois: National Textbook Co.

Grove, Cornelius (1984) *Dynamics of International Host Families*, AFS Research Report No. 27, New York: AFS Intercultural Programs.

Chapter Twelve

THE HISPANIC ADULT LEARNER IN A RURAL COMMUNITY COLLEGE

René Diáz-Lefebvre

There has been considerable media attention given to the fastest growing minority group in the United States: Hispanic Americans. According to the US Hispanic Market Study, of this group of nineteen million, 58 percent are of Mexican descent (US Hispanic Market Study 1987).

Despite their rapidly growing numbers, people of Mexican descent are vastly under-represented in higher education. Research has indicated the majority of Hispanics enrolled in institutions of higher learning are found in the community college (Ferrin 1972; de los Santos 1980). Review of the literature on the Mexican American adult learner is limited, with articles ranging from teacher assessment in the principles and practices of adult education (Condi 1983), to a resource guide on the Hispanic elderly (Lacayo 1981). Fewer than twenty articles have been written specifically addressing Mexican American adult education issues.

A profile of the 'typical' adult learner in formally organized education is described in surveys of the literature conducted by Cross (1981), Shippe and McKensie (1981), Darkenwald and Merriam (1982), and Long (1983). The typical adult learner is a relatively affluent, well-educated, white, middle-class individual. Research conducted by Johnstone and Rivera (1965) on adult learners over twenty years ago reported similar results. Adult learners were viewed as young, well-educated, white-collar workers of moderate income. It would appear that not much change has taken place in characterizing the adult learner.

Gavilán College, a small, rural community college in Gilroy, northern California, provided the setting for a community-based project for different adult learners during the 1979-80 school year. The average age of students at Gavilán was nearly thirty years, which means it serves an adult population. The college district includes the communities of Gilroy, Morgan Hill, and Hollister. The population of Mexican descent in these communities was significant: Gilroy, 48 percent; Morgan Hill, 34 percent; and Hollister, 55 percent. Yet, despite the large Mexican American population from which it could draw, Gavilán College was only reaching 25 percent of the Chicano community.

Why did such a small percentage of Hispanics attend the college? Was it recruiting in the right places? Did it take into account the large number of migrant/seasonal workers? Was the curriculum designed to meet the needs of these adult learners? I became interested in exploring ways to reach this large segment of the adult population, and wrote a proposal which was funded by the California Postsecondary Education Commission (CPEC). The program was designed to develop and facilitate a bilingual counseling/human development class in the Chicano community within the college district, in order to close the gap between it and the college.

The gap I speak of is not political or generational, but rather attitudinal. Prior to offering this course, my hypothesis was that the college environment — location and atmosphere — deterred the type of non-traditional Chicano student I was hoping to reach. We were not doing very much to help students with suspicion, fear of failure, and lack of self-confidence, to develop self-esteem and a sense of their own potential.

PURPOSE AND ORGANIZATION OF THE COURSE

The objective of the course was to explore the development of self-concept, self-confidence, acculturation, biculturality, and academic/personal/social support systems within the Mexican American community. The two-unit course was offered through the college Office of Continuing Education. Realizing the heterogeneity within the Mexican American community, my goal was to include all segments within the community, to reflect a rich diversity: individuals with generational differences, educational and political differences, those who had married individuals outside their ethnic group, and youth of the counter-cultures (cholos and lowriders). A few non-Mexican Americans wanted to take the class, because of their interest in working in the Chicano community. I spent many hours speaking and socializing with the various groups I wanted to bring together. I wanted to be accepted as belonging in the community too. Potential students were approached in most unusual places: bars, the cannery, migrant farm worker camps, shopping centers, Sunday mass, the local lowriders club, and through the Spanish-speaking radio station.

The time spent with each group of people enabled me to share ideas, develop rapport, and to establish trust between us. My approach was to invite individuals to participate in a 'class' where, in small groups, we could explore 'quienes somos y adonde vamos' (who we are and where we are going). Even though the previously mentioned groups exemplified the diversity within the community of Mexican descent, the following characteristics seemed to be possessed by a large percentage of the target population: (1) limited educational success; (2) uncertainty regarding abilities; (3) limited success in proactively planning to facilitate success; (4) limited scope of reference for positive crisis coping; (5) very little participation in Gavilán College activities. In essence, the prevailing attitude was 'college is not for me.'

The class met two nights a week for six weeks. The first part of each session was spent explaining and discussing various philosophical, historical, political, social, and personal theories and issues. During the second part of the class, students participated in personal growth exercises to increase self-esteem.

THEORETICAL BACKGROUND

Ethnicity

Sotomayor (1977) defines ethnicity in terms of cultural and linguistic uniqueness that allows for membership in a particular group:

> Ethnicity refers to the character, the spirit of a culture, or more succinctly, to the cultural ethos. Specifically, ethnicity is related to the underlying sentiment among individuals based on a sense of commonality of origin, beliefs, values, customs or practices of a specific group of people.
>
> (p.202)

Sotomayor points out that, while ethnicity is primarily based on ancestry, there is also a sense that the present population is descended from a group that was independent in the past. It is important to note the mythic meaning of the unit of descent that provides a sense of historical continuity

213

for the development of the self-concept and social identity.

Parsons (1953) elaborates on the notion that the meaning of ethnicity is highly subjective, as it is concerned with the sentiment felt by the members of an ethnic group. He identifies a number of major types of collectivities, related to stratification, and linked by sentiment, that lead to a strong sense of solidarity among members. He categorizes 'ethnic groups,' along with local communities and kinship networks, as 'diffuse solidarities.' In this type of association, the elements of sentiment, solidarity, and loyalty, provide the context for the sense of belonging. It is the sense of belonging, together with the opportunity to participate, that allows for a process of self-perception and self-definition, both integral processes in the development of the self-concept.

The sense of ethnic identity and separateness, through the attribution of internal and external role expectations, influences the various forms of social interaction. The ethnic experience of Chicanos has resulted in a feeling of separateness and isolation from the majority community, until more recently when they have shared the feeling of rebirth of ethnic pride. The participation in nationalistic movements, such as the Chicano and Black movements in the 1960s, is an attempt to link with the past, in order to feel a sense of continuity of belonging so essential to the concept of self-worth.

Ethnic self-identity

Kurokawa (1971) asserts that the selection of an ethnic label can have important implications for the self-esteem (and presumably group esteem) of the members of an ethnic group. Each individual has a self-image, formed in a life-long process, through which a person interacts with others and acquires a sense of who he or she is, by what he or she sees reflected in the responses of others. For example, a sincere complimentary remark may make a person feel worthwhile, but a 'put-down' remark may make the person feel worthless. C.H. Cooley calls this the 'looking-glass self' (1964:184).

The persistence and dynamics of ethnic self-identity among populations of Mexican origin has been a major concern of many social scientists (Gutierrez and Hirsch 1973; Hayes-Bautista 1974). Self-identity within a variety of ethnic group labels has been associated with the process of assimilation and acculturation (Teske and Nelson 1976), political participation (Welch 1977), and cultural maintenance (Driedger

1976). For the most part, research has indicated that the absence of ethnic identity represents assimilation, as well as a lack of consensus on any ethnic label, such as Mexican American, Chicano, or Mexicano.

While culture deals with symbolic generalities and universals, ethnicity deals with the individual's mode and depth of identification, by providing a sense of belonging to a reference group.

Maldonado (1975) points out that the phrase, 'ethnic self-identity' refers to

... the integration of ethnicity or race into self-concept or self-image. It is the full recognition of one's ethnicity and the subsequent self-identity that flows from the values, ways and styles of that ethnic background, instead of from a self-concept based upon the opinions and prejudices of the larger society toward that ethnic group.

(p.621)

Self-identity studies

Group identification connotes awareness of ancestry and historical experiences, language use, social interaction (Driedger 1976), as well as other cultural projections through associational preferences, and cultural loyalty (Teske and Nelson 1976; Carlos and Padilla 1974). Self-labeling can also play a role in political consciousness, e.g., participation of an individual in a movement, and activism for social change (Gurin and Epps 1975; Hall and Freedle 1972), as well as the holding of a political ideology and political participation (Gutierrez and Hirsch 1973; Verba and Nie 1972).

The diversity within populations of Mexican origin — differences in language use, cultural ties to Mexico, and personal interaction — may affect label choices, with different generations preferring certain ethnic labels over others (Alvarez 1971; Martinez 1966).

Garcia (1976) suggests that, in addition to individual background traits affecting selection of ethnic labels, situational and psychological factors affect the presence and intensity of ethnic labels. He further suggests that the importance of ethnic loyalty for people of Mexican origin is linked to intergroup associations. Cultural loyalty and geographic circumstances, such as place of birth (urban/non-urban, etc.), affect attitudes and behavior in a variety of sociopolitical situations. For the most part, geographic circumstances serve to determine ethnic label preference. One's situational condition interacts with socio-demographic status and psychological predispositions to influence the type of ethnic label used.

Garcia, in his 1976 study on ethnic identity and background traits of populations of Mexican origin in the southwest, reports that the term 'Chicano' was selected by more younger respondents (thirty years and under), while older respondents selected 'Mexicano' and 'other Spanish' labels. The 'Mexican Americans' were predominantly in the thirty-five to fifty age range. 'Other Spanish' identifiers were predominantly New Mexico residents. While persons from California use 'Mexican' as a more prevalent choice, 'Mexicano' is used in Texas. The small numbers of 'Chicano' identifiers were primarily residents of Colorado and New Mexico. At the same time, 'Mexican American' was a more prevalent choice among Arizonans and Tejanos. Educationally, Chicanos fell into the higher educational levels (college) than any other group. 'Mexican American' and 'other Spanish' were more likely to have a high school education.

Garcia believes background traits are important in determining ethnic self-labeling. He suggests the search for additional factors, e.g., other background traits — religion, barrio versus non-barrio residence, generation — should serve to expand the relevant 'world of critical factors' interacting with ethnic group labels.

Garcia believes the variation in group labels among the populations of Mexican origin in his study can be seen as evidence of cultural diversity, or variations along some assimilationist continuum, or a fluid labeling choice dependent on the context in which ethnic identification is retrieved. In addition, an understanding of the multi-dimensionality of the ethnic cultural experience (cultural awareness, loyalty, pride, language use, ethnic interaction, and ethnic distance) should help clarify the interaction of ethnic self-labeling with behavioral and affective aspects of the Mexican cultural experience in any specific context.

In the major nationwide survey conducted by Carlos Arce, of the University of Michigan's Institute of Social Research (1979), a significant number of data have been collected from 911 bilingual interviews, designed to generate a probability sample of all people of Mexican descent in the United States. The survey is representative of approximately 88 to 90 percent of the US Chicano population, as defined by the 1970 US Census (Arce 1979). Preliminary findings from the survey indicate that, although respondents were given complete freedom to indicate which labels they used and which they believed others used in several different social situations to describe people of Mexican descent, the respondents generally (83 percent) used one of three names: 'Mexican,' 'Mexican American,' or 'Chicano.' The language of the interview seemed to be related to label selection: those interviewed in English differed from those interviewed in Spanish in the frequency with which a given label was supported. Of those interviewed in English, the overwhelming choice (46 percent) was 'Mexican.' The second choice was 'Mexican American,' preferred by 21 percent. The third choice was 'Chicano,' specified by 16 percent. The rest chose a variety of other labels or none at all.

Of those interviewed in Spanish, the top three choices were the same, but there was an even stronger preference for just 'Mexican' (or 'Mexicano' in Spanish), as compared with those questioned in English. The study also found that the support for the 'Chicano' label came primarily from those under thirty years. With few exceptions, it is also true that people of Mexican descent do not call themselves 'Hispanics,' contrary to popular belief.

Cultural preferences among all respondents who selected any of the three labels were remarkably similar. An overwhelming proportion (75 percent) of the English and Spanish interviewees identified bilingualism as the aspect of Mexican culture they hoped their families would maintain. Virtually all respondents (90 percent) expressed the desire that their children maintain Mexican traditions when they grow up. It is clear that culture is deeply valued by most respondents. Neither the language of interview nor preferred identity label tended to have an effect on the overall cultural preferences expressed by respondents.

Another interesting facet of this monumental survey dealt with the thoughts and perceptions by the respondents as to the causes of their inability to become upwardly mobile, e.g., why they receive less education and fewer promotions. Half attributed the current plight of Mexicans in the United States to faults in the system, and half to the Mexicans themselves. On the whole, 'Chicano' respondents in the group tended to recognize inequities in the socio-political system. 'American' respondents were more apt to attribute inequality to individual shortcomings.

Blending in

Acculturation is the process of adapting to a new or different culture. Assimilation is the cultural absorption of a minority group into the main cultural body.

The debate between those favoring acculturation over assimilation is not a new one. It has been debated in this country ever since the first immigrants gained a footing on this continent and began to call it their own. Breiter adds the idea of the melting pot: 'The concept is based on a "melting pot" theory, a vague nationalist dream of an America where all diverse groups are welcome and where all melt into a new nation, a new nationality, an American' (1980:2).

Prior to the Civil Rights Movement of the 1960s, becoming American meant 'melting' into the mainstream of society. De la Garza (1979) indicates that during the 1920s, the only way Mexican Americans could be fully accepted in American society was to acculturate and become 'Americanized.' If they behaved, dressed, and spoke like Americans, Mexican Americans hoped to achieve equality and dignity. Because of the strong impact and influence of acculturation, many sought to deny and disregard their Mexican and Mestizo (Indian and Spanish) background. Many persons tried to act as if they were accepted by the mainstream society. This self-rejection focused on skin color and nationality and, hence, community. For the light-skinned (güeros) Mexican Americans, it was relatively easy to pass for white. It was not uncommon for the darker Mestizo to say that he was Spanish or Italian, not Mexican. He introduced himself as Spanish, because that was synonymous with white (Casavantes 1969:1).

Acculturation and psychological stress

Ruesch, Jacobson, and Loeb (1948) have discussed the problems of American ethnic minority groups in terms of their 'cultural distance' from the core values of the dominant society. When the newly arrived immigrant is confronted with the established white, middle-class values, the individual experiences difficulty or greater 'cultural distance.' For the individual from a Spanish-speaking, lower-class, agrarian, Catholic background, the cultural distance has been historically great. The process involved in adjusting to the dominant culture is a stressful one.

According to Maslow's classification of human needs, aside

from some very basic needs, the individual's behavior is modified in the satisfaction of these needs by the society and by the culture in which the person functions. After the satisfaction of the basic needs, such as food and shelter, the individual operates within the confines of his or her society and culture. Each individual, then, lives within a culture and within a society, each complementary to the other. The two converge on the individual, to develop in him or her a given personality with definite needs and aspirations.

Horacio Ulibarri (1968), of the University of New Mexico, presents some important insights on the problems of acculturation for Mexican Americans. In explaining the problem of culture conflict, he indicates that, when an individual is asked or is required to perform certain roles within given statuses, that person will become emotionally committed and play the role according to the norms he or she has been taught. A role is the function an individual has to perform within each given position he or she occupies. For instance, there are the roles of mother, father, son, daughter, husband, and wife. Status is defined as a series of positions an individual occupies in his or her life space. An individual may be an attorney, Den Mother, head of the family and/or a member of the Rotary Club, and may occupy several other positions as well.

A problem arises, however, when there is an incompatibility between the social and cultural system in which the individual has been socialized and the new roles the person is expected to play in the new social and cultural system. When this takes place, the individual experiences culture conflict. The statuses and roles he or she learned, and to which he or she became emotionally committed, were vastly different from those he or she has to occupy and play in the United States. The individual may not know or fully comprehend the new role. The individual will tend to define his or her new status or role according to the cultural norms in which he or she was raised.

Ulibarri defines acculturation as a process by which the individual moves in his or her behavior from one sociocultural setting to another. There are several accompanying phenomena which affect the personality of an individual involved in acculturation. There is a diffusion, or the aspect of cultural change which includes the transmission of techniques, attitudes, and concepts from one cultural group to another. This could be a two-way process. However, the dominant culture usually undergoes less change with more selectivity than the minority group. Ulibarri also indicates that another factor in acculturation is assimilation. When a value system has been assimilated, it becomes a functional part of the belief system, and is taught through the culture's own process enforced by the mechanism of internal social control. Another aspect of acculturation is acceptance, acceptance by the members of a minority group of the values and practices and behavior patterns of the new culture with which the group has come into contact, and consequently, the losing of the old belief system together with the totality of its function.

Ulibarri suggests that the problems of acculturation for the person of Mexican descent basically arise because of the dysfunctions between the social system in which the individual is forced to operate and the value system to which the individual is emotionally committed. For some individuals the disparity between the demands of the Anglo society and basic values to which the somewhat traditional person of Mexican descent adheres creates schizophrenic or schizo-cultural conditions in which the individual must function. Thus, for many people of Mexican descent, difficulty arises when they do not understand or accept roles meeting Anglo norms. The individual can adapt if he knows and understands the roles and norms of the Anglo socio-cultural setting. Once the individual moves into a Chicano or Mexican socio-cultural setting, the norms of the Chicano socio-cultural system are in operation. For some individuals, this schizo-cultural situation gives rise to personality dislocation, to confusion and complete disorientation of values. Stonequist (1964) defined these as 'marginal people.'

> The marginal man as conceived in this study is one who is poised in psychological uncertainty between two (or more) social worlds; reflecting in his soul the discords and harmonies, repulsions and attractions of those worlds....
> (p.329)

According to Stonequist, the 'life cycle' of marginal man follows three stages: (1) positive feelings toward the host culture; (2) conscious experience of conflict; (3) responses to the conflict which may be prolonged and more or less success-ful in terms of adjustment. He suggests that the third stage may encourage the individual to adopt one of three roles: (1) nationalism — organization of a collective movement to raise the status of the group; (2) intermediation — bringing the two cultures closer to promote accommodation; and, (3) assimila-tion. For the most part, his concept focuses on conflict and implies that the only 'healthy' resolution is assimilation into the dominant culture.

Earlier writings by Park (1951) and Stonequist (1937) suggest that members of many racial and ethnic groups suffer from the ambivalence of values created by their longing for the old and their increasing desire for integration into the new. Such persons have been defined as 'cultural hybrids.' One result of this marginality, it was suggested, is personal maladjustment.

Critics of the Park-Stonequist thesis have argued that minority status in and of itself does not necessarily predispose one to inner strain, personal disorientation, psychic and neurotic difficulties, and various types of deviant behavior, such as crime (Golovensky 1952).

In a reformulation of the notion of the 'marginal man,' one sociologist modifies the concept of 'marginality' as follows:

If (1) the so-called 'marginal' individual is conditioned to his existence on the borders of two cultures from birth, if (2) he shares the existence and conditioning process with a large number of individuals in his primary groups, if (3) his years of early growth, maturation, and even adulthood find him participating in institutional activities manned largely by other 'marginal' individuals like himself, and finally, if (4) his marginal position results in no major blockages or frustrations of his learned expectations and desires, then he is not a true 'marginal' individual in the defined sense, but is a participant of a marginal culture, every bit as real and complete to him as is the non-marginal culture to the non-marginal man.

(Goldberg 1941:52)

Ethnic identification, or the individual's values, attitudes, and preferences representative of a particular cultural group, is an integral part of the totality of identification formed by all people of Mexican descent. Ruiz *et al.* (1977, 1978) present a model of ethnic identification which is divided into four basic types: traditional, non-traditional, bicultural, and marginal. Traditional ethnic identification, according to the authors, consists of high Mexican affiliation and low Anglo affiliation. Non-traditional ethnic identification consists of high Anglo affiliation and low Mexican affiliation. High Mexican and Anglo affiliation constitutes biculturalism and, conversely, low Mexican and low Anglo affiliation is referred to as 'marginality.' Stoddard (1973) suggests that Mexican Americans are removed from the cultural patterns of both groups (Mexican and Anglo) in a distinctive way:

The traditional approach (which has assumed that Mexican Americans are merely transplanted Mexicans, saturated with Mexican values, but subject to Anglo influences) would consider Anglo and Mexican values as opposite poles on a continuum. Mexican American values would lie somewhere between these polar types. Yet, two social scientists reject this model, proclaiming instead that Mexican American values do not merely mix Mexican and Anglo values, but comprise indeed a distinct culture. Nall (1962:37) in comparing Mexican, Mexican American, and Anglo students found that Mexican Americans expressed values with a distinct cultural dimension, often representing a more extreme position along the continuum than those of either the Mexican or Anglo samples. Another comparison of university students in Mexico City and Austin with Mexican Americans from the border land zone resulted in similar findings. The American attitude toward respect, for example, was one of detached, self-assured equalitarianism, whereas, Mexican students displayed a close-knit, highly emotionalized reciprocal dependence and dutifulness within a firm, authoritarian framework. Mexican Americans, rather than combining the two attitudes, were further removed from the core-culture pattern of the other two than they were from each other's.

(p.45)

In terms of the Ruiz *et al.* (1977, 1978) model, this change in approach can broaden the interpretation of a person's ethnic identity and group membership. For example, second- or third-generation Mexican Americans may be knowledgeable of, and adequately versed in, the American culture and yet not strongly identify with 'Anglo-ness.' They may also be relatively uneducated in, and removed from, the Mexican tradition; that is, they may speak limited Spanish, thus reflecting a low commitment. At the same time, they primarily identify and interact with persons of a similar background. This places them somewhere between the bicultural and marginal categories used in the Ruiz model.

Ulibarri (1968) suggests yet another view on the acculturation process, as it affects the person of Mexican descent. He views acculturation as a continuum. At one extreme, one finds the individual in a state of confusion and possibly in a state of cultural shock. In the second stage, the individual is striving to be more Anglo than the Anglo. In the third stage, the individual engages in a pseudo-cultural regression, trying to be more Mexican than his or her Mexican forefathers. At the fourth stage (the most important and desired stage), the individual develops an objective perspective of the intrinsic values of the cultures in which he or she is operating, and develops an inner direction for himself or herself, basically knowing to which values he or she is emotionally committed and knowing which culture is dominant at a given moment when he or she is playing a given role. As a result of variation in exposure to one or both cultures, there is a potential for change in ethnic identity throughout an individual's lifetime.

EXERCISES BASED ON THE THEORY

The individual's particular potential must not be overlooked. Otto defines potential as 'the total sum of capacities and qualities which, in the human race and in every individual, exist but have not been brought out and used (actualized)' (1977:12). Potentialities, therefore, are individual hidden capacities and qualities. In many instances, people are unaware of the talents they possess and, therefore, rarely develop them. I found this to be true of the individuals of Mexican descent enrolled in the class. By encouraging, nurturing, and developing a sense of trust, I saw emerging in them a more vibrant and affirmative attitude to life.

I found it important to take an active role in exercises designed to develop self-confidence and to bring to the surface hidden talents.

A facilitator might consider presenting a history of his or her own self-esteem as an introduction to the growth exercises, or at some later point. This will serve several purposes: (1) It will present an example of self-disclosure, an attitude and behavior which the facilitator wants to model as early and as often as possible throughout the exercises. (2) It will give a personal example of how self-awareness and self-esteem have contributed to one person's personal growth, productivity, and happiness. (3) It will help students realize that even the facilitator is still working on the problems of self-esteem, since the enhancement of self-image is a lifelong process. (4) It will help create a safe and non-threatening atmosphere in which openness and authenticity are the hallmarks. (5) It will provide a convenient way to begin the course in a personal, meaningful, and open fashion.

A willingness to engage self-disclosure means the facilitator will actively interact with other class members. I found that students considered me a friend, who could be trusted, because I was willing to disclose my personal concerns and share my life experiences with them. This was especially true of the older students of Mexican descent. Even though I represented the college, I was also perceived as a member of the community. I believe the 'gap' was beginning to be closed.

In one class I was challenged by an older Chicana, who said my knowledge of Mexican people was based on books, and that her knowledge was based on life. I asked her to explain what she meant. She responded by sharing and explaining different 'dichos,' or Mexican proverbs, with the rest of the class. She had a third grade education, yet was contributing a tremendous wealth of knowledge and life experience. The reaction of the others, especially the younger ones, was very positive. I discovered that this was a good method for involving the older members of the class and for giving the younger ones the opportunity to learn the dichos used by their parents and grandparents.

Before presenting the structured exercises, I explained the diagram shown in Figure 12.1 to students.

Figure 12.1 Self-concept components

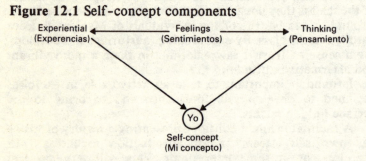

In general, student reaction to the fifteen personal growth exercises was favorable. Three of the most enjoyable ones, according to student oral and written communications, were: '¿Quienes Somos?' (Who Are We?); 'No Le Hace Lo Que Me Digas, Soy Alguien y Soy Muy Importante' (It Doesn't Matter What You Say to Me, I Am Somebody and I Am Very Important); and, 'El Arbol' (Self-esteem Tree).

'¿Quienes Somos?' was developed to demonstrate the diversity and potential of people of Mexican descent. I saw a great need to bring together different and sometimes opposing factions within the Mexican American community. My goal was not only to raise people's awareness of themselves but also for them to look at misperceptions, stereotypes, and negative and positive descriptions of others.

Students wrote descriptions and characteristics of people

of Mexican descent, such as farm worker, 'boracho,' 'familia,' 'musica,' 'comida,' religion, pride, 'cholos,' and 50s music. It was exciting to watch them try to agree on descriptions. Students were reluctant to mention descriptors, such as college graduate, bank officer, professor, lawyer, doctor, engineer, or Chicano astronaut! They have difficulty seeing themselves in these types of positions. After general discussion I introduced two or three role models, persons who held professional positions within their community. They shared their perspectives with the class and described their vocations. This interaction between the 'community' and the 'educados' (educated ones) also helped to close the gap.

The exercise, 'No Le Hace Lo Que Me Digas,' was developed to help students identify situations in which they felt demeaned or 'put down.' I wanted them to become aware of the feelings they have had from such experiences. The exercise elicited some strong emotional testimony from a significant number of them. A young Chicano high school student stated that he was tired of being 'put-down' by other persons of Mexican descent, because he was dating an Anglo and because he did not hang around with other Chicanos at school. He had recently moved into the area from Nebraska, where there were very few Chicanos. He did tell of his fond memories of his family visits to see his grandparents and cousins in Texas. His ability and willingness to share such a personal and emotional experience impressed us. After a few moments of silence, I said, 'No matter what you say to me, I am somebody and I'm very important.' I asked him to repeat what I said aloud. Soon the whole class was sharing their unique situations and receiving group support and validation. This was a successful exercise, because an awareness had been developed of the painful and long-lasting consequences of 'put-down' experiences. The sharing of these experiences helped students feel more open and comfortable.

The exercise 'El Arbol' was very popular with all students. It is intended to help them identify their abilities, skills, talents, accomplishments, hopes, and dreams. The students enjoyed developing the roots and branches of their trees. On one occasion a re-entry student, who had not been to school in fifteen years, said it was difficult for her to identify skills or talents she had. As she shared more of herself with the class, she realized that she had many skills and talents, because she had raised five children. The exercise helped her look realistically at her hopes and dreams for the future and to realize that she was spending all her time helping others and not doing enough for herself.

STUDENT REACTIONS

Of the 75 adult learners enrolled in the class, 71 completed the course, 60 continued studies at either Gavilán College or San José State University. The following are some student assessments. The names are fictitious, but the people are real.

Rafael

Older farm worker, politically active in the Chicano community. 'I am very happy this type of class has been developed. For the first time, we can come together and discuss our differences and similarities. I enjoyed all the exercises, especially "El Arbol" and "Soy Alguien." I am somebody.'

Nelly

Older Mexican American woman, a teacher's aide in the school district. 'During the weekends, I shared some of the articles from the class with my daughters, who don't speak Spanish. I would translate them and we would discuss our thoughts and feelings. I also had them do their "tree." They really enjoyed it. This class helped me to be the kind of Mexican my father is and not to be ashamed I'm Mexican.'

Mary Lou

Re-entry student married to an Anglo. 'I have gained quite a bit of insight from the exercises. The class has allowed me to express myself in areas that I have never discussed with anyone. It feels great, almost a relief to find out that other Mexican women feel as I do. I have always felt like an outsider and not quite fitting in a society of non-Mexicans. The written exercise, "El Arbol," was very self-revealing. It reinforced my goals and self-confidence. All those little hurts and insecurities about being a Mexican have slowly been surfacing. The exercises have helped me deal with them. I feel good about myself and my belief that I have a beautiful heritage and love my "familia." How stupid of me to have ever had doubts or regrets about them.'

Raúl

Chicano student working on a Master's Degree in Counseling. 'I've taken so many classes on self-examination in college. But there was something different with this class. The exercise on put-downs really hit home with me, especially regarding my relationship with my father and other people who were influential in my life. The thing I liked the most was that the class was taught by a Chicano with similar experiences. I also enjoyed the group support. Thank you for letting me be myself — again.'

Daniel

High School drop-out. 'By participating in the exercises and discussions, I learned I wasn't the only one that felt like I did. I like the exercise on pronouncing Spanish. I have always liked my name and been proud of it. My parents gave it to me for a reason. I know my name is hard to pronounce, especially for Anglo people. I feel bad inside when they don't pronounce it right. I always try to correct them, but if they can't help it, that's all right. This exercise has made me realize that my name really means a lot to me.'

Irma

Single parent working in the cannery. 'I really liked the exercise on put-downs. This exercise has made me realize something about myself that no one person has ever made me realize. For years at home, school and work I had been convinced I was a nobody. I actually believed I wasn't going anywhere in my life. In school I was called stupid for little mistakes I would make. I finally quit. I was always put-down at home, too. No one has ever told me I'm somebody and very important. After the exercise, I felt all that load of put-down words were gone. For the first time in my life I felt good about myself. I also enjoyed the exercise on speaking Spanish. It has been very embarrassing for me when another Mexican at work asks me something in Spanish; I can understand but I can't speak it. The exercise helped me identify my feelings better.'

Virginia

Single parent working in the cannery. 'The exercises were most valuable to me because I was made aware and got in touch with emotions and ideas I wanted to repress because I was always made to feel put down. I enjoyed the exercise, "Soy Alguien." For the first time, I felt my fellow students' strength in helping me believe they saw me no different and believed I could do anything; ignoring all the put-downs that were drummed in my head from family, friends and experiences at school and at work. Even my last name I changed because the Anglos could not pronounce it, and they'd embarrass me. I felt anger and resentment because I wasn't being accepted. I had to assimilate to this culture. Now I'm proud of me and my name without changing it.'

Juanita

Older Mexicana coming back to school. 'All the exercises were excellent. I believe that this is one of the best methods that helped me in knowing and appreciating myself as a person, for I have always had a lack of self-esteem. There were times when I felt like crying. The experiences we had were things that are "us" in so many ways. All of us shared our inner feelings with a sense of oneness. I will never think less of a cholito; but I will try to understand that his problems are my problems too. In taking this class, I have gained much wisdom about my own people. It has given me courage and not to fear what I am. I have a right to feel important.'

CONCLUSION

The challenge was to provide a process and environment where honest, open dialogue and exchange of ideas and feelings could occur among a group of diverse representatives of the Spanish-speaking community. Four of the five classes were held in Chicano neighborhoods. The adult learners felt at ease and comfortable in their own environment. I especially wanted to attract older students who could contribute wisdom and life experience. I remember the comments of a 68-year-old farm worker who was very happy that the class was offered in his neighborhood. He had not been in school for fifty-eight years. He had worked in the fields next to the college for ten years without entering, even though he wanted to learn. He now felt comfortable and accepted.

Through small group discussions and participation in individual and group experiential exercises, reflecting cultural values, the adult learner of Mexican descent developed a more realistic and positive attitude and could say 'college is for me.'

REFERENCES

Alvarez, R. (1971) 'The unique psycho-historical experience of the Mexican American people,' *Social Science Quarterly*, 52.

Arce, C. (1979) *National Chicano Survey*, Ann Arbor: University of Michigan Chicano Research Network, Institute for Social Research.

Breiter, T. (1980) 'A blending — not a melting of cultures,' *Agenda: A Journal of Hispanic Issues* 10.

Carlos, M.L. and Padilla, A. (1974) 'Measuring ethnicity among Mexican Americans: preliminary report on the self-identification of a Latino group in the United States,' paper presented at the XV Inter American Congress of Psychology, Bogotá, Colombia.

Casavantes, E.J. (1969) *A New Look at the Attributes of the Mexican American*, Albuquerque, NM: Southwestern Cooperative Education Laboratory.

Condi, G.J. (1983) *Analysis of Scores on Principles of Adult Learning Scale for Part-time Faculty and Recommendations for Staff Development*, Research Report No. 143, Austin: Texas A&M University.

Cooley, C.H. (1964) *Human Nature and the Social Order*, New York: Schocken.

Cross, K.P. (1981) *Adults as Learners: Increasing Participation and Facilitating Learning*, San Francisco: Jossey-Bass.

Darkenwald, G.G. and Merriam, S.B. (1982) *Adult Education: Foundations of Practice*, New York: Harper & Row.

de la Garza, R.O. (1979) 'The politics of Mexican Americans,' in A.D. Trejo (ed.) *The Chicanos as We See Ourselves*, Tucson: University of Arizona Press.

de los Santos, A.G. (1980) *Hispanics and Community Colleges*, Topical Paper No. 18, Tucson: University of Arizona College of Education, Center for the Study of Higher Education.

Driedger, L. (1976) 'Ethnic self-identity: a comparison of in-group evaluation,' *Sociometry* 39.

Ferrin, R.E. (1972) *Access to College for Mexican-Americans in the Southwest*, New York: College Entrance Examination Board.

Garcia, J.A. (1976) *Yo Soy Mexicano ... Self-Identity and Sociodemographic Correlates*, Department of Political Science, University of Arizona, Tucson.

Goldberg, M.M. (1941) 'A qualification of the marginal man theory,' *American Sociological Review* 6.

Golovensky, D.I. (1952) 'The marginal man concept: an analysis and critique,' *Social Forces* 30.

Gurin, R. and Epps, E.G. (1975) *Black Consciousness, Identification, and Achievement: A Study of Students in Historically Black Colleges*, New York: Wiley.

Gutierrez, S. and Hirsch, H. (1973) 'The militant challenge to American ethos: Chicanos and Mexican Americans,' *Social Science Quarterly*, 53.

Hall, W., Cross, W., and Freedle, R. (1972) 'Stages in the development of Black awareness: an exploratory investigation,' in R.L. Jones (ed.) *Black Psychology*, New York: Harper & Row.

Hayes-Bautista, D. (1974) 'Being Chicano: a disassimilation theory of transformation of ethnic identity,' unpublished doctoral dissertation, University of California, San Francisco.

Johnstone, J.W.C. and Rivera, R.J. (1965) *Volunteers for Learning: A Study of the Educational Pursuits of Adults*, Hawthorne, NY: Aldine.

Kurokawa, M. (1971) 'Mutual perception of racial images: White, Black, and Japanese Americans,' *Journal of Social Issues* 27.

Lacayo, C.G (1981) *A Research, Bibliographic and Resource Guide on the Hispanic Elderly*, Washington, DC: Administration on Aging.

Long, H.B. (1983) *Adult and Continuing Education: Responding to Change*, New York: Teachers College Press.

Maldonado, D. (1975) 'Ethnic self-identity and self-understanding,' *Social Casework* 56.

Martinez, J. (1966) 'Leadership and politics,' in J. Samora (ed.) *La Raza: Forgotten Americans*, South Bend, Indiana: Notre Dame University Press.

Nall, F.C. II (1962) 'Role expectations: a cross-cultural study,' *Rural Sociology* 27.

Otto, H.A. (1977) *Developing Your Potential*, North Hollywood, Cal.: Wilshire Book.

Park, R.E. (1951) *Race and Culture*, Glencoe, Ill.: Free Press.

Parsons, T. (1953) 'A revised analytical approach to the theory of social stratification,' in R. Bendix and S.M. Lipset (eds)

Class, Status, and Power: A Reader in Social Stratification, Glencoe, Ill.: Free Press.

Ruesch, J., Jacobson, A., and Loeb, M.B. (1948) 'Acculturation and illness,' *Psychological Monographs* 62.

Ruiz, R.A., Casas, J.M., and Padilla, A.M. (1977) *Culturally Relevant Behavioristic Counseling*, Occasional Paper No. 5, Los Angeles: University of California Spanish-Speaking Mental Health Research Center.

Ruiz, R.A., Padilla, A.M., and Alvarez, R. (1978) 'Issues in the counseling of Spanish/speaking/surnamed clients: recommendations for therapeutic services,' in L. Benjamin and G.R. Walz (eds) *Transcultural Counseling: Needs, Programs, and Techniques*, New York: Human Services.

Shipp, T.R. and McKensie, L. (1981) 'Adult learners and non-learners: demographic characteristics as an indicator of psychographic characteristics,' *Adult Education* 31.

Sotomayor, M. (1977) 'Language, culture, and ethnicity in developing self-concept,' *Social Casework* 58.

Stoddard, E.R. (1973) *Mexican Americans*, New York: Random House.

Stonequist, E.V. (1937) *The Marginal Man*, New York: Charles Scribner's Sons.

—— (1964) 'The marginal man: a study in personality and culture conflict,' in E. Burgess and D.J. Bogue (eds) *Contributions to Urban Sociology*, Chicago: University of Chicago Press.

Teske, R. and Nelson, B. (1976) 'An analysis of differential assimilation rates among middle-class Mexican Americans,' *Sociological Quarterly* 17.

Ulibarri, H. (1968) 'Acculturation problems of the Mexican-American,' paper presented at the Conference of Adult Basic Education, Albuquerque, NM.

US Hispanic Market Study (1987) Miami, Fl.: Strategy Research Corp.

Verba, S. and Nie, N. (1972) *Participation in America*, New York: Harper & Row.

Welch, S. (1977) 'Identification with ethnic political community and political behavior,' *Ethnicity* 4.

INDEX

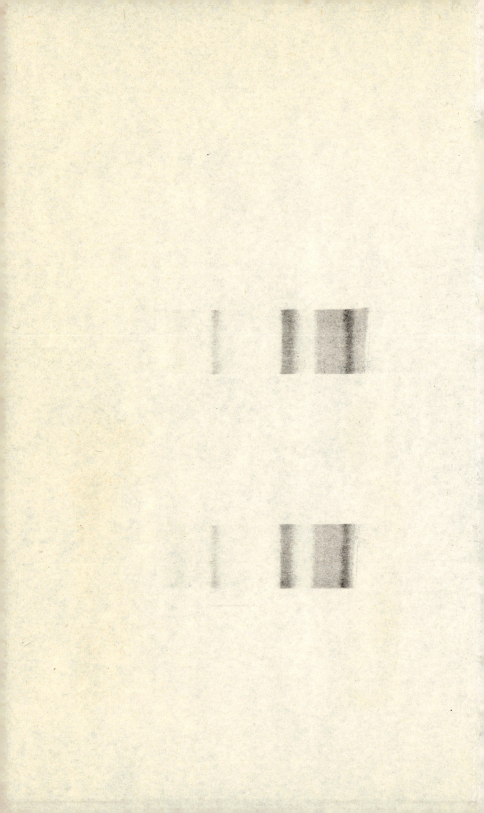